EDUCATIONAL ADMINISTRATION AND ORGANIZATION

General Editor *W. G. WALKER*

School, College, and University

The Administration of Education in Australia

edited by W. G. WALKER

Professor of Education, University of New England

University of Queensland Press

Set in Baskerville 11/12. Text paper is 100 gsm Unglazed Woodfree. Printed and bound by Dai Nippon Printing Co., (International) Ltd., Hong Kong
Designed by Cyrelle

Distributed by International Scholarly Book Services, Inc. Great Britain – Europe – North America

National Library of Australia card number and ISBN 0 7022 0735 7

What can the managers of educational systems do on their own? The one most vital thing they can do is to overcome their own inherent inertia in the face of a clear and immediate challenge to the relevance of their systems. No more than a grown man can wear the clothes that fitted him as a child can an educational system stand still and oppose making changes within itself while a world of things is on the move all around it . . . It would pay imperfect homage to the truth to suggest that the teaching profession itself—viewed in the mass—is avid for professional self-criticism, or is alive to opportunities for innovations that will help teachers achieve more in the classroom, where now they have little chance to think. Indeed, one must note an ironic fact about the worldwide educational crisis. It is that, although the crisis has occurred amid a universal expansion in knowledge, education, as the prime creator and purveyor of knowledge, has generally failed to apply to its own inner life the function it performs in society at large. It has failed to infuse into the teaching profession, for transmittal into the classroom, the new knowledge that is both available and is needed if the present disparity between educational supply and demand is to be corrected. Education thus places itself in an ambiguous moral position—it exhorts everyone else to mend their ways, yet seems stubbornly resistant to innovation in its own affairs.

PHILIP H. COOMBS
*International Conference
on the World Crisis in Education,
Williamsburg, Virginia,
5–9 October 1967*

Contents

Preface

The administration and organization of education in Australia have long attracted the attention of critics both from overseas and from within Australia itself. No sector has escaped the lash. The government schools are accused of breeding mediocrity and conformity, of emphasizing efficiency rather than "education", of authoritarianism and bureaucratic control. The non-government schools, on the other hand, are accused of shirking responsibility for that leadership which their freedom should grant them in producing change. Indeed, they are accused of remaining islands of conservatism in a sea of change.

Nor has higher education escaped. Teachers' colleges are described as inward looking, inbred, merely leading their students to become departmental stereotypes. The technical and agricultural colleges are often seen as low level training institutions dominated by the government departments which are responsible for them.

The institutes of technology and colleges of advanced education are as yet new institutions, and thus have been relatively free from criticism, but the same cannot be said of the universities, which have been constantly under fire in recent years.

Are such criticisms justified? If so, what can be done about them? And *who* can do something about them? These were the questions asked a year or two ago by members of staff of the University of New England who were concerned with that University's courses in educational administration and with editing the *Journal of Educational Administration*.

Obviously, the answers to the questions asked had implications for a great many Australians, ranging from politicians to teachers and parents. However, the answers also had clear implications for administrators or managers of schools and school systems. In discussion, an extraordinary fact emerged: there had apparently never taken place in Australia a meeting of administrators from the various sectors of education, and there certainly had been no meeting with university teachers and researchers in the field.

It was decided to arrange a conference of administrators from the various sectors, not in the hope of solving major problems— such a goal would have been too ambitious—but with a view to providing a forum for the exchange of ideas, opinions and, perhaps, research results. The conference was held in January 1968.

Because the entry of the Commonwealth Government into the field of education is of much significance, but is as yet so poorly understood, one of Australia's best known academic lawyers, Professor Zelman Cowen, was invited to present an introductory paper on the subject.

With the exception of a paper from Dr. George Baron of the University of London, who in view of the growing Australian interest in "decentralization" was invited to describe how policy making was approached by local authorities in England, the week's programme in Armidale was devoted to symposia on four issues. The first three issues reflected areas of direct concern to critics of Australian education: the impact of bureaucracy, the operation of channels of communication, and the processes of recruitment and retention of staff.

In each area a similar approach was adopted—a "position" paper setting out certain principles and theoretical constructs was prepared and circulated to a number of administrators from education departments and individual schools, colleges, and universities, who were asked to relate those principles and constructs to their own institutions.

The same pattern was followed with a fourth issue of growing concern in Australia, though one rarely referred to by her critics—the question of the preparation or training of educational administrators.

The conference was attended by more than one hundred administrators representing not only schools, colleges and universities, but also the armed services, colleges of nursing, and teachers' associations.

Three overseas participants were invited: Professor Richard

O. Carlson of the Center for the Advanced Study of Educational Administration at the University of Oregon, Dr. G. Baron of the University of London Institute of Education, and Mr. J. Ewing of the Victoria University, Wellington. The assistance provided by each of these participants' home universities is gratefully acknowledged, and in the case of Dr. Baron the generous support proffered by the British Council deserves special mention.

Within the University of New England the Department of University Extension played a major role in organizing the conference, while the Vice-Chancellor, Emeritus Professor Zelman Cowen (now Vice-Chancellor of the University of Queensland) took an active interest in the whole project. The contribution of two teaching fellows in the Department of Education of the University, Mr. R. Teasdale and Mr. P. Rich, went far beyond the normal bounds of duty.

This volume reproduces the papers read at the conference, though reports of group discussions are not included. It is worthy of note that the six "in-baskets" on school administration developed for the conference have now been published by the University of Queensland Press under the title *Schools of Mapleton.*

While the number of problem areas in the administration of Australian education which could be discussed at a one-week conference was small, and shortage of time prevented the inclusion of topics relating to all sectors of education, the quality of the papers presented amply justifies the publication of the book.

These papers will be especially rewarding if read in conjunction with those presented at the UNESCO Seminar on Educational Planning held in Canberra in September 1968 (see G. W. Bassett, *Planning in Australian Education* [Melbourne: A.C.E.R., 1970]) and the as yet unpublished papers presented in Armidale at the Conference on Planning in Higher Education in Australia during August 1969.

In the future this volume will be recognized, I am sure, as a catalyst in the development of professional and academic contacts among educational administrators in Australia.

W. G. WALKER
Armidale, 1970

Part	THE GOVERNANCE OF EDUCATION–
One	FEDERAL PARTICIPATION

1 The Growth of Federal Participation in Australian Education

We start with the Australian Constitution. That instrument is nearly seventy years old and came into operation on 1 January 1901. It is wholly silent on the subject of education in the sense that it makes no explicit reference to it. The constitution expressly spelled out the *specific* powers assigned to the new central authority, the Commonwealth, and no power with respect to education was specifically assigned to the Commonwealth. The constitution provided further that save so far as powers were assigned to the Commonwealth or their exercise expressly denied to the states, the state constitutions and the powers of the states under those constitutions remained operative. The various states were given powers to legislate for their peace, order, and good government (the precise formula varied from state to state), and under this general power the states were left with their powers over education, and it was not necessary in the Commonwealth constitution to say so explicitly.

The proposition that the Commonwealth was given no power over education requires qualification in respect of Commonwealth Territories (outside the area of the states). In these territories, the Commonwealth was assigned general authority, and so it followed that provision could be made for education in such places as the Australian Capital Territory, the Northern Territory, Papua and New Guinea, and the other territories of the Commonwealth.

Then again, through the exercise of particular powers over other matters the Commonwealth might deal with matters of education. For example: the Commonwealth was assigned a defence power. This meant that repatriation benefits could be provided for ex-soldiers and for the children of soldiers. These benefits could and do include education benefits. Then again in the major wars of this century it has been found necessary to provide for military and civil conscription. In fixing exemptions, there was some power to deal with matters affecting education and educational institutions.

There has, however, been a major source of indirect power attracted to the Commonwealth to deal with matters of education. This comes from an unexpected source. It is Section 96 of the Constitution which provides that,

During a period of ten years after the establishment of the Commonwealth and thereafter until the Parliament otherwise provides, the Parliament may grant financial assistance to any State on such terms and conditions as the Parliament sees fit.

This is known as the Commonwealth Grants power and it means what it says: that the Commonwealth may make grants to states on terms prescribed by it. It has proved to be a very important source of power, somewhat surprisingly, because its opening words contemplate that it was intended only to have a transitional and limited operation. There can be little doubt that it was thought that for a limited period of time after the Commonwealth came into existence, there would be some need for specific and limited financial adjustments, but that this would phase itself out. Section 96 has, however, proved to be a permanent and potent source of power, and its scope has been considered on a number of occasions in the courts. It was first examined in the twenties in the High Court in connection with Commonwealth legislation providing grants to the states for the construction of roads. A young lawyer, Mr. R.G. Menzies, argued against the validity of the legislation which required the states to put up money and to do many other things besides. Mr. Menzies said that whatever Section 96 authorized, it did not allow the Commonwealth simply by virtue of making a grant of money to regulate road making and road making procedures and activities within the states. This, he argued, was an unconstitutional encroachment on state powers. The High Court, in a short and perfunctory judgment, said that the legislation was valid, and that the terms were authorized by Section 96.

In other cases, the High Court reaffirmed what it had said in the Road case. In the early 1940's and the latter 1950's, the High Court, in the two Uniform Tax Cases, gave the broadest scope and operation to the power. In the early years of the second world war, the Commonwealth desired to become the sole income-taxing authority, whereas previously income taxes were raised separately by the Commonwealth and the states for their separate purposes. Without going into overmuch detail, one of the major acts in the scheme (the term is not used technically) was the States Grants Act which provided that if the Commonwealth Minister was satisfied that in any year a state had abstained from imposing an income tax, the Commonwealth would pay sums of money to the state, calculated by reference to a formula which originally had close regard to what the state had previously raised by its own income tax. The states challenged the legislation, and in respect of this particular Act, it was argued that there must be a limit to the "terms and conditions" which the Commonwealth might impose on a grant to the states. Specifically it was said that it was not constitutionally permissible to impose a term or condition which required a state to abstain from the exercise of a fundamental, a basic governmental power such as the power to impose taxes. That argument failed; it commanded the support of only one judge on the bench of the High Court. The majority said that there was no warrant for reading down the "terms and conditions" in this restrictive way.

The Uniform Tax legislation was originally devised as a wartime expedient, but the bases upon which a number of its major provisions were sustained were not simply wartime defence and emergency factors. In fact the Uniform Tax legislation was maintained during the post-war period. There was much grumbling on the part of some of the states. A new challenge was directed against the legislation by the states of Victoria and New South Wales in the 1950's. The Chief Justice of the High Court, Sir Owen Dixon, had been absent from the court on wartime duties as Minister to Washington when the legislation was first challenged in the forties and it was hoped that his views of federalism might produce a differing interpretation. The new challenge failed substantially and the renewed argument about Section 96 directed against the States Grants Act failed altogether. Sir Owen Dixon considered the history and interpretation of Section 96 at length; he pointed to its seemingly transitional and limited character. In substance, however, he said that earlier interpretations of the power by the High Court made it impossible to sustain the argument that the "terms and conditions" could be limited in the manner argued for by the states of Victoria and New South Wales. So it has come about that by the attachment of terms and conditions to grants of money the Commonwealth power has a very wide and extensive reach.

As a result of the decision upholding the Uniform Tax scheme, the states became dependent on the Commonwealth by way of reimbursement for a very large part of their resources. From time to time, the reimbursement formula was revised to correct patent anomalies and injustices at least to some extent. And by another interpretation of the constitution, the states, already effectively denied access to independent income taxes, were also shut out of other important sources of tax revenue. From the very beginning, customs duties were exclusively reserved to the Commonwealth, though states had imposed and collected them before federation. There was another provision of the constitution which declared that the imposition of excise duties was exclusively reserved to the Commonwealth. The definition of excise duties was evolved in a number of cases, and it was held that a sales tax was an excise within the meaning of the constitution. So the states were denied power to levy sales taxes.

Without power in practice to impose income taxes and without power in law to impose sales taxes, the states' sources of independent revenue by way of tax are meagre and often quite unsatisfactory; so that the states' access to an independent revenue is severely restricted at a time when the demands upon them for the provision of various social services and notably education at all levels are growing ever greater. The states, it must be remembered, have the prime constitutional responsibility for education within their geographical areas.

In the very earliest days of federation, Alfred Deakin prophesied that the states would find themselves financially chained to the chariot wheels of the Commonwealth. And that has certainly proved to be the case. In the context of education where the demand is great and ever-growing this has had significant implications.

Late in 1966, honouring an election pledge, the Commonwealth government formally established its own Ministry of

Education and Science with Senator John Gorton as Minister. He had formerly been Minister in Charge of Commonwealth activities in education and research, and that was a sub-department within the Prime Minister's Department. The new department had as its permanent head Sir Hugh Ennor, formerly of the Australian National University. I pause to observe that the Commonwealth had formally established a ministry and a department in an area in which the constitution assigned it no specific or direct power. And it is important to bear in mind that the ultimate source of authority to establish the department was money. Section 81 of the Constitution authorizes the Commonwealth to appropriate money for the purposes of the Commonwealth. In this case, it appropriated funds for the establishment of a department.

The establishment of the department was, however, a step taken after substantial intervention by the Commonwealth had already occurred in the educational field. It is worth tracing out the steps by which the Commonwealth became involved in education.

In the very early 1920's the Commonwealth made provision for the education of returned servicemen's children. That might have been sustainable as an exercise of its defence powers; it was certainly supportable as an exercise of the Grants Power. In 1930, the Commonwealth established the Canberra University College. There was no constitutional problem there, for there is direct and general authority to deal with matters within Commonwealth Territories. Then between the wars, the Commonwealth made grants to state universities for particular purposes: aeronautics in Sydney, meteorology in Melbourne. There was some small provision for medical research.

During the second world war, there was a financial assistance scheme for university students and some provision was made for the supervision of their enrolment and courses of study. With the end of the war came the Commonwealth Education Act, 1945. It contemplated various Commonwealth activities in the educational field, for aiding students, for providing funds for assistance to various educational bodies, and for promoting research in education. This legislation established the Commonwealth Office of Education.

Major steps were taken by the Commonwealth in providing assistance to students at university and tertiary level. There was first of all the Commonwealth Reconstruction Training Scheme, and then the major Commonwealth Scholarship Scheme for education at universities and other tertiary institutions. That scheme has been recently replaced by two schemes: the Commonwealth University Scholarship Scheme and the Commonwealth Advanced Education Scheme. The Commonwealth has also moved into the postgraduate field. In 1959 it established its postgraduate scholarship scheme. During 1965, the Commonwealth made its first significant move into the field of sub-tertiary education with the establishment of the secondary scholarship scheme. There are also Commonwealth technical scholarships at the sub-tertiary level. In 1967 under these various Commonwealth scholarship schemes, some 50,000 held awards, and in 1967 there were, in aggregate, some 22,000 new awards.

Thus the first major aspect of Commonwealth entry into the field of education has been by way of financial provision to students: a substantial scholarship scheme at secondary, technical, tertiary, and postgraduate levels.

What is more significant in the context of Commonwealth entry into the field of education is the development of aid to universities. From 1951, the Commonwealth began to make what were then "marginal" grants to universities. These were minor, and the great change came with the Murray Report. The constitution of that commission was a Commonwealth initiative, and Murray in 1957 proposed a very much greater measure of support for Australian university education. If this was to be a reality, it called for substantial Commonwealth subvention. Following the Murray Report, the Commonwealth government announced its intention to make grants to the states for university purposes.

The proposals contemplated matching grants by Commonwealth and state governments for capital expenditure and for recurrent grants. The Commonwealth by legislation established an Australian Universities Commission. The Australian Universities Commission Act of 1959 established the Commission as an instrumentality of the Commonwealth to advise it on the needs of the universities. The Commission has a full-time chairman and part-time members. The functions of the Commission are to furnish information and advice to the Commonwealth government on matters in connection with the grant by the Commonwealth of financial assistance to universities established by the Commonwealth and of financial assistance to the states in relation to universities, including information and advice relating to (a) the necessity for financial assistance and the conditions on which any financial assistance should be granted and (b) the amount and allocation of financial assistance. It will be seen from this that a prime function of the Commission is to advise the Commonwealth on the financial needs of state universities.

Section 14 is interesting. It provides that the Commission shall perform its functions with a view to promoting the balanced development of universities so that their resources can be used to the greatest possible advantage. For the purpose of the performance of its functions, the Commission shall consult with universities and with the states upon the matters on which it is empowered to furnish information and advice. A Vice-Chancellor answering a multitude of "please explain" missives from the Commission on details of building programmes and on an enormous range of matters relating to the university may perhaps look a little askance at the interpretation which the Commission has placed upon the word "consult"!

The Commission, then, is a Commonwealth instrumentality established by Commonwealth legislation to advise the Commonwealth on the financial support appropriately to be given to Commonwealth and state universities in Australia. The Commission's recommendations are just that; we know from recent history that those recommendations will not necessarily be accepted in full, and that is what happened when the Commission reported in 1960 on the universities' programmes for the 1967–69 triennium.

Following the Murray Report, the Commonwealth government also announced that it proposed to make grants to the state universities for research. Out of that has come angry dispute. Until the mid 1960's the contemplation was that there should be matched Commonwealth and state grants for research. These sums would be given to the universities which would then determine the allocations of the research funds.

In 1965, the Commonwealth government established the Australian Research Grants Committee as part of a scheme to back particular research projects by particular workers on the basis of their evaluation by the Committee. For the present triennium the Commonwealth said that it was prepared to support a research programme under which $6 million would be made available for *general* research to be controlled by the universities, while a substantially larger sum would be made available for the A.R.G.C. to administer and allocate to specific projects. The whole scheme, in the Commonwealth view, rested upon matching grants by Commonwealth and states, dollar for dollar. The states said in substance that they desired to have the research funds provided for general research administered by the universities and that they were not willing to support, dollar for dollar, the A.R.G.C. project. The Commonwealth then said that it proposed to support the A.R.G.C. allocation in full up to $9 million and that it was for the states to decide what they proposed to do about the general research funds. From the standpoint of a number of universities, this has worked out very badly because in some states, including New South Wales, the state governments have said that they will not provide the general research funds. The general research grants, they say, were allocated on the footing that Commonwealth and states would contribute dollar for dollar. The states say that they will now only pay their one dollar. In New South Wales, this means that anticipated resources from this source are cut in half; and the consequences for the universities, already in financial difficulties, are very serious.

The Commonwealth has also shown considerable interest in the development of non-university tertiary education. I refer now to the Colleges of Advanced Education. These had their genesis in the Martin Committee report on Tertiary Education. The Martin Committee gave its approval to diverse forms of tertiary education and recommended the establishment of institutions which are taking shape as the Colleges of Advanced Education. In March 1965, Sir Robert Menzies, in a debate on the Martin Committee Report, announced that the government approved of the concept of Colleges of Advanced Education and said:[1]

These Colleges would provide for those students who, though

qualified, do not wish to undertake a full university course, or whose chosen course is not considered appropriate for a university, or whose level at passing matriculation indicated a small chance of graduation from a university in minimum time or minimum time plus one year.

The report contemplated that the Colleges of Advanced Education would provide not only technical and technological education but also education in the field of liberal arts. Later in 1965 the Commonwealth government set up the Commonwealth Advisory Committee on Advanced Education under the chairmanship of Dr. Wark. One of the members of this committee is Professor McClymont, Dean of the Faculty of Rural Science in the University of New England. The Wark Committee examined in some detail what was involved in the provision of advanced education in this particular form, and also the appropriate methods of financing the operation. In the Wark Committee report, there was special emphasis on the *teaching* role of the new colleges; while research would be conducted, it would not be a primary field of endeavour, and not the basic research which was more appropriate to universities. The Wark recommendations were substantially adopted by the Commonwealth government late in 1965. The Wark Committee said that it wished the new colleges to provide for the community graduates with professional qualifications which had a strong bias towards the application of qualifications to immediately practical ends, and graduates with a tertiary education which had involved the study of liberal arts subjects in equal depth but not over as wide a field as in the university. Senator Gorton, in adopting these principles on behalf of the government, acknowledged that there was some uncertainty in the definition of the precise lines of development of the colleges, and announced a Commonwealth unmatched grant of $250,000 to provide for research on the definition of the tasks and role of the colleges. Legislation made provision for Commonwealth support which broadly finances the Colleges of Advanced Education in respect of grants for capital expenditure and recurrent funds in broadly the same way as the universities.

I turn now to teacher training. The Martin Committee proposed substantial Commonwealth support for teacher training. At first the Commonwealth rejected this proposal, but later reversed its attitude. In 1966 Senator Gorton held discussions with state Ministers for Education and announced a Commonwealth-state agreement under which the Commonwealth would make capital grants for teachers' colleges, and in 1967 agreement was reached on specific projects. Legislation in 1967 made $24 million available for the period 1967–70 for projects in six states under which teachers' colleges would be built to plans and standards drawn up by the states and approved by the Commonwealth minister. It was agreed that the states should not reduce their own expenditure on teacher training and that at least 20 per cent of the places made available as a result of the Commonwealth offer should be available to non-bonded trainees.

The consequence of all this is that the Commonwealth is now providing financial assistance throughout the whole range of tertiary institutions for which the Martin Committee proposed support.

In a more limited way, the Commonwealth has entered the field of education below the tertiary level. From 1964 to 1968, the Commonwealth provided an unmatched $40 million to the states to provide buildings and equipment for technical training in all states; and this extends to agricultural colleges. Since 1964, the Commonwealth has made $10 million per year available to the states for science buildings and equipment in schools. This is allocated to the states for government schools and to independent schools direct on the recommendation of the Commonwealth Advisory Committee on Standards for Science Teaching Facilities in Independent Schools. Within its own territories, the Commonwealth has given direct aid to independent schools in the A.C.T. and the Northern Territory and since 1965 has accepted direct responsibility for the payment of approved construction costs of independent primary and secondary schools in these Territories.

From this, it appears that the Commonwealth has assumed some responsibilities in education at levels from the lowest up to postgraduate education. In the tertiary field, of course, Commonwealth activity in universities and C.A.E.'s has been particularly significant.

Viewed from the standpoint of the universities, it is clear that the growth which has taken place would not have been possible on the post-Murray scale without Commonwealth support. A little time ago, Sir Robert Menzies after his retirement gave a series of lectures on the growth of central power in the Australian Commonwealth at the University of Virginia. He spoke specifically about Commonwealth grants and their implications which, as he pointed out, gave the Commonwealth great sources of increased power. As to this he said:[2]

I believe the overall results to have some good elements. A very recent example is the system of grants to the States for State universities. This is a development which probably was not foreseen in 1901, or even at a much later date than that.

He went on to trace the scheme under which the Australian Universities Commission made recommendations and said:[3]

The whole development is one which has affected what was then thought to be the federal distribution of powers between the national Parliament, which had been granted no general power over education, which remained a State function, and the Parliaments of the States. But it undoubtedly has had the effect of saving the State universities from financial disaster, and of enabling new universities to be established. The whole matter is a very good illustration of how something which was not anticipated in the Constitution when it was first enacted can come into existence by judicial interpretation and the inexorable demands of new circumstances.

That is one view, and there is another. That was expressed by Mr. Cutler, the New South Wales Minister of Education:[4]

I have no doubt whatever in my mind that the Commonwealth is increasingly using its financial control to force its way into the functions of the State—functions laid down under the Constitution. If the Commonwealth government wishes to enter any of these fields that are the responsibilities of the States under the Constitution it can do so by way of agreement between the States or by referendum of the people. It cannot be doubted that if the Commonwealth endeavoured to enter the constitutional fields of the State by means of a referendum that referendum would be defeated—as most have been in recent years.

Mr. Cutler said what is undoubtedly true, that the Australian people will not formally grant additional powers to the Commonwealth. But they will and do acquiesce in a *factual* sense. The Minister went on to say this—and the contrast with Sir Robert Menzies' words is striking:[5]

One of the outstanding fields into which the Commonwealth has intruded is education. In recent times we have seen the setting up of a Commonwealth Ministry of Education and Science. If the system is to continue as it is and the Commonwealth is increasingly to come into the field of State rights I see some reason for setting up this Commonwealth ministry, but I can see no reason for it if we are to adhere to the federal system in Australia. I must be quite plain and outspoken on this matter. I do not deny for a moment that the various fields into which the Commonwealth has entered with grants to the States are needy ones, but the intervention by the federal Government goes far beyond the mere making of grants, whether matching or unmatched, for specific purposes. The federal authorities are demanding that the States provide all sorts of details. In the Ministry of Education we have had officers of federal departments visiting the offices of the State department and asking for details to be supplied. Officers of the federal departments have written letters, not signed by the officers themselves but by a clerk on behalf of an officer, delivered by hand to a clerk in the Department of Education asking for details which neither I nor the Director-General have authorized. I cannot allow this sort of intervention by financial control to go on without raising my voice in protest.

In 1967, the New South Wales Minister for Education announced the establishment of a State Universities Board, the function of which was to advise the Minister on matters on which the Australian Universities Commission gives advice to the Commonwealth, and more generally to advise the Minister on the needs and problems of the universities in New South Wales. So that in that state, a Vice-Chancellor has *two* authorities with which to meet, deal, and negotiate.

It is not difficult to understand the frustration of the states. The states continue to be substantial contributors to education at the various levels at which the Commonwealth has intervened. In the capital grants field, in university financing, the Commonwealth and states match dollar for dollar. Under the recurrent grant formula, the state contribution (which takes account of various fees paid by students) aggregates $1.85 for every $1 contributed by the Commonwealth. The state finds these moneys from a limited pocket upon which increasingly heavy demands are made. Sometimes the situation is extraordinary. For example, a salary increase was given recently to university staff which operated retrospectively to 1 July 1967. The announcement of the increase was made by the Commonwealth Minister and the Commonwealth got the kudos. The Commonwealth said that it would pay the increase in full in universities in its own Territories, but would support them in the states on the recurrent expenditure formula, if the states agreed to come in on that basis. The states had no choice but to come in, and the tax implications were most interesting. Many university people now found themselves in a tax bracket in which the Commonwealth in respect of each $2.8 of increased salary took back at least $1 in income tax, and so (having regard to the fact that it contributed only $1 of each $2.8) got back at least as much and in some cases more than it put in to the increased salaries. For the states, the university salary increases only worsened their position, while the Commonwealth suffered not at all.

There are other problems which the universities (and doubtless others in good time) face through Commonwealth intervention. One of the major current functions of universities is to supply mountains of detailed information, many estimates and many more "guess-timates" to the A.U.C. The preparation of a triennial submission is an appalling and in many respects an unsatisfying task, and what the universities are called upon to do scarcely measures up—in terms of plain English meaning —to the "consultation" about which the Act speaks. We get questions on all manner of things and they range from detailed building enquiries to basic issues of academic policy: we are asked to supply details of academic performance; we are asked questions about possible transgressions of rules denying us power to embark on new developments which, unless expressly authorized, are to be regarded as forbidden fruit. The emergence of the new Ministry of Education and Science adds a new dimension of horror: Monday to Wednesday are now allotted to A.U.C. questions, Thursday and Friday to satisfying the appetite for information of the new department.

It all gets back to that Section 96 of the constitution. The Commonwealth gets the answers because it is the source of money and grants. It is interesting to note that in this field the workings of Section 96 are somewhat special. The terms and conditions are not imposed directly in the states, but Commonwealth officials now by-pass the state offices and officers and go straight to the universities with their requests, demands, and questions. This is one of the things Mr. Cutler complains of. It will be so, very likely, with the Colleges of Advanced Education, too. Section 96 on its face gives no warrant for this sort of activity. But no one takes the point.

There are fundamental questions to be asked. There are very real problems which arise from such detailed controls. The Australian Universities Commission is not surprisingly interested in a cost-benefit analysis. I do not think any responsible person would deny that cost-benefit questions *are* appropriate in financing universities and in making judgments as to the quantum and direction of university financing. But how far does control go? I have said in correspondence with a former chairman of the Australian Universities Commission that in the relations between universities and the Commission there must be a proper balance between autonomy and accountability. I cannot think that our universities are likely to have a tolerable, let alone a great, future if they are to be called upon to account, explain, and proliferate paper in the way they have been required to do in these immediately past years.

The point will doubtless grow in significance as Commonwealth entry into the education field spreads further and further. If the needs of education, and they are ever growing, are to be met, then short of a fiscal revolution there will be increasing appeals to and demands on the Commonwealth purse. That purse, too, has heavy competing demands upon it. One cannot face the future, as a Vice-Chancellor anyway, with too much cheer, for both the resources available and the terms on which they will be made available will pose difficult and uncomfortable problems.

Part Two   BUREAUCRACY IN EDUCATIONAL ORGANIZATION

2   An Overview

We live in an organizational society.

Rousseau's fateful complaint of 1762 may be of even more significance today, two centuries later:

Man is born, lives and dies in a state of slavery. At his birth he is stitched in his swaddling-clothes; at his death he is nailed in his coffin, and as long as he preserves the human form he is fettered by our institutions.

In the late twentieth century the scholar concerned with the place of the individual in society is constantly impressed by the number and variety of organizations which in one way or another impinge powerfully upon the social, political, economic, ethical—indeed, upon all—aspects of human life. We may cite the example of John Smith, born amid the sparkling antisepticism of one complex organization, the hospital; educated amid the not so sparkling walls of another, the school; married amid the pomp and mystery of another, the church; employed amid the clatter and bustle of another, the factory; and ultimately buried amid a flurry of macabre organizational activity which involves funeral organizations, religious organizations, insurance organizations, trustee organizations, banking organizations, and hospital organizations—all of which, while keeping one eye discreetly directed towards the dear departed, keep the other eye even more discreetly directed towards the dear present—that great super-organization the state, which, in one way or another, subtly and sometimes not so subtly, limits the power of them all.

One striking feature of these systems is their *power*. The reality of the power they exercise over the lives of people is evidenced in the chill, almost apprehensive way in which some of us react to a request to present ourselves at *the* Department, or the feeling of frustration we experience when told that *the* administration has refused our request. No more convincing demonstration of the trepidation with which some of us at least regard this power is the consistent demand for the appointment in Australia of an ombudsman to look after the rights of citizens aggrieved by the actions of bureaucrats.

Another obvious feature of many of these systems is their *impersonality*. For many people, the abrupt decision of someone "higher up" not to allow a student protest march or the terse telegram directing a teacher to report for duty at Mulligan's Tank East within two days demonstrate convincingly a depersonalization which is difficult to understand and even more difficult to oppose.

For the student of organizations an even more obvious feature is their *complexity*. The specialization of functions to be observed in the great university, the large independent school, or in its extreme form in the gargantuan Australian state education departments, is fascinating—though by no means as fascinating as the behaviour of the human functionaries upon which not only the success, however defined, but the very survival of the organization depends.

Barnard[1] in his classic *The Functions of the Executive* defines organization simply as "a system of consciously coordinated activities". Such a definition, though commendably brief, helps little in an attempt to understand the complexity of organizational structure. A useful definition is that given by Corwin[2] who points out that

a complex organization is an arrangement for coordinating the activities of subdivisions having a common identity, which consists of a status system, rules and procedures and a division of labour. The way it functions somehow depends upon its recruiting practices, how it deals with non-members, the allocation of status and the division of labour, and the degree of stability and control it is able to maintain over its direction. Responsibility for these processes is assigned to various roles.

Some of the terms used in this definition may need further comment, for it is essential to remember that organizations are systems not merely of structure, but of *humans*.

It is clear that an education system, for example, consists of a number of sub-systems (administrative departments, colleges, and schools) which have, or should have, some common identity and common goals. It has an official status system ranging from Director-General to student-teacher, and the authority to issue commands or to exercise control over the work of others is delegated to a hierarchy of positions. However, the status system goes well beyond that officially designated. There is also an informal *prestige* hierarchy which reflects the relative importance assigned to each position by members of the organization and a power hierarchy which reflects the actual opportunity which positions provide for members to control others. Clearly the distribution of power and authority affects decision making by setting limits of discretion, defining the extent of routinization, and determining the degree of centralization and decentralization.

Rules and procedures ("the usual channels"), the bearers of organizational authority,[3] co-ordinate the various parts of the organization and regulate the conduct of its members. The number, scope, specificity, and enforcement of rules and regulations establish the degree of standardization and conformity throughout the system—and may, of course, also establish the degree of apathy in the system.[4]

Stability of control depends largely upon the patterns of interaction among people occupying positions in the organization. Positions in turn are comprised of work *roles* which are the product not only of legal job definition but of norms arising from the expectations of others and the sanctions imposed for conformity, or lack of conformity.

Complex organizations are often described as *bureaucracies*—a term which will be used here not with its vulgar connotations of cups of tea by the gallon and red tape by the furlong, but in its scientific sense of an organization designed to achieve rational decision making, and based on the four factors of *specialization, hierarchy of authority, a system of rules,* and *impersonality.*

The concept of bureaucracy is not new. It existed in a rudimentary form in ancient Egypt, where the complex task of constructing and regulating waterways demanded large scale organization; it flourished in Rome, first in the Empire and later in the Catholic Church which survives as the longest-lived bureaucracy in the world.

Weber[5] regarded bureaucracy as the most efficient form of organization known to mankind. The members, chosen for their specialist knowledge, work with speed, precision and discretion, following rules and regulations which minimize the personal, the irrational, and the emotional in decision making. Weber's ideal bureaucracy—a model widely adopted in Western democracies—is characterized by the following:

1. A well defined hierarchy of authority in which higher officials supervise lower ones
2. A division of labour based on functional specialization and full-time, trained officials
3. A system of rules, policies, regulations, and by-laws covering the duties and rights of officials
4. A system of procedures based upon written documents to deal with particular work situations
5. A fundamental impersonality in dealing with work situations
6. A system of promotion plus selection based solely on technical competence.

The purpose of bureaucracy is to create social conditions which lead each officer to pursue rational *organizational* objectives, irrespective of how rational or irrational those objectives might seem to him personally.

In due course we shall return to this theory; meantime we may note Blau's[6] pungent comment: "To administer a social organization according to purely technical criteria of rationality is irrational, because it ignores the non-rational aspects of social conduct."

One formal organization which either directly or indirectly influences the lives of nearly every member of our society and which consequently has received more than its fair share of criticism from scholars is the organization we know as "school". For good or ill nearly all schools and school systems, and all universities, in Australia increasingly display symptoms of the growth of bureaucracy. This is so whether the schools are part of the great state systems, the loosely organized Catholic "systems", or the independent "system", and the symptoms are likely to become even more obvious as these institutions grow in size, complexity, and staff specialization, as the need is felt for codification of rules and procedures, and as more and more subordinates intervene between the chief executives of the organization and those operating at the "cutting edge" in the classroom.[7] The same is likely to be true of universities which, already under fire in some quarters for bureaucratic procedures,[8] have become increasingly involved in, and influenced by, federal and state planning. Recently, quoting Perkins of Cornell University, Cohen[9] asked "Who is going to 'manage' integrity?"

What is the likely impact of burgeoning bureaucracy upon educational organizations?

First, let us lay down some ground rules.

The argument to be developed in this paper depends upon the acceptance of a number of assumptions about organizational behaviour. These assumptions are:

1. An organization is a system, a complex of elements in mutual interaction[10]
2. The behaviour of participants in the system is shaped not only by personal role expectations but by institutional role expectations,[11] i.e. the organization does something *to* the individual
3. The climate of the organization is shaped by the role expectations of individual participants, i.e. the individual does something *to* the organization
4. In a bureaucratic organization, because the most substantial power is exercised by a few, the climate of the organization is shaped chiefly by the role expectations of members of the oligarchy
5. In a bureaucratic organization the climate of sub-systems is likely to be strongly influenced by the climate of the system itself.

From these propositions it is possible to extrapolate certain propositions referring specifically to educational organizations:

1. The prime measure of the effectiveness of an educational organization is the effectiveness of its impact upon the behaviour of individual students
2. The educational organization has its impact upon individual students largely through the interaction of those students with individual teachers
3. The behaviour of individual teachers—the product of personal and institutional role expectations—is largely determined by the organizational climates produced in the system and sub-systems by educational administrators.

The essential point arising from these propositions is that organizational climate, a facet of organization largely influenced by individual administrators, is assumed to have an important bearing on teacher-pupil interaction and hence on the learning function which is the prime concern of the organization.

This assumption appears to be strongly supported by recent theorists and researchers working in the fields of teaching and learning, if the contributors to Gage's classic *Handbook of Research on Teaching*[12] are any guide. "Climate" factors in teacher-child relationships are referred to elsewhere by workers such as Remmers,[13] Biddle,[14] Flanders,[15] Campbell,[16] and Dunkin,[17] for example. Some writers have worked specifically in the field of climate. Withall[18] has developed a "Climate Index", Wright and others[19] have examined the psychological ecology of the classroom, and Halpin[20] has pioneered a number of important studies of the organizational climate of schools rather than classrooms.[21]

In a recent important study John B. Miner[22] of the University of California at Berkeley demonstrated that "school districts develop very disparate organizational characters". He concludes:

The Hawthorne studies started out to study the effects of environmental conditions, including illumination, on performance; they ended by stressing human relations, because they could not be explained in other terms. In the same way, the current research started out in an attempt to establish selection procedures for school administrators; it ended by stressing *organizational* character because the data could not be explained in terms of the occupation based models.

The assumptions about organizational climate or character which underlie leading current thinking have been well stated by Professor Enns[23] of the University of Alberta:

Learning is active and individual. It takes place only when the individual is ready and when he is motivated. The individual can be helped to learn, but it is doubtful that he can be "taught" very much. Thus, learning can take place best in an atmosphere of stimulation, freedom from restrictive influences, and in a psychologically supportive climate . . . Good teaching in this sense requires great skill, sensitivity, adaptability and flexibility. It depends upon intimate, subtle interaction between learner and teacher. It requires all the professional ability and art that a teacher can muster. This kind of teacher behaviour is highly individualistic and can flourish only if and when the over-all atmosphere is sufficiently permissive and stimulating. In response to social and economic trends we have tended to develop large, centralized school systems. While the large system has more resources and can use them more effectively and efficiently than the small one, it nevertheless does develop some aspects which tend to reduce the warmly intimate relationships and rapport which are so important in teaching and learning. It therefore becomes one of the functions of administration to counteract the impersonal, demanding, often threatening aspects of the large organization—the bureaucracy—so that the professional person can exercise as much of his professional talent and skill as possible, in spite of the restrictions which may exist. Rather than hold the teacher to the requirements of the system, the administration should attempt to free the teacher from at least the extraneous organizational demands and to take these demands upon itself. The professional needs to be free to practise his profession.

If the criticisms implied by Enns are correct, then those of us who are concerned with education at all levels—Commonwealth, state or local—will need to devote particular attention to our own organizations, for it is clear that the impact of bureaucracy is growing as the populations and complexity of educational systems increase.

The questions the educational administrator needs to ask himself in the cold light of dawn are: "Is the climate in my institution an *educative* climate? Is it conducive to learning, generative of zest, open to change? If it is not, what should I be doing about it?"

If something does need to be done about climate we might turn for useful concepts to Warren G. Bennis of the Massachusetts Institute of Technology, whose recent book *Changing Organizations*[24] provides an excellent framework from which to attack our discussion.

Bennis' hypothesis is that bureaucracy as a form of organization is becoming less and less effective, that it is out of joint with contemporary realities and that within twenty-five to fifty years we should see the end of bureaucracy as we now know it and the rise of new social systems more capable of coping with twentieth century demands.

One immediate reaction to this statement is that one hopes changes will, in fact, lead us to cope with *twenty-first* century demands! The year 2000 is only thirty-two years off, and as educators we are only too keenly aware of the fact that the children now in school, indeed the students now in universities, are the executives and administrators of the twenty-first century.

Bennis goes to some pains to point out logical weaknesses in Weber's theory, many of which are obvious to the most junior student of bureaucracy. Clearly the very factors which Weber claims enhance efficiency may also detract from it. For example, strictly impersonal relationships are unlikely to produce high morale in the work group, promotion based solely on merit deprives many employees of advancement in the organization, strict exercise of authority may militate against effective upward communication and hence informed decision making, and so on.

Thus, in Weber's model the very processes regarded by him as functional might well have dysfunctional consequences. In other words, the very nature of bureaucracy leads to organizational pathologies.

Bennis presents a number of major criticisms of bureaucracy as a system of organization. The criticisms seem so fundamental for the administrator of educational institutions that they deserve analysis in terms of the earlier discussion of teacher-student interaction and organizational climate. His criticisms are:

1. Bureaucracy does not adequately allow for personal growth and the development of mature personalities
2. It develops conformity and "group-think"
3. It does not take into account the "informal organization" and the emergent and unanticipated problems
4. Its systems of control and authority are hopelessly outdated
5. It has no adequate judicial process
6. It does not possess adequate means for resolving differences and conflicts among ranks and most particularly among functional groups
7. Communication (and innovative ideas) are thwarted or distorted because of hierarchical divisions

8. The full human resources of bureaucracy are not being utilized because of mistrust, fear of reprisals, etc.
9. It cannot assimilate the influx of new technology or scientists entering the organization
10. It will modify the personality structure such that man will become and reflect the dull, grey, conditioned "organization man".

Yet Bennis does not appear to be advocating, or expecting, the end of bureaucracy as defined by Weber so much as the development of a different kind of bureaucracy which has come to terms with changing concepts and values in society. He points out that already we may observe some fundamental changes in administrative philosophy which have influenced organizational behaviour in recent years, viz.:

I. A new concept of *man*, based on increased knowledge of his complex and shifting needs, which replaces the over-simplified, innocent, push-button or inert idea of man.

II. A new concept of *power* based on collaboration and reason, which replaces a model of power based on coercion and fear.

III. A new system of *organizational values* based on an humanistic existential orientation, which replaces the depersonalized value system.[25]

The acceptance of these changes, while by no means universally adopted, has clearly influenced policy formulation by large organizations in Australia as well as in U.S.A.

A major study of the normative world of the elementary school teacher conducted recently by Dr. Foskett of the University of Oregon illustrates Bennis' first point very well. Foskett's study showed that in a sample school system in U.S.A. teachers' roles, far from being simple, "push-button" roles, were complex and ill-defined. Marked differences were revealed in teachers' and principals' own perceptions of their roles—in fact, the average level of agreement was below 50 per cent. Foskett concludes:

The normative world surrounding teachers is less rigid than teachers are aware. To the extent teachers are constrained in their behaviour as a consequence of the alleged rigidity, they are being constrained by something that actually does not exist.[26]

Would replication of Foskett's study in an Australian school system lead to similar conclusions?

Few of us would disagree with Bennis' proposition that the nature of bureaucracy must change: the more fortunate among us see this happening around us every day. The important question for us is: Is bureaucracy changing rapidly enough— and in the right direction? Is bureaucracy providing organizational climates in which teachers and children can maximize their relationships, in which professors can *profess* rather than administer, and in which human needs[27] are met?

If, as seems likely, most of us are only too conscious that our schools, departments, or universities are far from perfect, we may turn to theories of organizational behaviour for insights which might affect our own behaviour as leaders. Most of the theories known to this author originate in the United States, a few in Europe. It is, of course, possible that some of the theories do not apply to Australian culture. However, we will not know whether that is so or not until we have tested them. As Getzels[28] has put it: "To be sure, theories without practices, like maps without routes, may be empty, but practices without theories, like routes without maps, are *blind*."

Theories, of course, are of prime importance for the administrator: as John Dewey pointed out, theory is in the end the most practical of all things—a point of view this author will defend to the death. Just as the researcher depends upon theory for the generation of hypotheses, the administrator relies upon theory for the generation of guides to action and for sources of prediction and explanation of organizational behaviour. The wider his sources of theory, the larger the variety of theories available to him, the better are his chances of understanding and influencing the human organization.

The most valuable section of Bennis' book and the one providing the best available model for the discussion of theories of organizational behaviour is his table of the core tasks confronting the contemporary administrator. This table, which presents the tasks in terms of the human problem involved, the likely "bureaucratic" (by implication, nineteenth century) solution to the problem, and the twentieth century conditions which render the bureaucratic solution inadequate, appears to the present author to have widespread application, irrespective of the "adjectival" organization involved or the Western democracy in which it is situated.

TABLE 1 Human problems confronting contemporary organizations

Problem	Bureaucratic Solutions	New Twentieth Century Conditions
Integration The problem of how to integrate individual needs and management goals.	No solution because of no problem. Individual vastly over-simplified, regarded as passive instrument or disregarded.	Emergence of human sciences and understanding of man's complexity. Rising aspirations. Humanistic-democratic ethos.
Social influence The problem of the distribution of power and sources of power and authority.	An explicit reliance on legal-rational power, but an implicit usage of coercive power. In any case, a confused, ambiguous, shifting complex of competence, coercion, and legal code.	Separation of management from ownership. Rise of trade unions and general education. Negative and unintended effects of authoritarian rule.
Collaboration The problem of managing and resolving conflicts.	The "rule of hierarchy" to resolve conflicts between ranks and the "rule of coordination" to resolve conflict between horizontal groups. "Loyalty".	Specialization and professionalization and increased need for interdependence. Leadership too complex for one-man rule or omniscience.
Adaptation The problem of responding appropriately to changes induced by the environment of the firm.	Environment stable, simple, and predictable; tasks routine. Adapting to change occurs in haphazard and adventitious ways. Unanticipated consequences abound.	External environment of firm more "turbulent", less predictable. Unprecedented rate of technological change.
"Revitalization" The problem of growth and decay.	?	Rapid changes in technologies, tasks, manpower, raw materials, norms and values of society, goals of enterprise and society all make constant attention to process of firm and revision imperative.

From *Changing Organizations* by W. G. Bennis. Copyright 1966, McGraw-Hill, Inc. Used with permission of McGraw-Hill Book Company.

In this paper we shall take Bennis' five "core tasks" and discuss them in the light of certain theories and empirically-derived evidence relating to organizational behaviour. In the process many important theorists—Merton,[29] Selznick,[30] and Parsons,[31] for example—will not be referred to, though this does not mean that they have no relevance to Australian educational organizations. It has been necessary to select only a few theories for discussion in each task area, but it will be obvious that most theories overlap several, if not all, areas in one way or another.

Integration

The problem of how to integrate individual needs and management goals

This is a problem which has long confronted practitioners and theorists. Reacting against the mechanistic concept of man and the impersonal rationality of measurement reflected in the theories of Weber,[32] Taylor,[33] and Fayol,[34] writers like Mary Parker Follett[35] and Ordway Tead[36] sought to find means by which the individual could become involved in and identified with the organization while preserving his independence and integrity.

The problem seems to be one of major importance for Australian education if the reports of overseas observers and the constant complaints of teachers' federations and to a lesser extent, university staff associations, are any guide.

A theory of major importance which relates to personality and organization is that presented by Chris Argyris.[37] Writing not only as a theorist but as a researcher in banks, hospitals, and industrial organizations, Argyris comes directly to grips with the fundamental man-organization problem.

In fine, Argyris hypothesizes that the needs of the individual and the demands of formal organization are basically incompatible. Man, he says, is constantly striving towards "self-actualization", a process which seeks need-satisfactions as one's personality matures. Man matures along a number of dimensions—from passivity to activity, dependence to independence, behavioural inflexibility to flexibility, subordination to superordination, and so on. Formal organizations, however, by their very nature stultify such growth. Task specialization, chain of command, unity of direction, span of control and the like push the work force into a dependence relationship in which individuals are dependent upon, passive towards, and subordinate to appointed leaders. There is thus a basic lack of congruence between the needs of mature individuals and the demands of formal organizations.

While the lack of congruence can never be entirely overcome, it may be minimized, in the long run interests of both individual and organization, by job enlargement, employee centred leadership, and reality leadership (the last of which is a very difficult concept to grasp—for this author at least). He appears to be arguing for "participative" leadership—a process which, it is hypothesized, is most likely to produce both self-actualization in individuals and goal-achievement in organizations.

Diametrically opposed to Argyris is McMurray's[38] view that most personnel are children, and that this is the only way they can be and want to be. Man, he claims, is slothful, wants to be dependent, is incapable of taking responsibility and prefers to be a follower rather than a leader.

Of these two points of view, which like all theories are over-simplified, Argyris' is the only one acceptable to the educational administrator, for the educator *cannot* accept that man's needs are fixed and immutable at the level of childhood. The whole of the educator's value system is oriented towards developing growth, maturity, and independence. If he rejects change, he rejects improvement and the very bases of our culture.[39]

Most theories of organization relate to the problem of man and organization. Bennis, for example, looks beyond the theories of both Argyris and McMurray and himself puts forward Robert Kahn's conception of "role set" as a moderator between personality and organization. From our point of view the existence of multiple theories is a good thing, since it provides us with a variety of approaches in diagnosing and treating our organizational ills—as we shall see in the discussion of the following task areas.

Social influence

The problem of the distribution of power and sources of power and authority

Here, if such observers of Australian education as Butts,[40] Kandel,[41] Jackson,[42] and Sanders[43] are to be believed, lies a major weakness in the administration of Australian schools and universities.

Interestingly, this particular "core area" has produced more empirical research than any other. The poorest-read of students of organizations are familiar with the findings of Mayo[44] and Roethlisberger and Dickson,[45] with their implications for human relations, involvement, and leadership in the informal organization. In the field of education most administrators will know the work of Halpin,[46] Hemphill,[47] and Gross,[48] for example.

One theory which appears to be of more than ordinary importance for Australian education, and one which overlaps in many ways with the previous core area of Integration, is that presented by Robert Presthus.[49] Crane has referred to this theory in chapter 5 of this book, but it appears to be so important for this discussion that the theory is developed here in some detail. Presthus is chiefly concerned with the behaviour of individuals in large organizations, especially bureaucracies as described by Weber. Accepting Harry Stack Sullivan's interpersonal theory of psychiatry he argues that each person's personality is the product of his accommodation to people significant to him; indeed, that most behaviour is the result of the individual's search for relief from tension—especially *anxiety*—induced by conforming to authority; human personality is formed largely from efforts to get along with people in authority, to reduce anxiety, in fact, and this method of accommodating is brought by the subject to the big organization when he joins its staff.

The very nature of big organizations induces anxiety in their participants. The bigger the organization the more unimportant the individual feels. Specialization militates against interpersonal relationships. Hierarchy assigns and validates authority through a constant display of scarce status symbols. The oligarchy—the few running the bureaucracy—have a marked preponderance of power, and their presence tends to accentuate the anxieties of other members.

Individual members accommodate in one of three ways—upward mobility, indifference, and ambivalence. *Upward-mobiles* are the most successful organization members. They experience little difficulty in reaching decisions because they accept the organization's values and act in terms of the organization rather than of the individual. Such members enjoy organizational life, learn to play and succeed at the "organization game", and reap the rewards of status and salary. *Indifferents* refuse to compete for the organization's favours. They accommodate to the organization by doing a routine job, but at the same time develop their major interests *outside* the organization. Organizational anxieties are reduced because indifferents do not compete for its favours or rewards. As Presthus puts it, "He sells his time for a certain number of hours and jealously guards the rest."

Ambivalents, the minority, can neither resist the appeals of power and success nor play the role necessary to achieve them. They cannot play the "organization game", for they resent high authority and the impersonality of the organization. As Griffiths[50] says, "His is indeed a miserable lot in the modern, large organization."

The implications of this theory for organizational climate and teacher-student interaction are obvious. Many of Presthus' anguished comments upon bureaucracy are obviously inspired by his own experience as a university professor. Questions which we might ask include: How are administrators to tap the resources of today's "organizational teacher"? Is the upward-mobile "organization man" the most valuable teacher? Is the indifferent a common figure in Australian education? Is not the ambivalent a likely source of change and innovation?

Presthus' theory, like Weber's, clearly sees man as a rational being but differs from Weber's in that the latter ignores the personal and informal relations while over-emphasizing the infallibility of rules.[51] A major implication of this theory appears to be that in order to play down the dysfunction between the needs of the organization and the anxieties of the individual one role the leader must play is that of facilitator—of providing situations in which individuals will feel involved in the organization, identify with it, and be encouraged to act creatively within it.

Presthus' theory has not been as widely tested as one might hope, though the results of Zeigler's[52] fascinating study of the political world of the high school teacher appear to support some hypotheses which might have been derived from Presthus' writings.

Other research supporting Presthus' theory in certain ways was the study of the New York City System, referred to by

Crane[53] and conducted by Griffiths and others[54] in 1965. To climb up the New York ladder, it appears, one must "G.A.S."—Get the Attention of Superiors. Teachers of this type (almost one in eight males) exploited the visibility system—getting promoted was more important than good teaching. Further, the major study of the elementary school principalship conducted by Gross and Herriott in the same year may relate directly to this discussion as well as to the previous discussion on *Integration* and the following discussion on *Collaboration*. One of the most rigorous sociological enquiries of education ever reported, it examined the leadership role of the principal. The leadership exercised by the principals was designated Executive Professional Leadership (E.P.L.), i.e. "the efforts of the executive of a professionally staffed organization to conform to a definition of his role that stresses his obligation to improve the quality of staff performance". The authors hypothesized: "The more a principal permits his teachers to share in his decisions, the greater his Executive Professional Leadership." When the hypothesis was tested, the relationship between E.P.L. and teacher involvement was strongly positive and statistically significant. "In short", they conclude, "the evidence provides support for the hypothesis that there is a positive relationship between the staff's involvement in the principal's decisions and his professional leadership."[55]

The question of involvement in decision making naturally leads to the question of managing and controlling conflict, referred to by Bennis as "collaboration".

Collaboration

The problem of managing and resolving conflicts

Administrators no longer regard a measure of conflict in an organization as a sign of lack of organizational health. Today conflict is recognized as an inevitable aspect of organization without which innovation, for example, is unlikely of achievement. Conflict often arises from questions of authority, and one major source of conflict growing in significance in education these days is the dichotomy between *professional* authority and *administrative* authority.

One theorist, Gouldner,[56] claims that the classical Weber

theory in fact incorporates these inconsistent types of authority, one based on technical competence, the other on power derived from the position itself. Such a theory is clearly of importance at a time when teachers in most states are claiming to be professionals competent to make decisions—indeed, in New South Wales, to make major policy decisions involving both "fact" and "value"[57] decisions in the role of *professionals* rather than of *bureaucrats*. The whole question of the proposed N.S.W. Education Commission is haunted by the obvious conflicts arising from these two role perceptions.

An understanding of Gouldner's theories (and many others) depends upon some familiarity with role theory. According to the latter theory organizations are social systems made up of people who occupy positions in hierarchical or horizontal relationship to one another. The behaviour of an individual in a position is explained in terms of expectations, i.e. how the individual thinks he is expected to behave and how others expect him to behave. Such expectations are termed "roles".

According to Gouldner a role may be "manifest" or "latent". A manifest role is the overt role—e.g. Professor of Sociology, principal of a primary school. A latent role is a secondary or underlying role which, however, has important implications for behaviour in the overt role, as indicated by Crane. Latent roles of importance for organizational behaviour are those of "local" and "cosmopolitan". The "local" derives his rewards from manipulating power within the hierarchy; the "cosmopolitan" his from inward standards of excellence, internalized and reinforced through professional, usually scientific, identification.

Etzioni[58] too has raised this significant area of role conflict. Briefly, Etzioni hypothesizes a typology of organizations according to three dimensions:

1. The sanctions which they employ to induce members to participate: *coercive* (the use of force), *remunerative* (use of monetary rewards), and *normative* (reliance on ethical and moral involvement of members)
2. The involvement of members, described as *alienative* (members are negative towards the organization), *calculative* (members are neutral but participate because of contractual

bargains), and *moral* (members are involved in the values and activities of the organization)
3. The congruence of dimensions (1) and (2) above, described as *order-type* organizations, which are alienative and coercive (e.g. prisons, labour camps), *economic-type* organizations, which have a remunerative-calculative pattern (e.g. factories, retail stores) and *culture-type* organizations which have a moral-normative pattern (e.g. universities, schools, clubs).

Schools are thus, like general hospitals, predominantly *normative, culture-type organizations, with coercion in varying degrees as a secondary pattern*. It is instructive to note the impact of professionals within these organizations. Bureaucracy, of course, assumes a power hierarchy in which the higher in rank have more power than the lower and can control them. But knowledge and creativity are essentially individual properties, and the application of these is essentially a matter of conscience, not a matter of rule, regulation, or decree.

Some organizations are more professionally oriented than others. Etzioni claims that the primary school, for example, like the social work agency is a *semi-professional* organization since its goal is largely to communicate rather than to create knowledge. However, semi-professionals tend to adopt the full-fledged professions as their reference group in the sense that they view themselves as fully-fledged professionals and feel that they should be given more discretion and be less controlled than they are.

While Etzioni's typology is not without its critics, and while his classification of schools might be suspect in terms of United States teacher commitment, his theory may well have greater relevance to the Australian than to the United States environment, because of the career commitment of Australian male teachers.[59]

It is certainly worthy of discussion.

Adaptation

The problem of responding appropriately to changes induced by the environment of the firm

The introduction of change and innovation into Australian

education has concerned many observers, especially those from abroad who have expressed horror at the lack of so-called "grass roots" policy making. Whether or not we agree with the specific criticisms made by our colleagues from abroad (the grass roots theory has its critics even in America[60]) few of us will deny that the introduction of change is by no means an easy exercise for the Australian educational administrator. Most of us are only too well aware of the in-built inertia in educational systems which was recently criticized so skilfully by Coombs[61] at the International Conference on the World Crisis in Education.

If we consider that bureaucracy as we now know it is not working in the best interests of individual children in classrooms or of researchers in laboratories, it behoves us as administrators to do something about reforming bureaucracy or replacing it with something better. In other words we need to concern ourselves with *strategies* for change.

The problem of introducing change to social systems is not, of course, a new problem. Jesus, Luther, and Florence Nightingale, for example, were all concerned with the introduction of change. Bennis describes eight traditional types of change programmes: *exposition and propagation* which rest on the assumption that knowledge is power and that men who possess "truth" will lead the world; *elitism* which recognizes that ideas by themselves do not constitute action, that "the right man in the right job" is necessary for ideas to be implemented; *human relations* training which seeks to inculcate into key executives insight, wisdom, and sensitivity; *"staff" resources* which provide a source of intelligence within the client system; *scholarly consultations* which include exploratory enquiry, analysis of the problem, and scientifically based advice to clients; *circulation of ideas to the elite*, which assumes that change will follow the circulation of ideas to men in power; *developmental research*, which is not directed toward a particular operational problem or client, but to helping people to see through theoretical insights how something could be done differently or better; and *action research* which, unlike other forms of applied research, actually involves the client in the solution of his own problems.

The criticisms which can be made of these strategies are

obvious: knowledge *about* something does not lead automatically to intelligent action, the presentation of a programme by an expert does not necessarily mean that the client will carry it out, the possession of insight does not guarantee control of strategic variables which will produce action. Clearly, a theory of change must concern itself with many more variables than those implied in the above list.

Robert Chin[62] has set out some prerequisites for a theory of change. These are:

1. It must provide for influencing variables that are accessible to control, i.e. variables must be manipulable
2. It must not violate the client system's values
3. It must take into account cost of usage
4. It must provide a reliable basis for diagnosing the strengths and weaknesses of the conditions facing the client system
5. It must account for phases of intervention so that the change agent can decide points for terminating his relationship with the system
6. It must be able to be communicated to the client system with a minimum of distortion
7. It must be able to assess its own appropriateness for different client systems.

The introduction of change into an organization, educational or otherwise, is carried out by *change agents*. These may be researchers, teachers, consultants, or administrators. One theory claims that significant change in an organization depends upon the outsider who can approach his task with detachment and vigour. Another theory, however, postulates that it is the insider who possesses intimate knowledge of the systems, does not generate suspicion and mistrust, and whose acceptance is guaranteed by membership in the organization who is the most effective change agent.

One such theory which seems to have particular relevance to the study of innovations is systems theory. Derived from engineering and the field of cybernetics, this theory is now attracting considerable attention especially among the students of von Bertalanffy at the University of Alberta and Maccia at Ohio State University.

A system is a complex of elements in mutual interaction. An

open system is related to and exchanges matter with its environment. All systems except the smallest have sub-systems and all but the largest have suprasystems, which are their environments. System theory deals only with *open* systems, i.e. those which exchange energy and information with their environment. To make a long story short, this theory can be used to explain, describe, and predict a wide range of human behaviour within organizations. Griffiths[63] of New York University has presented a number of hypotheses derived from this model which have obvious implications for our centralized systems. These are:

1. The major impetus for change is from the outside
2. Change is more probable if the successor to the chief administrator is from outside the organization rather than from inside
3. When change in an organization does occur it tends to occur from the top down, not from the bottom up
4. The number of innovations expected is inversely proportional to the tenure of the chief administrator
5. The more hierarchical the structure of an organization the less the possibility of change.

As yet, little significant research has been conducted in this area, but Carlson's[64] work is relevant. Carlson's study of school superintendents who come from "inside" or "outside" the system shows the instrumental role that turnover plays in accelerating or retarding organizational adaptation and lag. The insider, attached to a specific place, his home system, puts place of employment above his career as superintendent. The outsider, on the other hand, is career bound and is willing to leave the system for a job elsewhere. From his observation of a number of school systems Carlson concluded that school boards appointed outsiders when they were dissatisfied with the status quo, insiders when they were satisfied.

So far, however, we have not discussed any strategic models. One of these is R. R. Blake's[65] "managerial grid", based on an analytic framework of managerial styles. Blake attempts to change the organization in the "high concern for people, high concern for production" direction through a variety of procedures including feedback experiments, T-Group sessions and team training, goal setting, and stabilization of changes.

A more complex strategy, and one which might be employed in large systems, is described in the next task area.

Revitalization

The problem of growth and decay

Bennis' concept of revitalization is closely related to *adaptation*. To achieve revitalization, he says, we need theories not simply of change, but of changing, i.e. operational theories which provide for the control of strategic variables.

One such theory (or near-theory), though Bennis does not mention it, is the schema presented by Clark and Guba[66] of the National Center for the Study of Change in Education, which can be used either to explain or predict change behaviour or, as proposed here, to devise a strategy for the introduction of change.

The schema or model attempts to classify the processes related to and necessary for change specifically in education. Four processes are hypothesized: Research, Development, Diffusion, and Adoption. The *objective* of each of these processes is described, as is their *relation* to change.

The first process is, of course, *Research* which provides the basis for invention by presenting *ideas*.

The second process is *Development* which is sub-divided into *invention* and *design*. The objective of invention is to *innovate*— to formulate a new solution to an operating problem or to a class of operating problems. It is this stage which produces the invention. The objective of design is to *engineer*—to order and to systematize the components of the invented solution; to construct an innovation package for institutional use.

Thus far we have been concerned with those who research, engineer, and package. An analogy in medicine is the invention of the Salk vaccine and in the engineering which produced it in large quantities at an economic price. The research stage is the concern of the egg-head, the development stage of both the egg-head and the engineer.

The next process primarily concerns the "leg" men, those concerned with spreading the word—the agricultural extension officer in rural industry, the advertising agency in business,

FIGURE 1 A Classification Schema of Processes Related to and Necessary for Change in Education

	Development			Diffusion			Adoption	
	Research	Invention	Design	Dissemination	Demonstration	Trial	Installation	Institutionalization
Objective	To advance knowledge	To formulate a new solution to an operating problem or to a class of operating problems, i.e. *to innovate.*	To order and to systematize the components of the invented solution; to construct an innovation package for institutional use, i.e. *to engineer*	To create widespread awareness of the invention among practitioners, i.e. *to inform*	To afford an opportunity to examine and assess operating qualities of the invention, i.e. *to build conviction*	To build familiarity with the invention and provide a basis for assessing the quality, value, fit, and utility of the invention in a particular institution, i.e. *to test*	To fit the characteristics of the invention to the characteristics of the adopting institution, i.e. *to operationalize*	To assimilate the invention as an integral and accepted component of the system, i.e. *to establish*
Criteria	Validity (internal and external)	Face validity (appropriateness) Estimated viability Impact (relative contribution)	Institutional feasibility Generalizability Performance	Intelligibility Fidelity Pervasiveness Impact (extent to which it affects key targets)	Credibility Convenience Evidential assessment	Adaptability Feasibility Action	Effectiveness Efficiency	Continuity Valuation Support
Relation to Change	Provides basis for invention	Produces the invention	Engineers and packages the invention	Informs about the invention	Builds conviction about the invention	Tries out the invention in the context of a particular situation	Operationalizes the invention for use in a specific institution	Establishes the invention as a part of an ongoing programme; converts it to a "non-innovation"

the drug companies' medical representative in the vaccine analogy referred to above, the demonstration schools attached to the teachers' colleges in the case of education. This is the process of *Diffusion*, the first stage of which, *dissemination*, seeks *to inform*, to create widespread awareness of the invention among practitioners. The second stage, *demonstration*, seeks *to build conviction*—to afford an opportunity to examine and assess operating qualities of the invention.

The next process, that of *Adoption*, involves the practitioner himself, since it is now necessary to put the innovation to the test of practice. The first stage of adoption is *trial*, in which the practitioner *tests* the invention in particular contexts in order to provide a basis for assessing its quality, value, suitability, and utility. The second stage is that of *installation*, in which the practitioner *operationalizes* the invention by fitting it to the characteristics of the institution in which he works. The third stage is that of *institutionalization*, that in which the invention ceases to be an innovation, when it is established and assimilated as an integral and accepted component of the system.

Examples of the third process, adoption, are everywhere to be seen: the medical practitioner has tried and adopted the Salk vaccine; the Queenslanders years ago tried and adopted the cactoblastis insect to defeat prickly pear; teachers everywhere—for good or ill—have tried and adopted the Herbartian steps.

It is a sobering thought that at one time in our history the formal institutions we now call "school" were themselves innovations. By what stages did the school change into a "non-innovation"? At the present time we are watching an interesting innovation in the field of politics—the gradual adoption of substantial state and federal aid for independent schools. This innovation remains largely an innovation: it still is in the process of adoption, and then only in certain areas. Why is this innovation moving so slowly? At what stage in the schema is the blockage taking place? Is it perhaps at the stage of demonstration in the *diffusion* process? Have its proponents *built conviction* about the invention?

Has this schema relevance for the adaptation of bureaucratic procedures in Australian schools and universities? In what way might it be employed as a strategy for making use of insights gained from organization theories in such a way as to produce appropriate organizational climates?

Conclusion

This paper began with the assertion that we live in an organizational society. It concludes with the prognosis that we shall continue to live in an organizational society—but in a society in which organizations, influenced by new conceptions of man, power, and social values might, with good leadership, seek ways and means of retaining efficiency and productivity while providing for man's needs and satisfactions.

Such good leaders could do no better than turn to Sir Geoffrey Vickers[67] who, in his *The Art of Judgement*, vividly points to the real challenge facing the innovator—*the ability to envisage as possible what has not yet been experienced in fact*. Vickers urges the planner, the ideas man, to envisage the possible: "Any alternative which the planner suppresses or fails to notice goes unconsidered by the policy maker and may indeed be lost for ever." Soberly, he adds, "this danger is latent not only in decisions based on formal planning. It is latent in all decisions." There is certainly a lesson in this for the strategist who hopes to reform bureaucratic processes.

Such action may require sweeping changes. So be it. There is no point in attempting to revive organizational cadavers. Irrespective of how achieved, educational organizations tomorrow no less than today will need to develop organizational climates in which teachers and pupils, lecturers and students will not merely be told they are free, but will in fact *feel* free to teach, learn, and research in a climate in which those two compulsive absentees from Australian education—creativity and audacity—might tip-toe in, take their seats, and flourish.

3 The Government School

Introduction

Professor Walker's thesis is that our educational institutions today are complex organizations with all the features of bureaucracies—rational efficiency, rule by experts under a hierarchical structure operating according to definite rules and regulations and standard procedures.

The success of these educational organizations is measured in terms of the growth or changes brought about in individual children. And the chief agent in ensuring this growth is the individual teacher. But the complexity of the organization, its rules and procedures, do not favour the kind of pupil-teacher relationship or administrator-teacher relationship that is necessary for the most effective teaching and learning.

To improve the organization so that creative teaching and effective learning can occur he sees the "core tasks" as:

1. Reconciling needs of individuals and the goals of the administration
2. Distribution of power and authority
3. Resolving conflicts
4. Adaptation to changing situations
5. Revitalization.

My task is to apply this thesis to state education departments and schools under their control, and to show whether these improvements are being made or can be made in these bureaucratic organizations.

The examples in this paper will be taken from the Education Department of South Australia.

We agree that state education departments in their organizations have the features of bureaucracies, but we also believe that these organizations have evolved as the best available method to achieve the educational goals—to see each child develop to his full stature—of the society that has produced them according to the values it holds.

In response to historical and geographical facts, Australian education has developed these structures which have been criticized by visitors from other countries, where in turn they are proceeding to produce similar organizations. "The greatest single obstacle to revamping of education lies in the fact that control of schools is in the hands of thousands of local boards", says a Texan.[1]

We agree, too, that inherent in complex educational organizations there are features that can well react against the creative teacher, but that means are available to alleviate the problems or eliminate these negative influences on educational goals.

Why have state school systems been set up and given their present structure?

State school systems have been established over the years and assumed their present form because the people of the state saw that the objectives they had for education in an increasingly complex and growing society could not be achieved if left to the individual entrepreneur. The marshalling of the scarce resources in finance, equipment, skills, and creative energy and their disbursement through a vast but thinly populated area in the interests of children's educational development needed a structure and organization.

In the words of Corwin the need was for "a stable pattern of interaction among coalitions of groups having a collective identity, pursuing interests and accomplishing given tasks, and co-ordinated by power and authority structures".[2]

As these state systems have developed they have acquired their own dynamism and mechanism and the following favourable features:

1. An efficiency in disseminating education justly over wide geographical areas with economy of effort and within the resources that the community is prepared to provide
2. Great expertise in a hierarchy of officers performing special functions

3. Rules and regulations concerning rights, responsibilities, and duties built up not only from precedent, but from research, experiment, and advice from specialist officers and groups, which are in the main acceptable to all involved in the educative process
4. Impartiality in making appointments and reaching decisions affecting children in the schools coupled with a minimum of conflict
5. Means of identifying and rewarding the innovative teacher.

They also have certain unfavourable features:

1. In achieving efficiency over a whole state, some standardization and sameness accrue—set texts, lesson plans, and teachers' handbooks which support the conforming teacher and restrict the lively teacher and consequently his pupils. Effectiveness in that what is achieved is done with the full committal of all concerned is lost. The inert structure has inherently in its makeup the capability of cramping the exercise of diverse talents of individuals within it.[3] A system that demands efficiency runs the risk of stifling ideas by demanding conformity rather than experiment and change.[4]
2. Through its size, hierarchical structure, its rules and procedures, its rationality and impersonal decisions, it can easily become static, and teachers become passive and spiritless. This should never happen in an educational organization which by reason of its purpose is committed to the notion of change in individuals and in society.
3. The rules and procedures become ends in themselves, rather than means to educational ends, leaving no room to bend the regulations when professionally desirable. The question of why these rules exist ceases to be asked.[5]
4. Upward communication from the teacher becomes more difficult as the organization grows, and the teacher feels that he is not participating in the construction of policy. He feels that he is no longer valued by the organization and he has no incentive to proceed with his own life-long learning, a prime function of all schooling.
5. Other bureaucracies can limit the effectiveness of the education department. The South Australian Education Department under a Minister of the Crown operates within

the state public service, and the majority of its teachers are members of the South Australian Institute of Teachers. The Public Examinations Board and the Universities also have a restricting effect. While these institutions are ostensibly complementary organizations, they can in fact be in opposition to and in competition with the Education Department. For instance, the following position could arise: the Public Service Board sees teachers' aides in schools as expensive; the Education Department sees them as necessary to make effective use of teachers in the interests of children; the Institute sees them as an insufficient service not providing enough relief to teachers, or possibly sees them as an intrusion into the professional field by unqualified persons, with deleterious effects on teachers' status. The influence from these other organizations can push individuals into unacceptable behaviour leading to defensive decisions by the Education Department and eventually rigid application of regulations.

How education departments bring about changes

The processes needed for change in education have been classified by Clark and Guba as Research, Development, Diffusion, and Adoption. The criteria on which the changes are judged are validity, feasibility, intelligibility, impact, adaptability, effectiveness, continuity.

Let us consider on these grounds the introduction of modern mathematics into South Australian primary schools.

The basis for the change was the *research* of Professor Z.V. Dienes and its validity was checked against the opinions and judgments of mathematicians and educators the world over.

The *development* was carried out in two demonstration schools, where its feasibility, viability, and impact were tested.

Diffusion was carried out through the snowball effect of in-service training, particularly of consultants who trained other teachers to be consultants. They put the work into intelligible booklet form for teachers and children and consequently showed its credibility, and built conviction in the course.

Adoption is nearing completion in some grades with the production of text-books for children and their universal use in these grades.

We must not overlook the alienating forces that inhibit or even thwart such a change. The mere size of the project, the number of widely spread schools and teachers involved, invite attempts to fragment and thwart the change. But this project shows bureaucracy at its best. Because of its resources and facilities in communication the change has been achieved with the greatest economy of effort and little disruption.

The change has been effective in that it has been accepted by all teachers who have been brought into active participation at all stages. The parents, too, can attend Adult Education classes and evening sessions provided by the schools to give them an understanding of the new mathematics. Nothing is hidden from them. They, too, are brought into the exercise.

What has the Education Department of South Australia done to improve its organization to undertake the five "core tasks" set by Professor Walker if the bureaucracy is to meet the challenges ahead of it?

Reconciling the needs of the individual and the goals of the administration

The South Australian Education Department has been reorganized into five Divisions under a Director-General of Education and a Deputy Director-General of Education. The Divisions under Directors are Primary Education, Secondary Education, Technical Education, Teacher Education and Services, and Administration and Finance.

The Director-General, the Deputy Director-General and the five Directors meet regularly at a Management Conference. It is an advisory body, as by Act of Parliament the ultimate responsibility for decisions rests with the Director-General. But it affords an opportunity for horizontal communication as well as upwards and downwards communication. The whole service can see itself as a whole.

Each Director speaks for the teachers in his division and he is given the opportunity to see that departmental policy and objectives are acceptable to and consistent with the needs of teachers as individuals. The professional officers are sure to watch the procedural policy of the Administration and Finance

Division to see that they do not cut across the professional freedom of teachers and the interests of children.

The individual teacher has the right to communicate through the orthodox channels or directly to the Director-General.

The Publications Section to be set up in terms of the reorganization, too, will provide another medium for communication of ideas both up and down in the service. An official *Gazette* contains largely downward communication, but an Educational Magazine can provide opportunity for communication from teachers to administrators as well as from administrators to teachers. Other publications will be composites of ideas and ideals of both teachers and administrators. At present a supplement to the *Gazette* carries reports of pilot studies and researches by teachers such as team teaching, programmed learning, and assessment of progress of classes studying alternative courses.

The members of the Management Conference also conduct massive public relations exercises when groups of headmasters and teachers are met face to face for question and answer and for suggestion and counter-suggestion for adoption or rejection.

In-service education touching three-quarters of the teaching service annually is not a one-way affair. The annual In-service Training Programme of the Department, involving approximately six conferences a week, one of which is residential, is developed through a representative In-service Training Advisory Committee which ensures that in-service education meets the real needs of teachers who tell the administration what kind of courses they need. I shall mention a few of these— Improved Liaison between the Inspectorate and the Teachers' Colleges, School Administration for Deputy Headmasters, Regional Conference of Craft Teachers to Associate with Industry, Resources of Raywood for Nature Science, Production of an Alternative Secondary Mathematics Course and a Handbook for Teachers.

From each conference there is a feedback by means of a report. Again, the experience of teachers living in residence at the In-service Centre with administrators assists in reconciling different points of view, and in making objectives coincide.

The Getzels model has been fed widely to inspectors in an attempt to have them review their human relations with

teachers, to headmasters to analyse their relations with assistants, to teachers to see relations with pupils laid bare. This conceptual model, too, has been made more useful for our purposes by adding arrows at the behaviour end to show:
1. Desirable changes to bring about better behaviour, i.e. better human relations
2. The suggested means to bring about these changes. It is thus a practical instrument and not just a conceptual model used for theoretical analysis.

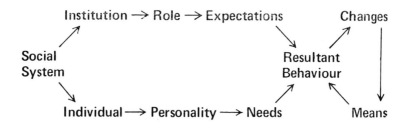

Headmasters, too, have been shown how to use the model for introspection, to analyse the conflict within themselves as representatives of authority in a bureaucracy and as professional persons. For instance, regulations concerning leave and rules for supply of equipment are expected by the bureaucracy to be followed specifically and in all cases, but the professional in a headmaster urges him to bend the regulations and rules to meet deserving individual cases.

Teachers holding half-time release scholarships for a year are brought into the central administration half-time to share in it, to work with the people involved in it, to offer advice concerning it and to return to the schools to tell their colleagues that administrators share their aspirations.

Distribution of power and authority

The new organizational structure of the Education Department means much delegation of authority from the Director-General to the Directors of the Divisions—approval to employ, to travel, to experiment, to vary time-table, to implement curriculum, and so on. In the reorganization there is provision for appointing two regional officers who will have delegated authority to transfer staff, to incur expenditure to certain levels, and to make decisions on educational needs in schools under their control in particular geographical areas. They will be focal points for communication near to the source, the teachers in the field.

In-service training conferences are asked to end the conference with recommendations to the Director-General. Hence, individual teachers in representative groups have the power and the authority to recommend changes in policy. At these conferences teachers share in setting the goals and planning the activities in which they are to be interested participants. For instance, one conference to plan a new mathematics course for slow learners in secondary schools involved an agriculture teacher, a primary teacher, a social studies teacher, mathematics teachers, a headmaster, a teachers' college lecturer, and an inspector.

Raywood Conference Centre represents an invitation to all to share in profound changes in teaching and administration of education, but offers no guarantee that they will come about, for it is still much easier to be authoritarian, defensive, and repetitious than it is to be liberal, versatile, a sharer, and a learner. Nevertheless, the following statement from a craft teacher after attending a residential course augurs well: "For the first time in all my years of teaching, I have been made to feel that I am a partner in a great enterprise."

More and more authority is given to headmasters to make decisions on staff, curriculum development, their equipment and building needs. The administration, too, wants headmasters to solve their problems with parents without reference to them.

Resolving conflicts

Conflict encourages innovation; it generates uncertainties and spreads ideas, and means that more than one group is at work looking for solutions to problems.[6]

How does the Education Department set about resolving conflicts that occur between teachers and administrators or Teachers' Institute and Education Department, or Public Service and Education Department, or Universities and Education Department, and hence create conditions that favour acceptable behaviour by all parties and lead to good teaching and learning?

Shephard and Blake[7] suggest some solutions:

1. Develop relationships between and within these groups
2. Generate mutual confidence and trust
3. Share responsibilities and control, and depend on one another
4. Use bargaining and problem-solving methods to reach compromises.

The South Australian Education Department uses all of these methods to seek out the cause of conflict and to resolve it. It has teacher representatives on all of its boards—the In-service Training Advisory Committee, the Teachers' Classification Board, the Teachers' Appeals Board, the Teachers' Salaries Board, Boards of Studies of the Teachers' Colleges Diplomas in Teaching, all Advisory Curriculum Boards and Subject Sub-committees.

Induction courses for new inspectors, teachers, college lecturers, and others make these people aware of the significance of discussion and representation, or in other words, the importance of adequate communication in resolving differences.

The Public Service Board, the Education Department, and the South Australian Institute of Teachers, have different priorities for various matters important to teachers and children. These are resolved by discussion, with the benefits to children as the basic criteria on which any compromise is reached. Informal lines of communication, too, are used to inform the groups and reach compromises. Headmasters and administrators, too, are conversant with the Guba-Getzels models and extensions by Thelen for dealing with community relations and the influence of pressure groups within our society, with its particular customs, traditions, social and moral values.

Methods of dealing with particular pressure groups vary with the social and industrial pattern of a country. For instance, relations between a Director of Education and teachers in Scotland, where there is a General Teaching Council but no Teachers' Appeals Board, must be different from those between a Director-General and his teachers in Australia where statutory Appeals Boards exist. The different pressure groups and, indeed, members within pressure groups will have different views on the role of the administrator and have different expectations about any particular problem. The administrator can solve them by sound administration—good communication, frequent consultation, clear thinking and delegation, and keeping the good of children ever before him. His decisions, then, may not always bring affection, but they will bring respect.

Mutual confidence and trust is enhanced by face-to-face discussion and using informal channels of communication. This comes about when the man at the top is a technical-generalist, and a man who has come through the ranks and the system and is known widely and well. In the Australian setting the top administrator who comes from another system is not usually a "viable proposition".

This mutual trust is brought about by setting up liaison committees, for instance between the Inspectorate and Teachers' College Lecturers, between the Education Department and the Public Buildings Department, between the Education Department and the South Australian Institute of Teachers, and between the Education Department and the Public Service Commissioner's Office. Barriers between parties holding conflicting views, too, dissolve at residential conferences under the influence of propinquity and other solvents.

Representatives of the University of Adelaide, Flinders University, the Education Department, and independent schools met for an informal weekend at the Raywood Residential Centre to deal with the thorny problem of matriculation. Not only were points of view known to all at the end of the conference, but the gaps between them had closed considerably.

The *bargaining and problem solving methods* are used to resolve conflicts. The expanded Research Office in the reorganization of the South Australian Education Department will provide personnel and a framework for problem-solving. In the bargaining process any Education Department policy affecting teachers is, in its planning stage, submitted in draft form to the South Australian Institute of Teachers and to the Public Service Commissioner if it is likely to run counter to public service regulations. The differences are finally resolved at a conference.

The Land Acquisition Committee has among its members representatives of the State Planning Office, Transport Authorities, Highways Department, and Engineering and Water Supply Department, as well as educationists.

In short, efficient communication with everyone who may have a stake in any decision is the best method of resolving conflicts.

Adaptation

How does a state education department adapt itself to changing ideas, ideals, and environment?

The climate for change and adaptation is certainly hastened and facilitated by a large and diverse programme of in-service education and the possession of a residential conference centre.

As far back as 1955 Professor Freeman Butts told us: "The vitality of education rests in the long run upon the vitality of the public opinion that supports it."[8]

Consequently a centralized system of education must embark on a massive public relations programme, to get parents' goodwill and make more effective use of talents of teachers and pupils.

The two management instruments available to facilitate adaptation to change are *decentralization* and *delegation*. The two methods available in the schools are *action research* and enlightened *inspection*.

In this paper you have seen the proposals for decentralization and increased delegation.

Action research and *inspection* are indispensable for teacher growth, and teacher growth is fundamental to any change in education.[9] Recently South Australia has taken steps to liberate the inspector and liberalize inspections. Assessment has become biennial and is shared with the headmaster. In terms of this paper, his role as a representative of authority is reduced and his role as a professional valuing the uniqueness of each teacher is heightened. The inspector can now show genuine educational leadership.

Teachers, too, are encouraged to experiment in the classroom, for the liveliest teachers are those who participate in innovation, enquiry, and change, and they will be enthusiastic if they know that their pioneering endeavours will assist other teachers. Teachers' college lecturers have been seconded to schools, full-time and part-time, to carry out special classroom research such as study habits, creative craft, physical education and music, matriculation biology and seminar methods in English. Teachers have been enthused and in primary schools alone over one hundred projects worthy of attention by press and television are in progress.

The reformed Research Section and Publications Section will assist to disseminate the results of teachers' own classroom investigations and will, we hope, bring about adaptation of the system.

Revitalization

New life is always being added to a state education department; it is always evolving, for teachers are people, and people staff our schools, people plan the curriculum, people teach it, and if something needs to be done about our system it is done by and through people.

The top decision maker is a person; if he is a corner-cutter, a risk taker, one who trusts teachers, a man of sharp judgment or reliable intuition, a man with insights and creative imagination who grasps the crux of an issue, and a good communicator, the climate for new life in the system is set.

If he uses teamwork across lines of responsibility to advise him on problems, help him reach decisions and to share his worries and aspirations, he develops an atmosphere of freedom, confidence, and cooperation far removed from the classical rule by a hierarchy in a bureaucracy. Indeed, many of the strengths and weaknesses of a bureaucracy result from people and not from structure and procedures. The man is just as important as the power of the position he occupies. He must be selfless, and use his power only to seek the effective achievement of the goals of the organization.

He must create an open climate and accept advice and criticisms from anywhere—the parliamentary question, the parent, the teacher, and influence groups. He must tolerate disagreement, he must let teachers know that he appreciates creativity, he must plan to get a regular flow of ideas from teachers, he must endeavour to make schools exciting and adventurous places. He must at all costs avoid in his bureaucratic role being insulated from people and losing contact with schools and teachers.[10]

To use the current word, he must demonstrate his authenticity, which will make him acceptable to a wide range of people holding dissident views.

But perhaps it is the nature and quality of leadership in the final analysis which contributes most heavily to the final character of bureaucracy.[11]

The education department, to perform its true function, the dynamic growth of human beings, must be more than an organization, it must be an organism tingling with life. "If the leadership has a fresh view-point and one that is attuned to social forces and social change, then there is at least hope of carrying the bureaucracy along with it."[12] To keep it charged with life the man at the top must be at one time both educationist and administrator. To encourage learning he must administer people rather than a system. As South Australian headmasters have been told by their top administrator, "You will get freedom till it hurts".

A.J. DAVIES

4   The University

Organizations, some say, have no utility in themselves. In general, they are instruments designed to assist us in the realization of desired ends or values. They need not be valued in themselves; indeed they may be negatively regarded and yet be accepted as necessary to the age or the culture. They may be accepted as part of the "system", just as most of us accept taxation because by paying taxes we buy civilization (or so Mr. Justice Holmes claimed).

Universities, in our Western culture, *are* valued institutions. If ideas mean power then universities are power houses. Moreover the power of these ideas penetrates and permeates an international society. For example, Weber's ideal type of bureaucracy has influenced generations of scholars and organization men. In the ideological sense universities are essentially non-bureaucratic. Where bureaucracies conform, universities criticize. The spirit of critical enquiry is a fundamental feature of the ethos of a university.

Bureaucratic organizations typically are hierarchical in their authority system. Universities, as far as their academic community is concerned, are collections of peer groups organized in departments, faculties, or schools. Academic policy is supposedly a product of departmental discussions and faculty fraternals. The Professorial Board is a peer group laying down educational guide-lines and supplying advice on academic matters to the legal sovereign, the University Senate or Council. The Vice-Chancellor, to paraphrase Walter Bagehot, represents the buckle which clasps the legal governing body to the professoriate, while he simultaneously heads the "administration" (the university bureaucracy).

The preceding paragraph is normative or prescriptive in tone, as is much of administrative theory. Bureaucracy, like beauty, may lie in the eye of the beholder. To the clerk in the fees office, to the student complying with enrolment procedures, to the supervisor of university examinations, to the catering officer or the library officer or the deputy gardener, the university may appear to be just as bureaucratic (in the Weberian sense) as the high school, technical college, or hospital. In the large Australian metropolitan university, e.g. Sydney, Melbourne, or Brisbane, the individual student in a class of hundreds foregoes the educational experience (mentioned in Professor Walker's paper) of interaction with the individual teacher. What could be more impersonal or anonymous, or more likely to engender in the student the feeling of being a very insignificant cog in a vast teaching machine? Has the traditional community of scholars been transformed into the "degree factory"?

Here we may state the obvious: the term "university" does not denote a uniform type of organization, even in Western society, and it does not imply an identical organizational "climate". An example from West Germany will illustrate the point:

The student population more than doubled in the fifteen years from 1950 to 1965, from about 120,000 to 250,000; this situation led to a terrible overcrowding of all university faculties ... The expansion took place primarily in the large urban universities like those in Munich, Cologne and Hamburg, where the anonymity of student life aroused much complaint; on the other hand, the older traditions of student social life—including alcoholic conviviality and the revival of duelling—remained strong in small university towns like Marburg and Heidelberg.[1]

In Australia alcoholic conviviality and duelling are not necessarily found in small university towns, one reason being that the University of New England at Armidale is the only autonomous university institution located in a relatively small centre of population. The same university is the only one in Australia which is fully residential respecting internal students, although La Trobe University in Victoria is proceeding on the basis that all staff and students will be affiliated to or live in one of the ten colleges planned to be built. Fairly clearly the type of organization required for a fully residential university is likely to differ from a university such as Sydney where only a fraction of the student body lives in college, and where the enrolments number some 17,000. There is not necessarily "one best type" of organization equally suitable to realize the purposes of all universities.

Britain, in Oxford and Cambridge Universities, has systems of administration unlike all other British universities. There is nothing bureaucratic about the following description of Oxford's administration:

In a real sense . . . the University is controlled by the whole academic staff. They directly elect to the main administrative bodies, and the authority of those bodies is delegated from the sovereign assembly, Congregation, which also retains a right of review which can be exercised with great freedom. This democratic structure, though it has its roots in the long history of the University, is closely related to the autonomy of the colleges.[2]

One further reference from the Franks Commission Report on Oxford University will emphasize the informal nature of its institutional arrangements:

This change in relationship between Council and the colleges [on methods of joint working] has not been given any institutional form. The constitutional framework remains unaltered and the new patterns of co-operation in policy and action depend for their existence and success on the will to make them work rather than on any administrative or constitutional basis.[3]

One suspects that the organization of Oxford University is an administrative theorist's nightmare. We quote the example to emphasize that organizations must be related to purposes and place. There is one allied matter which arises here and that is the question of organizational membership. Corwin's definition of a complex organization, quoted by Professor Walker, referred to "a common identity". Professor Walker reminded us that organizations are "systems not merely of structure, but of *humans*". All university graduates are members of the Convocation of their university. To the extent that they retain their feeling of common identity they may be regarded as members of the university, and many of them continue to support their alma mater through financial and other means. In this respect universities conform closely to Etzioni's concept of normative institutions relying on ethical and moral involvement of their members. Even when many of these members have physically departed the campus they remain emotionally, morally, and legally linked—like officers on the reserve list. The latter analogy is defective however because a reservist officer can be recalled to the colours whereas the member of Convocation can scarcely be coerced to support his university; he supports it because he thinks he ought to do so. Indeed, even university "drop outs" may continue to identify with their university as in the reputed cases of those who write "B.A. (failed)" with pride after their names.

One marked dissimilarity between universities and bureaucracies of the Weberian ideal type is that the latter are run by trained, expert administrators whereas universities typically do not have trained professional administrators in the top positions. As Dr. J. A. L. Matheson, Vice-Chancellor of Monash University, Victoria, put it, "the government of universities is, by and large, government by amateurs".[4] This government by amateurs is a characteristic also of the Australian and British cabinet systems and, to a lesser degree, of the administrative class of the British civil service in which Oxford and Cambridge graduates predominate.

Presthus' The Organizational Society and the universities

What are we to make of Presthus' hypothesis that in any organization the role incumbents may be classified as upward-mobiles, indifferents, and ambivalents? One criticism is that the typology does not fit well with Etzioni's theory in *Modern Organizations* of the dichotomy between administrators and professionals in organizations and their different attitudes towards "authority". Some observers of organizations have found that differences between administrators and professionals arise from the distorted image, the stereotype, which each holds of the other, the "failure to understand and accept each other's roles and codes of behaviour".[5]

Most students at universities would be upward-mobiles because education is a valued social good and universities are prestige institutions. Some students are indifferents who try to skate through their courses at the bare pass level. The ambivalents of an organization, Presthus says, are idealistic, independent, often introverted, honouring "theory, knowledge and skill". They represent a challenge to conventional wisdom and to bureaucratic authority. This prescription could apply to some good, honours students at university. The objection could be raised that Presthus is not considering students as members of the university considered as a big organization. But students are subject to the university's systems of authority (both professional and bureaucratic) and they contribute in many ways to the corporate life and the public image of the university as a social institution. It is not uncommon for a representative of the students to be a member of the University Council in Australia. Students assess the performance of their teachers (the reverse is also true). Student newspapers and societies help to socialize their fellows. Students participate in college government. Students in sporting activities contribute to the public "image" of the university. At New England University students are represented on the Student Health Committee, the Sports Union, and the Union Board. Moreover in all Australian universities the numbers of postgraduate students are growing, being expected to exceed 10 per cent of total enrolments by 1969 (according to the Third Report of the Australian Universities Commission, 1966). Perhaps the relationship of the student body in the university in terms of Presthus' categories will provide a theme for useful discussion.

What of the university academic staff and Presthus' tripartite membership classification? At first sight university administration appears to be conciliar rather than bureaucratic. Decisions are taken and policies are evolved through a process of discussion in a network of committees, councils, meetings, boards, and subcommittees. Not all professors wish to profess only. Some professors and non-professorial staff have (or consider they have) a flair for administration, including the ever-present task of fund-raising. Professor Harry Messel of Sydney University is a case in point. There are seeds of conflict within universities among academics over the allocation of resources between teaching departments or schools, between teaching and research, between Science and Arts, and between academic goals and overall university goals. For example the A.U.C. Committee on the Future of Tertiary Education in Australia (1965) noted that the percentage of professors to sub-professorial staff in state universities had declined from

21.3 per cent in 1939 to 9.5 per cent in 1962. It commented:

One cause of hesitation in the establishment of multiple chairs in a department when funds are limited is the competition between the two ideals of an improved staff-student ratio and an improved ratio of senior staff to junior staff. It is natural for an administration to hesitate to provide multiple chairs when the cost of one chair might provide two lectureships or three tutorships; but an adequate proportion of senior staff should be maintained, if necessary at the expense of the arithmetical staff/student ratio.[6]

If an academic conforms to the administration's view that multiple chairs should not have priority over additional teaching staff at non-professorial level is he behaving as an upward-mobile? In one sense he is because he is identifying with the administration, he is fusing his personal goals with the administration's interpretation of overall university policy. In another sense he is not because he is denying the prospect (or at least the immediate prospect) of his own personal ascendancy in the hierarchy of his discipline. Our feeling is that Presthus' categories are too sweeping. Surely the type of behaviour exhibited may vary with the particular situation, i.e. the person who is upward-mobile on one issue such as university salaries, may be indifferent on another such as student parking, and he may be ambivalent and anti-administration on a third issue such as an easing of standards of matriculation entry. On reflection this may mean that most academics, viewed over time, are ambivalents because Presthus claims that the ambivalents oscillate "between defiance and submission".[7]

Presthus writes of "the" bureaucratic situation and the three personality types which he associates with it. It is not clear how one differentiates between a bureaucratic situation and a non-bureaucratic one, especially in a university. Even in a governmental bureaucracy, the classic case envisaged by Weber, people do not behave as do ideal Weberian types. Government architects, like their non-governmental confrères, have a habit of obtaining their own way despite the "authoritative" commands of their clients, including university administrators.

A more serious criticism of Presthus' theory is that he does not appear to allow for group loyalties and influences within his large organization. One is reminded of Herbert Spencer's

Man Versus the State. Presthus' individual confronts the organizational colossus without apparent realization that his professional association, his trade union, his learned society, his faculty, his department, his graduate seminar group, his Staff Club, his Senior Common Room, are all group instruments for abating anxiety in institutional life. In a university peer group recognition and status seem to be powerful factors in shaping individual norms. If indifferents refuse to compete for the organization's favours it may not be because they "develop their major interests *outside* the organization" but rather that they are more concerned with their department or their faculty or their school as the prime focus for loyalty and support. A university, it has been said truly, is a complex organization containing many interacting organizations within a moving perimeter. Yet Presthus recognizes this fact because he says at one point: " . . . big organizations are composed of many subhierarchies, each bound together by authority, interests and values in a way similar to the total organization."[8]

If our criticisms are valid then there appear to be internal contradictions in Presthus' work which reduce its expository and explanatory value.

Universities as organizations

Organizations involve both cooperation and conflict between the individuals and groups which constitute them. Organizations exhibit regularities of behaviour, recurrent patterns of action and interaction, and a degree of independence from other organizations and their environment. Universities began as "an association of scholars and teachers who formed themselves into a sort of guild to regulate and protect their profession of learning".[9]

On conflict, the present Vice-Chancellor of Macquarie University in Sydney has had some interesting comments on his former University of Sydney (founded in 1852).

I was led to think of the time when the University of Sydney was new: of the controversies, the manoeuvrings, the formulation of rival principles, the invocation of different models and precedents, the clash of great personalities and the oratory that were its beginnings . . . There were struggles between ecclesiastics and secularists, conservatives and radicals; contentions about the balance between general liberal education and professional training, about the relations between the university and society, about the extent of opportunity that should be held out to young people of a university education.[10]

These conflicts were between academics, between professionals, not between administrators (bureaucrats) and academics. Control of the top echelons of an organization by former academics rather than by non-academic administrators does not necessarily mean less conflict and more harmony over goals and purposes. For these goals and purposes of the organization have to be defined and re-defined in operational terms. The consequence is that, as Etzioni has said, "Organizations are social units . . . deliberately constructed and reconstructed to seek specific goals".[11] Reorganizations (formal or informal), as all political scientists know, are difficult to implement because they disturb existing power relationships and "vested interests". They alter (or attempt to alter) the role-expectations of the constituent groups and individuals. Gouldner's study of strategic succession in the American gypsum plant, discussed by Professor Walker under the sub-head of "Collaboration", illustrates the point that organizational changes may have (and almost certainly will have) unintended or latent consequences. Good research as a preliminary to action and an intelligent communication structure will help in reducing organizational conflict but will hardly eliminate it. Only when conflict reaches a critical level will it threaten organizational survival. Of course different individuals and groups within the overall organization may have their own conceptions of what constitutes a "critical level". New South Wales public school teachers have been agitating for an education commission for more than twenty years, but successive governments have disagreed on the existence or nature of the crisis (and on the proposed remedy). Because teachers in schools and lecturers in universities are the line operators, the "cutting edge" of their organizations, in the long run our expectation would be that their views must be heeded by organizational leaders. But in a bureaucratic system authority lies at the top of the structure and short-term problems tend to take precedence over long-term innovation.

Whether universities are primarily bureaucratic organizations (in the Weberian sense) or not (and this author's view is that they are not, although some parts or sub-systems may be) they are, like schools, conservative institutions. Universities are governments of designated academic communities and

Any system of government which has been a going concern for many generations is permeated by long-developed attitudes, the results of all those political, social and professional factors which colour and shape institutional reactions.[12]

If it is agreed that universities are largely non-bureaucratic organizations, the fact remains that Australian universities are very similar, excessively similar as the Federation of Australian University Staff Associations put it a few years ago, "in scope, organization and methods". Why? F.A.U.S.A. suggested that universities were acting as "service stations" for the schools, that heads of departments combined control over teaching and administration (exhibiting oligarchical tendencies in the process) and that "the traditional professorial board [is] too large and too cumbrous to operate as a policy-forming body".[13]

Complexity of administration: Some comments on Etzioni's approach to organizations

To what extent is a university an organization with a normative compliance system relying on the moral involvement of its members? The answer will vary from university to university. Within a university some members will participate primarily because of remunerative considerations—one's family still has to be fed, clothed, and amused. Universities are organizations in competition not only with each other but with many other organizations for scarce, highly competent human resources. Is the orientation of University Staff Associations calculative or moral? Probably it is a mixture of both.

Schools and universities are culture-type organizations but the compliance structure of many schools is coercive and the involvement of many members is calculative. Most pupils are compelled to attend school, most students want to attend university. In other words it does not appear as self-evident to us that schools are "predominantly *normative, culture-type organizations, with coercion in varying degrees as a secondary pattern*".

Schools could probably be arranged along a scale ranging from normative at one extreme to coercive at the other: where the majority of schools would be found along this continuum would be likely to vary from region to region, state to state, country to country. We agree that schools *should* be primarily normative institutions, but are they? One must take account of *The Blackboard Jungle* as well as *The Loom of Youth*; of the authoritarian headmaster as well as the democratically inclined principal and the laissez-faire subject master. One must allow also that "schools" means anything from a one-teacher unit to the complex, comprehensive type and that the vast migrant intake has added to the complexities of educational organization (in the U.S.A. as in Australia).

Universities vary in complexity between themselves, e.g. the University of California dwarfs the University of Papua-New Guinea, but the same example illustrates that the nature of administrative problems is not just, or even primarily, a question of relative size. Practically any university involves much greater complexity of organization and problems than any kind of school. This seems evident if we accept the Hage-Aiken measure of "complexity" as the number of occupational specialities, the degree of professional training, and the amount of professional activity.[14] Greater complexity and greater professionalization is usually accompanied by greater decentralization of decision making, according to scholars such as Victor Thompson and Alvin Gouldner (cited by Hage and Aiken). If we accept this proposition then any university by its relatively greater complexity is likely to be more decentralized in its organization and administration than any school.

Yet even if we accept the above view the situation of Australian universities at least in terms of educational efficiency and excellence has been judged as less than optimal by at least one historian who is now a Vice-Chancellor. Professor Auchmuty, Vice-Chancellor of Newcastle University, has written of Australian university government: "The dominance of chancellors and senates, the influence of governments, the comparative weakness of academic bodies like the professorial boards, have resulted in a certain diminution of the true value of university education."[15]

To say that organizations are governed by professionals

rather than by administrators, that professionals have the primary decision making role and administrators the secondary one, helps us to classify types of organizations (including bureaucratic organizations). But to understand universities as educational organizations more fully we need to know *which* professionals decide and to *what ends* and with what degree of *feedback*, both inside the university, within the wider academic community, and within the society. Etzioni's theory, as others have remarked, is a partial theory of organizations, not one which explains the totality of organizational life.

Conclusion

In the Australian context the actions of Commonwealth and state governments towards universities and the shape of universities as organizations have been influenced greatly by the "appreciations" (to use Sir Geoffrey Vickers' term) furnished by the Murray Committee (1957) and the successive reports of the Australian Universities Commission (since 1959). If laying down general rules, common principles, regulating new developments, controlling growth patterns, emphasizing rational planning of buildings and courses, are the attributes of bureaucracy (accompanied by the associated paper work, approval and veto power and designation of "appropriate" staff-student ratios), then due to Murray, A.U.C., and governmental influences Australian universities today are more bureaucratic than in the pre-1957 era. Whether they are more audacious or more creative is an open question. There is greater political interest in them because they are absorbing a greater share of the public purse. There is also a greater integration of their activities and interests through the development of national academic and administration organizations such as the Australian Vice-Chancellors' Committee, the Australian Academy of Science, the Social Science Research Council, the Australian Humanities Research Council, the National Union of Australian University Students, F.A.U.S.A., and the Australian and New Zealand Association for the Advancement of Science.

Weber's theory of bureaucracy assumed that people would know what was going on in their organization, why it was happening, that functional responsibilities and lines of authority would be clear and rational, that the whole organization would be well articulated. In a university it is difficult to know who or which body decides what policies or is authorized to take which actions and what remedies are available to those who disagree. Weber's theory of bureaucratic organization assumes that policies are received by the organization (from governments, politicians, legislators) but much policy in all organizations is made internally. In universities many of us do not know the details of the administrative processes, and those who know the formal machinery may be ignorant of how power and decision making is shared in practice. Academic freedom may be interpreted as freedom not to involve ourselves with all that administrative work. Yet many of us may feel empathy with Professor Matheson who said of the organization of the University of Manchester, "It took me years to find out how it worked".[16]

Weber also assumed that people belonging to a bureaucratic organization would accept decisions because they came from above and therefore were (supposedly) rational and legitimate. But as Professor Matheson has also observed of universities the fundamental premise is lacking: " . . . there is no unanimity at all about the objectives and the purposes of universities."[17] Of course, a university is not the only organization to which this lack of clear goal definition applies and even when objectives are agreed there remain the difficult administrative problems of interpretation and of priorities. Professor K. F. Walker points to another lion in the path of organization practitioners and theorists in universities when he states: "It is very difficult to get any kind of objective measure at all in the case of universities, as the effectiveness of a university cannot be measured for generations."[18]

If then it is difficult to agree on objectives, on priorities, and to measure whatever it is that the organization is supposed to produce, it will not be surprising if we argue over the type of organization (or organizations) most likely to satisfy the community of scholars, students, and administrators within the university as well as the wider public associated with it.

Some goals and values are attainable only through organized effort: that is why we have a state, governments, pressure groups, political parties, and many other types of organizations.

Weber was wrong in claiming that a bureaucracy is the most efficient type of organization for all purposes. Before we can be efficient we have to agree on what we are to be efficient about. Modern administrative aids like computers and machine accounting can assist in building factual information as premises for judgment. Bureaucratic methods (in the value-neutral sense) can assist in the effective and expeditious execution of decisions. But bureaucratic standards rigidly applied to academic work represent the kiss of death, not the breath of life. Individual discretion, professional discretion, departmental discretion, faculty discretion, all point to a decentralized organization as preferable to centralized organization insofar as academics are concerned. The key questions are the limits of these discretions and who shall determine them (and review them) and what form of organization will preserve and sustain relative academic freedom with an efficient use of university resources (including time). Because the U.S.S.R. has a six-day formal working week in its universities it does not follow that Australian, British, or American academics (with no such formal requirement) will or do work for less than a six-day week. But if an organization where members value academic freedom attempts to prescribe a minimum work load or "darg", group pressures are likely to transform the minimum to a maximum. In any event the whole notion of prescribed work loads assumes that the organization must force (coerce) its members to work whereas the whole rationale of university staff is that they work because they want to—they are well-motivated; their vocational values are internalized. Any ordering of university life must be based on some such conception of academic freedom as that expressed by Sidney Hook: " . . . the freedom of professionally qualified persons to inquire, discuss, publish and teach the truth as they see it in the field of their competence, without any control or authority except that of the rational methods by which truth is established."[19]

Finally, it is worth reminding ourselves that a good deal of the rigidity and conformism of university behaviour is due to the jealousies and empire-building tendencies of some academics and some departments which display the classic bureaucratic attributes of hierarchy, specialization of function, written rules and regulations, careerism, and impersonality. Decentralization of organization may be dysfunctional when it operates in a mean and narrow manner to stifle originality and the spirit of critical enquiry. Some of the newer Australian universities, such as Flinders, La Trobe, and Macquarie, are experimenting with new forms of academic organization. The advent of Colleges of Advanced Education, Institutes of Technology, and the Institute of Colleges (in Victoria) leaves little doubt that the future will continue to involve the universities in searching problems of appropriate areas of teaching and research and of appropriate organizations to serve Australia's revolution of rising educational expectations.[20]

Part Three COMMUNICATION IN EDUCATIONAL ORGANIZATION

5 An Overview

A message will select its audience before it affects its audience.[1]

Over the past ten years there has been a veritable explosion of interest in the behaviour of people working within organizational frameworks: factories, hospitals, prisons, individual schools or whole school systems. This paper will direct attention to but one aspect of behaviour within educational organizations: the problems involved in the sending and receiving of messages.

Here we enter a very complicated and still barely understood field of human behaviour. However, it is now generally agreed that the communication process can be analysed into a finite number of basic elements,[2,3] viz.:

1. The sender
2. The purpose of the communicator in sending the message
3. The encoding of the message
4. The channel along which the message flows
5. The receiver
6. The receptive tuning of the receiver
7. The decoding of the message
8. The interpretation of the message by the receiver
9. The response of the receiver
10. Feedback from the receiver to the sender, i.e. some evidence that the message has been received.

Figure 1 might help to clarify the relationship between these several elements. This diagram can be read horizontally when the communication is between friends or those on the same status level in an organization. It can be read vertically when the two are superior and subordinate in an organization or are in some power relationship the one to the other (such as father and son). We must remember, however, that here we are

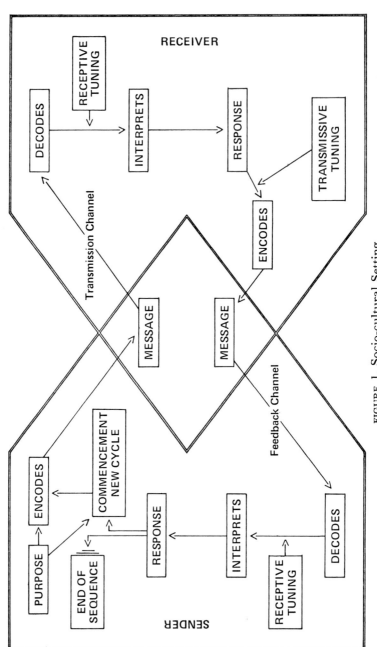

FIGURE 1. Socio-cultural Setting

concerned with behaviour of people within an organization; and here a further complication arises because communication acts can be described as either formal or informal.

By formal communication is meant the use of the established organizational channels by which decisions flow down the hierarchy from level to level and through which reports flow up the hierarchy. Included in informal communication is discussion about the implication of these decisions or reports amongst people both at the same or at different levels. A lot of informal communication will also be of a personal nature and will flow freely amongst friendship groups—just chit-chat which might or might not be about the job in hand. For purposes of analysis the two can be differentiated and separately mapped and discussed, but no organization can work without both.

Discussion in this paper will focus mainly on some aspects of formal communication within education organizations but before we can gain any real understanding of this facet of organizational behaviour it is necessary to look carefully at some characteristics of the organization within which people behave and communicate. Otherwise we are faced with a buzzing booming confusion in which messages and noise are so conglomerated that it is difficult to make much sense out of it all.

*   *   *

In the analysis of an organization the conceptual system of Talcott Parsons[4] is an indispensable tool. Parsons differentiates three qualitatively different levels in the structure of hierarchical organizations: the institutional, the managerial, and the technical levels of activity. This approach has been developed further by Haberstroh[5] who refers to the entrepreneurial, the organizational, and the operating levels. The terms to be used in this paper will be selected from both these sources: when discussing school systems it seems most appropriate to refer to the entrepreneurial, the managerial, and the technical levels.

The *entrepreneurial* level refers to those positions within the organization whose incumbents are centrally involved with the relationship between the organization and the publics outside the organization. Obvious examples of such positions are the American District Superintendent of Schools, the English Chief Education Officer, in Australia the Director-General of Education and heads of independent schools. (This does not mean that no one else in the organization ever engages in entrepreneurial activities.)

The *managerial* level is centrally concerned with the administration of the internal affairs of the organization and the work of those occupying these positions will be directed mainly towards mediating between policy decisions made at the entrepreneurial level and the technical level. Australian directors of primary and secondary education, inspectors of schools, and all school principals are clear examples of such positions.

The *technical* level is comprised of those whose work is mainly at the productive face of the organization—the salesmen, the miners, the teachers. Those filling technical positions are expected to possess the knowledge and skill necessary to bring plans made at the entrepreneurial level to fruition.

This is where Parsons' analysis stops, but when the organization being analysed is a school system and especially when attention is being directed to communication within that system, there would appear to be very good reason for adding yet another level. This might be termed the *production* level at which plans made at the higher levels are actually put into operation. We are now right inside the classroom and the main communication concerned is that between teacher and pupil. Why is it that in education the administrative chain is so often not followed below the technical level? Why do administrators often appear to behave as though they thought that once a teacher knows the job to be done, then it will be done? How much of our so-called "in-service" training has this assumption behind it? Whether or not you agree with the appropriateness of these questions, the fact remains that many who write on educational administration show a curious reluctance to go beyond the classroom door.

In any education system, then, there are these four levels of activity through which decisions might have to pass before reaching the production level. And now we return to Parsons for still another insight into what happens as these decisions are communicated downward. As they move from one level to the next there is a qualitative break: they must be reinterpreted and rephrased in terms of the activity appropriate at each successive level. This is where blockages and misunderstandings occur and when such questions as "just what does this mean in terms of my behaviour?", "what does this ask of me?" have to be faced and answered.

We can see now that in a school system there are at least three qualitatively different types of communication activity, each of which demands a qualitatively different type of receiving and sending skills. A person who proves adept at one level might not necessarily be so at another; conversely, because a person is unskilful at one level it does not necessarily mean he will be unskilful at another. We can also see why it is that the position a person occupies in the organization will determine his perception and interpretation of incoming information.

Parsons' approach to organizational analysis is molar. Other analysts are more concerned with characteristic ways in which individuals react to "organizational press", that is the demands made upon a person merely because he works within the system. Here the work of Presthus is of prime significance.

As Walker pointed out in his position paper Presthus[6] postulates (and he has supporting empirical evidence[7]) that there are three main modes by which individuals adapt to organizational press: the upward-mobile, the indifferent, and the ambivalent modes.

The upward-mobiles are those who identify with the aims and value system of the organization; they actively seek the rewards it offers to its successful members—bonuses, promotion, and such like. Their orientation is towards pleasing their superiors, their morale is usually high, they might generally be described as "ambitious", they think in strategic terms.

The indifferents seek self-realization outside the organization and are unmotivated by its reward systems, they are immune to appeals based on commitment to organizational values. Loyalty is not included as an ingredient of their membership.

The ambivalents are those who would like to be able to accommodate in an upward-mobile fashion but who are prevented or precluded from doing so by a lack of understanding of the appropriate ways to attract the organization's rewards or by their failure to do so for reasons that they either cannot accept or cannot comprehend. Ambivalents find it difficult, even impossible, to think in organization-wide terms. They can be highly competent in their own task area and cannot see why this in itself does not earn them recognition as being promotion worthy. Often they cannot believe that those who are promoted really merit their reward and speak of them in terms of "pull" and "apple polishing".

This analysis by Presthus can be integrated with Parsons' multi-level concept of the organization since presumably all three of Presthus' adaptation modes may be found in persons occupying positions at all levels of the hierarchy. In figure 2 this is shown at the technical level only, but this is merely to prevent the diagram from becoming too cluttered.

The implications of Presthus' work for the understanding of communication within an educational organization are clear: any message will be perceived and reacted to in accordance with the mode of the receiver's adaptation to the organization. We could look upon these three adaptation modes as producing three different maps of reality which guide an individual's orientation towards everything that happens in the organization. The upward-mobile, for instance, will tend both to send and receive communications in a way that he perceives as maximizing his status and demonstrating his promotion worthiness. In doing this he will demonstrate those tactics of ingratiation which have been so interestingly investigated by Jones and his associates[8,9] and which are briefly described in another paper.[10] The indifferent will both receive and send in a way that either least affects his own comfort or which expresses resentment at the possible disturbance of his extra-organizational life. The ambivalent's reception is likely to be suspicious and fraught with an anxiety that verges on the neurotic; he will be prone to question the motive behind any communication from a superior, especially if it is directed to him personally. One of the most difficult tasks any administrator has to face is to attempt to communicate to an ambivalent the reasons why he has not been promoted in seniority in the system.

Schools and school systems belong to a family of organizations which are marked by the fact that the workers within them are both employees and members of a profession involving a group

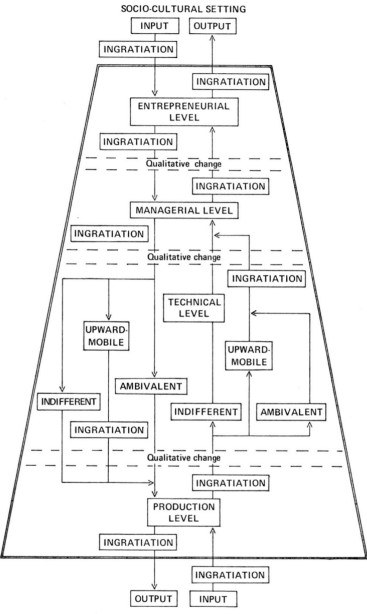

FIGURE 2. Contamination of Vertical Communication
in a Hierarchy

of people much wider than any individual organization. In a study of this state of affairs Gouldner[11] drew attention to two further modes of adaptation in the behaviour of professional employees: these he termed the local and the cosmopolitan. Locals are those who are committed to the immediate organization and who accept its value and reward system. They are interested in acquiring and manipulating power; they see success as the gaining of promotion up the hierarchy; they may be equated to Presthus' upward-mobiles. Cosmopolitans gain their satisfaction and rewards by achieving recognition from their professional peers rather than from their organizational superiors. Their decisions are on professional criteria rather than on organizational expediency. Such people are very often uncomfortable working within bureaucratic organizations and will resist receiving and acting on communications which they see as transgressing their area of professional action.

Walker has referred in his position paper to one of the most recent investigations into organizational adaptation, that of Dan Griffiths and his associates.[12] This study has particular significance because it was carried out amongst teachers in a school system. From an analysis of their data they present four modes of adaptation by teachers in the schools of New York City. About one-eighth of the teachers proved to be GASers because their main motivation was Getting the Attention of Superiors. These were clearly much the same as Presthus' upward-mobiles and Gouldner's locals and could be expected to receive and send communications in a way that showed all the ingratiation tactics discussed earlier.

The majority of Griffiths' sample, about two-thirds, he described as *pupil-oriented*; they wanted to stay in the classroom and shunned promotion to administrative and supervisory positions. (In interpreting the New York situation we must remember that the overwhelming proportion of the teachers were women.) A further 5 per cent of teachers, mostly in secondary schools, were *subject-oriented* and tended to move horizontally rather than vertically throughout the organization until they found either a congenial teaching position (with bright pupils and good facilities) or, if they were scientists, left teaching for industry. A further group of 15 per cent were *benefit-oriented*. These were content to continue teaching so long as it did not make too many demands on their time and energy. They also moved horizontally through the organization seeking a "good deal" where an adequate salary and comfortable conditions were available at the minimum effort on their part. Perhaps we could at least tentatively equate this group with Presthus' indifferents.

It still remains to be seen whether or not Australian teachers react in the same ways as this New York group. It probably depends somewhat on whether they are men or women or whether they are teaching in primary or secondary schools. It is, for instance, interesting to speculate about the fate of the recommendation in the Wyndham Report that "class teaching in a homeroom might be organized during first year".[13] This message has not been "heard". Is it because secondary school teachers are essentially subject-oriented?

Whatever the situation in New South Wales, it is not hard to understand why a memo from the principal which simply says: "There will be a Staff Meeting at 3.45 p.m. on Monday 26th at which a change in the method of teaching reading in the school will be discussed" will be received by members of staff in markedly contrasting ways and with different "noise" levels. For the practising administrator the problem becomes one of how to keep these noise levels at a minimum.

One of the most significant discussions of this problem is that by Gibb[14] who has analysed two contrasting climates of administrative action: defensive and supportive. In the context of this paper they may be termed "clear communication" and "noisy communication" climates and are contrasted along six dimensions that are worthy of some thought. The clear climate is characterized by:

1. Description rather than evaluation, e.g. the use of nonjudgmental expressions in supervision of and reporting on staff

2. Problem orientation rather than control orientation, e.g. putting the problem squarely rather than telling what to do

3. Spontaneity rather than strategy, e.g. being natural rather than "clever" or devious

4. Evidence of empathy rather than neutrality, e.g. showing respect for individual worth rather than taking an impersonal approach

5. Accent upon common task rather than superordinate status: the "Let us" rather than the "I instruct you" approach
6. Open to argument rather than a show of certainty, e.g. the aim is to solve a problem, not win an argument.

Likert[15,16] also has some very interesting things to say about the relationship between the administrative style of an organization and the clarity of the communications within it. His conclusion is that "participative" administration produces less noise than exploitive or benevolent authoritative styles and less than a consultative style.

A fuller discussion of the analyses of Gibb and Likert would take us deep into administrative theory and into the consideration of the results of research into administrative behaviour. It would not be out of place here to refer to Bassett, Crane, and Walker's publication *Headmasters for Better Schools*[17] where there is a discussion of participative administration.

Up to this point the paper has been discussing some of the factors that could aid an understanding of the problems surrounding vertical communication in a hierarchical organization. Nothing has been said about horizontal communication and, indeed, the tendencies to underemphasize horizontal communication and to underestimate its significance are fairly common. Yet it is by means of communication amongst organizational peers that the implications of communication from above (and below) are spelt out in operational terms. The "two level" conference is one way in which Parsons' "qualitative gap" can be bridged. Yet in school systems and even in individual schools, sub-organizations are allowed to grow up in virtual isolation from each other. The almost inevitable result is the appearance within the organization of subcultures and the fostering of loyalties towards subgroups and of commitment to subgoals rather than to the organizational goal. When this happens, each subgroup extracts a different meaning from communication they receive.

Australian schools and school systems have many examples of organizational fracture and fragmentation. There are Secondary Schools Divisions and Primary Schools Divisions, each with its own hierarchy, its own salary scale, its own sense of identity. The boundaries between the two can be so strong that they have very little communication with each other and consequently no strong sense of a common mission. The basic philosophy behind, say, the teaching of Oral Expression in the primary school could conflict with what is recommended for the secondary school. Such conflict is bound to happen unless horizontal communication between the two is not only encouraged but provided for by the planning of formal links and channels through which it can flow.

This same comment applies equally to all levels of the organization—directors, inspectors, principals, teachers, and even pupils. Principals' conferences and teachers' conferences, especially when any change is planned, are an essential part of the goal achievement strategy of the organization. For such conferences to be held in working hours is certainly no waste of time.

Yet, important as horizontal communication is for the organization's efficient and effective goal achievement, there are in many schools serious barriers against it. What Lortie[18] calls the "egg crate ecology of most schools", the absence of adequate common rooms, the geographical separation of school buildings, all militate against the flow of horizontal communication. The principal faced with a fragmented school plant has a major problem of vertical communication in his hands, but he should not be misled into thinking that this is his main communication problem.

One of the weaknesses of the bureaucratic organization is that it virtually ignores the importance of horizontal communication. It seems to be a fact that wherever superordinates have (in Thibaut and Kelley's[19] terms) either "fate control" or "behaviour control" over subordinates, teamwork is discouraged. (Fate control is a situation in which A can affect B's outcomes regardless of what B does. Behaviour control is a situation in which A can make it desirable for B to vary his behaviour.) What is encouraged is a positive diffidence to communicate "good ideas" to peers because to do so would be to abandon an advantage over one's colleagues when one is being considered for promotion to a coveted scarce senior position. Some upward-mobile, local, GAS teachers are markedly uncommunicative and tend to guard their classrooms as fiercely as a magpie guards her nest. In such an organizational atmosphere, attempts to introduce team teaching are destined to be stillborn.

So far we have been concerned with discussing some of the organizational factors which vouchsafe some insight into the complexity of communication within an organization, but this is by no means the full story. The organization also communicates with its surrounding publics, and there has recently appeared one of those stimulating theoretical analyses which is destined to become the basis for future empirical work. Litwak and Meyer[20] have presented a set of hypotheses concerning the relationship between the modes of communication between schools of various administrative styles and the community surrounding these schools.

This analysis categorizes administrative styles as rationalistic, human relations, professional, autocratic, paternalistic, laissez-faire, and nepotistic. However, it is suggested that these seven styles have but three approaches to school-community relationships: the "open door", the "closed door", and the "swinging door" approaches. By the last it is meant to imply that their communication mode is such that social distance can be reduced or increased at will based on a decision as to what is best for the school as a whole or for an individual pupil. Balanced relationships, they argue, are more likely to occur where the administrative style is professional. Litwak and Meyer also present a series of hypotheses concerning the most likely communication mode for any administrative style. For example, if the school is autocratic, communication is likely to be by means of mass media and common messengers (i.e. pupils taking information home). If you are wondering what other modes there are, could it be that in Australia we have accepted a certain administrative style so completely that we find it hard to conceive of the possibility (or at least the practicability) of other styles?

In attempting to understand the complications surrounding communication in educational organizations, we must keep firmly in mind the fact that "reality" is defined in different ways by different people. The school the inspector sees might not be the school the principal or the kindergarten teacher sees. Here, in a nutshell, is the endemic problem of communication.

P.W. HUGHES

6   The Government School

Any organization depends for both its existence and its usefulness on the clarity and effectiveness of its communication. This is especially true for an educational organization whose purpose is essentially one of communication: communication of the knowledge, skills, attitudes, and values felt to be desirable in the society represented.

The paper by Crane, interesting and valuable as it is, may even underrate the importance of its topic. The sending and receiving of messages is more than "but one aspect of behaviour within educational organization",[1] it is the central and most important aspect of behaviour. Another organization may still produce satisfactorily in spite of poor communication: good communication, on the other hand, *is* the desired product of an educational system and to fail here is to fail completely.

An educational organization, of whatever kind and size, is one which defines certain goals of desired student outcomes, and which seeks to achieve these through the processes of communication. The goals themselves relate to the needs of the individual and of society, and it is important for both individual and society to understand the goals, to agree with them, and to appreciate their relevance. All this occurs through the processes of communication, which are thus involved in both ends and means in education.

This paper will first comment directly on Crane's paper and then comment more generally on some of the issues involved for education departments.

The paper itself gives a thoughtful and detailed study of organizational theory. The comments on Berlo,[2] Presthus,[3] Talcott Parsons,[4] Griffiths,[5] and Gibb[6] include valuable summaries of the various analyses and models relating to organizations and the people of whom these are made up.

The most difficult feature, however, is the relationship sought between these analyses and the actual problems of communication in an educational organization. This relationship is general and tentative and allows very little of significance to be drawn as conclusions which relate to practice: very little, that is, which could not have been drawn from a more pragmatic approach. This is not to say that the approach is not valuable. The value lies, however, not in direct implications for practice but in introducing a theoretical framework which, through analysis and experiment, may eventually lead to useful conclusions.

The distinction made by Crane between formal and informal communication could well receive further emphasis. Formal communication is institutionalized, i.e. carried on according to established rules and procedures or explicitly recognized practices. While the direction of flow is principally vertical, there is also a substantial horizontal communication in formally established channels. Informal communication may be verbal in nature, or else a matter of informal social groupings, and of attitudes that are conveyed in non-verbal form. This form of communication owes little to established rules, or official channels, but is made through friendship groupings and may be expedited by such liquid aids as the tea-break or the club setting. As Crane has indicated,[7] "no organization can work without both"; the wise administrator will seek to use both forms for the promotion of organizational goals.

Crane has used a combination of the systems of Talcott Parsons[8] and Haberstroh[9] to describe the different levels in the structure of hierarchical organizations. Parsons' levels—institutional, managerial, and technical—have been linked by Crane with those of Haberstroh—entrepreneurial, organizational, and operating—to define four levels—*entrepreneurial, managerial, technical,* and *productive.* The distinction made between technical and productive levels does not seem entirely clear. It may be that the reference is to the distinction between the communication between principals and teachers at the technical level, and the communication between teacher and student at the productive level. In view of the comments on in-service training this may well be so, yet it is doubtful if such a criticism would be a valid one. In-service education for teachers is directed increasingly at changing behaviour, rather than simply changing knowledge.

In the discussion of hierarchical levels, the relevance of Talcott Parsons' institutional level deserves more detailed treatment. There are distinctions between this category as defined by Parsons and the entrepreneurial level in the sense used by Crane as those "centrally involved with the relationship between the organization and the publics outside the organization".[10] It would seem that a treatment of the institutional level may have been intended as separate from the entrepreneurial level, since Crane mentions "four levels of activity . . . before reaching the production level".[11]

Crane continues with two treatments of characteristic reactions to organizational press. Presthus[12] postulates three modes of reaction: the upward-mobile, the indifferent, and the ambivalent. Griffiths[13] identifies four modes of adaptation: GASers or Getting the Attention of Superiors, pupil-oriented, subject-oriented, and benefit-oriented. Crane identifies the upward-mobiles with the GASers, as those who tend to send and receive communications in a manner designed to maximize their own status and improve their own prospects. This seems too simple as an identification, lacking any of the complexity of actual human motivation. Upward-mobiles could presumably consist also of those whose motivation is, largely or partly, associated with the goals of the organization as well as with self-gratification.

This criticism may be irrelevant, since models of this kind are deliberate simplifications, designed to give a form to use for investigation. Nevertheless, some further consideration of the models would have been helpful. In consideration of the worth of such categorizations, two concepts from psychological measurement may be of use: reliability and validity. It would be of value to examine the reliability in a variety of educational and national settings, i.e. the extent to which agreement was obtained between different judges in their placing of persons in categories. The validity concept would relate to the extent to which the categorization permitted the prediction of defined types of behaviour in various situations, either concurrent with or subsequent to the categorization. The extent of such empirical testing of the accuracy and meaning of the categorizations is much too limited at present. Such a testing would make unnecessary the criticism of the categorizations as a matter of opinion. However, till this is done, such criticism is justifiable. Certainly such divisions as those by Gouldner,[14] into local (organizationally oriented) and cosmopolitan (professionally oriented), would seem at this stage too broad and undifferentiated to bear much resemblance to reality. In this regard, Gibb's[15] work on administrative climate shows much more promise and it would have been helpful to see this linked more definitely to the difficulties of communication.

As mentioned above, the major contribution of Crane's paper is in its analyses: of the processes of communication, of the structural levels within organizations, of the modes of response of persons within organizations, and of the climates of administrative action. The implications to be drawn from these analyses are necessarily limited. They relate to the occurrence of different levels of interpretation of messages, the high probability of "interference" with the messages and "noise" associated with them and the probability of "crossed lines" which result from a network of formal and informal communication within the organization.

The most evident implication for administrators is simply a realization of the possible distortions inevitably associated with their messages. This realization should lead the administrator to predict what kinds of interpretations will be placed upon such communications at the various levels, not merely to guide in the coding of messages but to enable the use of formal and informal channels to aid in the attainment of the goals of the organization.

It is evident that the present state of knowledge concerning the structure, processes, and personnel of organizations does not provide a sufficiently sound basis for such prediction and action as are clearly necessary. It does, however, provide the prospect for such a basis. In no field could it be felt more necessary than the education systems of Australia.

The views held on the state education systems owe more to slogans and stereotypes than to objective analysis and investigation. On the one hand they are pilloried as vast juggernauts without human concern, necessarily evil because of their centralization of authority and their size. On the other, they are upheld as the necessary instruments for obtaining both efficiency of administration and, more importantly, equality, and quality, of educational opportunity on a state-wide basis.

It is time the slogans and stereotypes were set aside, and the possibilities and difficulties of central state systems examined more objectively. Until a great deal more information is obtained, opinion must reign supreme. Such information, however, needs to be gathered on the basis of some framework of theory if it is to be of value in the formulation and testing of hypotheses. Aimless gathering of statistics can be of very limited value only. The paper by Crane is a useful beginning in a consideration of theory that may be of use.

There is, on the other hand, a growing body of information. A case in point is the paper by Sergiovanni,[16] reporting a New York investigation on the situations (and reactions to them) which teachers had felt to be particularly satisfactory or particularly unsatisfactory. The factors described in the first category were achievement, recognition, and responsibility, i.e. factors closely related to the teacher's actual work. The major factors described as unsatisfactory were interpersonal relationships with teachers, supervision, school policy and administration, personal life, and unfairness, i.e. those which focus on the conditions of work, but what might be described as the personal relationship conditions rather than the physical conditions.

A recent, as yet unpublished, investigation in Tasmania with a sample of some 655 teachers, is another example. A list was presented of some 65 problems experienced by teachers, classified as follows: Salaries, Promotion, Administration, Communication, Conditions of Work, Teacher Training, Human Relations, General. Space was left in each category for teachers to add three problems of their own devising. Teachers were asked to grade each of the problems on a 4-point scale ranging from "Not Severe" to "Very Severe", and also to indicate which of the problems listed was "Most severe of the very severe problems". Of the 17 problems rated in this way as being the major concerns, 3 related to Salaries, 1 related to Promotion, 1 related to Administration, 1 related to Communication, 6 related to Conditions of Work, 5 related to Teacher Training, none related to Human Relations or to

General. Only 27 teachers indicated any problems outside those listed as "Most severe of the very severe". The sources of dissatisfaction then, as in the New York study, related mostly to Conditions of Work and scarcely at all to Communication or Human Relations. The one problem identified under Communication was that of "Insufficient liaison between primary and secondary school staffs".

A number of such investigations has been made. The gap is obviously not in this direction but in the background of theoretical development which would permit the data to be related together.

At present administrators, whether in large state systems or in individual schools, do not have a verified body of theory on which to base their procedures. They must act on the basis of a mixture of intuition, tradition, common sense, and personal preference. The theory of administration is even more in its infancy than is the theory of instruction, which is gradually taking form. Papers such as the one we have considered, and conferences such as we are attending, can do much to contribute to the needs in the field. As research and analysis continues, however, it is important to remind ourselves that in education organizational structures and procedures are dispensable. The important elements are the purposes and the persons involved. Organizations exist for the achievement of certain aims and must be judged by the achievement of those aims and not by their success in enshrining particular forms or practices. The aims, however, must include the development and well-being of individuals and of society. However convenient it may be for us to use labels such as GASers or upward-mobiles, we are not dealing with categories but with human beings of almost infinite variability and of quite infinite value.

7 The Independent School

Not only is communication absolutely essential to organization but the availability of particular techniques of communication will in large part determine the way in which decision-making functions can and should be distributed throughout the organization.[1]

Whether one subscribes to the organization theory implicit in the above statement, accepts that communication exercises considerable control over decision making and that it is more important than hierarchical position in terms of furthering the objectives of an organization, it is certain that communication plays an important role in ensuring that the purposes of the organization are served and desired action or behaviour is obtained. Crane's paper wisely draws attention to many of the complications inherent in communication in educational organizations.

He first deals broadly with four levels of structure in an organization system (one of them somewhat arbitrarily though, as will be discussed later, reasonably included) and suggests that corresponding to these four levels are four types of communication activity. At each of these levels, individuals are subjected to "organizational press" and by citing the study of Presthus[2] he draws attention to three main ways in which individuals adapt to this "organizational press". The significant point here would seem to be that communication from a superior within an organization will be affected in accordance with the mode of the receiver's adaptation to the organization. Studies by Gouldner[3] and Griffiths[4] are also cited to lend weight to the argument that in any organization there are different modes of adaptation apparent in the behaviour of professional employees and these differences will have considerable influence on whether messages are "heard" or acted upon.

As well, the climate of administrative action within an organization will have an effect on vertical communication, and here Gibb's[5] analysis of "defensive" and "supportive" administration is cited to draw attention to "clear" and "noisy" communication climates which may exist in an organization.

Crane also draws attention to the importance of horizontal communication and suggests that lack of adequate communication channels of this nature can often lead to conflict and to organizational fracture and fragmentation. One difficulty involved in establishing satisfactory horizontal communication is that in bureaucratic organizations the importance of horizontal communication is either deliberately ignored or else the nature of the organization discourages it. This, he argues, is because "fate control" or "behaviour control" are antipathetic to good communication in that the control over subordinates is too strong.

A further complication to which Crane draws attention is the problem of communication between the educational organization and its public. Whilst there are probably several differing "styles" of administration, he suggests there are basically only three types of approach to the public, categorized as "open door", "closed door", and "swinging door", and that corresponding with certain administrative styles we have appropriate modes of communication. Whilst Crane's paper covers a wide range of communication difficulties, some of which are but sketchily referred to, there would seem to be considerable validity in the arguments, particularly in so far as they apply to the hierarchical structure of independent schools.

Before proceeding to a consideration of the implications of this paper as they apply to independent schools, one important point raised by Crane in reference to his analysis of administrative behaviour within the school organization specifically with regard to communication should be dealt with. He argues that "in education, the administrative chain is so often not followed below the technical level" and that "administrators behave as though they thought that once a teacher knows the job to be done, then it will be done". It is for this reason he includes a further level in the structure of hierarchical organizations as analysed by Parsons[6] and Haberstroh[7] which he calls the productive level. The argument here, though not supported by empirical evidence, does seem eminently reasonable and examples could probably be cited from the personal experience of headmasters. Why does this occur? It could be argued perhaps that headmasters, on the whole, believe that all teachers are professional in their approach, even though they may be frequently confronted with evidence to the contrary, and that teachers will, in general, act in a way which supports the organization. If this view is held, despite contrary evidence that teacher behaviour is often motivated by a number of factors not directly connected with organizational demands and that teachers are oriented in a number of ways,[8] is it because headmasters find it less complicated to pursue the administrative chain below the technical level and thereby avoid the risk of being considered unprofessional? Or is it because in educational organizations it is not considered necessary or desirable to make provision for the sort of supervision exercised by, say, works foremen in other organizations?

Without wishing to suggest that educational organizations ought necessarily to ape industrial or commercial organizations and employ supervisors at the "productive level" to ensure that the wishes of the administration are carried out, there does seem to be some need to examine more closely the operations which take place behind the classroom door. Probably many headmasters have been appalled to discover that a classroom teacher has acted in a way totally opposed to instructions believed to have been given clearly and concisely, and that information concerning such action has not been communicated to him until a considerable time has elapsed. Often such communications take the form of a complaint from a disgruntled parent dissatisfied with other aspects of the school organization. The question arises that if in our independent schools we appoint bursars or registrars to supervise the work of our ground, maintenance, or cleaning staffs to ensure that plans made are actually put into operation, ought we not also to employ similar methods where operations in the classroom are concerned? If we do this, who should act as supervisor—the headmaster himself, his deputy, the senior subject masters—and if the latter, what safeguards must be taken against the tactics of ingratiation which might be employed by the "upward-mobile, local, GAS" teachers who are most likely to be appointed as subject masters? Is the only solution to this interesting and disturbing problem raised in Crane's paper to develop what

Halpin calls the "informal way of knowing" and to develop as Crane[9] suggests, a "sensitivity to subtle cues and nuances of expression and behaviour, a second sight that detects both in himself and in his staff the tactics of ingratiation and the distortion that they introduce . . . " or do headmasters of schools need to borrow some of the administrative practices of other organizations and concern themselves less with the implications of a vaguely defined "professional approach"?

Let us return to the implications in this paper which refer specifically to independent schools. Because in almost all independent schools the headmaster has the right to hire and fire staff, the argument that his relationships with his staff must inevitably be coloured with what Thibaut and Kelley[10] term "fate control" and "behaviour control" would seem to carry some weight and it is probable that this relationship would tend to discourage teamwork. Furthermore unlike the situation which applies in state departments of education, opportunities for promotion within independent schools are limited and as well are very much in the hands of the headmaster who either decides or recommends promotion, or fails to do so. This factor must surely give weight to the argument presented by Presthus[11] and Parsons[12] that at each level of activity within the organization, i.e. entrepreneurial, managerial, technical, and productive, there are correspondingly four qualitatively different types of communication activity, and that messages will be perceived and reacted to in accordance with the mode of the receiver's adaptation to the organization. Thus we could expect a greater tendency in the independent system towards ingratiation, particularly in the case of the upward-mobile members of the staff who are interested in gaining promotion, and along with this phenomenon a marked tendency towards a qualitative change of communication and an interpretation of messages in the way in which the receiver thinks will please the sender. And yet in a hierarchical organization such as an independent school, it is very often with these upward-mobile members of staff or GASers that the headmaster will chiefly communicate, often because he is flattered by their seeming understanding of his problem or because their approach to the organizational problems would seem to be the most helpful. A further problem would seem to arise in the case of horizontal communication when, as the evidence suggests, these teachers tend to be markedly uncommunicative with their colleagues for fear that they will abandon an advantage over others when promotion is being considered. The dilemma for the headmaster would therefore seem to be that the teachers with whom he should logically communicate are likely to be less helpful than he imagines either in interpreting his messages or in spreading helpful ideas to their colleagues. How to overcome this would seem to be a major administrative problem, but at least if he is aware of the possibilities of the situation he will not be trapped into believing that all is well in his school and that his whole staff is "on side".

Another problem connected with horizontal communication which is raised by Crane's paper and which has direct relevance to independent schools is that there is often likely to be fragmentation of the organization when horizontal communication fails. Because of the comparative lack of mobility amongst members of staff in independent schools and the limited opportunities for promotion already referred to, older and more experienced members of the teaching staff tend to satisfy their desire for status by establishing an inner clique or "senior club" within the staff. This phenomenon is well known, I believe, to most of those who have taught in independent schools. Loyalties are more often then directed towards the subgroup and commitments are made to subgoals rather than to organizational goals. For instance, in the writer's experience, a verbal communication on his part to a group of sixth form English masters, on the subject of team teaching in English, was interpreted by two of the most senior men (both of whom had had over twenty years' experience in the one school) as implying that the object of the programme suggested was largely to allow younger men to show them how to teach—a clear illustration of commitment to the subgoals of seniority and comfort and a refusal to accept the organizational goal of more efficient instruction. This tendency to misinterpretation of a message would, one presumes, be more emphasized in situations in which the headmaster was not present to explain or re-phrase his communication. There would also appear to be a tendency for the subgroup to interpret the message in the terms in which they wished to see it and to pass this interpretation on to younger members of staff who might be only too ready to accept the interpretation of the more senior and "higher status" staff members. In this regard the point might well be made, though it was not mentioned in the paper by Crane, that "tactics of ingratiation" are also likely to affect horizontal communication in the hierarchical structure of the "common room" which is, in a sense, an organization within an organization, and when dealing with problems of communication it would be unwise to ignore this phenomenon which is a fairly common feature of independent schools. The study of Jones, Gergen, and Jones,[13] for instance, would seem to suggest that the line between leaders and subordinates is one firmly drawn within the organization and drawn chiefly by authority, but there may well be a less obvious but nevertheless important hierarchical structure drawn up in an organization as a result of custom and tenure which the headmaster should be aware of.

Another aspect of this fragmentation which is likely to be peculiar to independent schools is the frequent administrative division between senior and junior schools even when these exist on the same campus and Crane sensibly deals with this problem of breakdown in horizontal communication. In a study conducted by the writer[14] on communication within a private school it was found that though the senior and junior schools were separated spatially by only a few hundred yards, there was a serious lack of communication between teachers in these separate departments. A record of conversations on one day showed that there were only two conversations of up to five minutes held between members of the junior school and senior school staffs, both of them conducted by the head of the junior school, and there were no conversations of longer than five minutes between members of the two separate sections. One member of the junior school staff stated that he felt that members of the senior school staff were "stand-offish". This view would appear to be confirmed by a study by Homans and Simon,[15] who observed that:

in general the attraction of persons to each other tends to be greater among those who are in spatial locations that promote interaction, and liking tends to decrease sometimes turning to hostility as physical distance increases.

Whilst possibly the problem of spatial location can be overcome, there still remains the problem of providing adequate communication between two divisions of a school in which basically different work is being done. Crane's suggestions for overcoming the problem are eminently sensible and it would seem to be a most important requirement, particularly in independent schools with two separate departments, that horizontal communication be provided for by the planning of formal links and channels and by the holding of what he calls "two-level" conferences. In this way the whole education process can be furthered and misunderstandings between two departments avoided.

A most important point made towards the end of Crane's paper concerns communication between an educational organization and its public. This is a problem which has special application to the independent schools, dependent as they are on the "image" they present to the public. Though many headmasters of independent schools are acutely conscious of the need for presentation of a satisfactory image, in my opinion insufficient attention has been paid to this aspect of administration in terms of communication problems.

If it is assumed that independent schools operate on a fiscal policy that from one year to the next requires a stable enrolment, which at best can be either held at a certain level or at worst can be reasonably assessed by its headmaster, it follows that for successful operation the school must establish and maintain a satisfactory reputation in the community from which it draws its pupils. Put another way, because the members of the public have some sort of choice as to which independent school they will send their children to to be educated, administrative policy in an independent school must surely be geared towards preventing any appreciable drop in numbers from one year to the next. It will probably be agreed that the reputations of independent schools are too frequently based on criteria which have little to do with the sort of educative processes which operate in them. For instance, some members of the public may judge a school to be a worthwhile institution because its sporting teams win premierships, or others because its students generally wear their uniform neatly and correctly in public, and still others may judge a school to be unsatisfactory because they see some of its students misbehaving on public transport. The headmaster, knowing his school must establish and hold its reputation in the community, can be placed in an unenviable position if he is forced to accept these as the criteria for a good school (for he knows they have little to do with educational values), but on the other hand he cannot wholly reject them either if he is dependent on the attitudes of members of the community for success in recruitment. How then does the headmaster act in relation, say, to his parent body or "Old Boys' Association"?

If he allows himself to be too influenced by what some members of his public want, he will not be keeping faith with the educational ideals which (we presume) he holds, and if, on the other hand, he rejects the views of some of his public by showing impatience with their standards he is likely to reach a situation where no reasonable criticism will be brought to his notice for fear that he will be offended. In other words "the tactics of ingratiation" take over and he may shortly find himself in the position of knowing less about his school than he ought, and communication with his public may become more concerned with maintaining and enhancing the school's reputation by means which have little to do with education, than with providing a real educational service. In this regard, perhaps as Crane suggests "the swinging door" approach to community relationships may well be the most satisfactory approach—except that it is always difficult to know when to "swing the door"! The decision as to what is best for the school as a whole or for the individual pupil is not easy to make and is especially difficult when the headmaster's channels of communication with his public are such that feedback messages are distorted to please him. This view has been well expressed by Simon[16] who says

the possibility of permitting a particular decision will often hinge on whether there can be transmitted to him the information he will need to make a wise decision, and whether he in turn will be able to transmit his decision to other members of the organization whose behaviour it is supposed to influence.

What is the answer to this dilemma for the headmaster? Is it to make it quite clear that he has his own criteria by which his school should be judged, such as educational excellence, and that he listens to criticism only when these standards are in question? Or does he take the advice given by one headmaster[17] and say to his parents regularly:

This association exists to help the school in a number of ways and to provide for it things which the School Council cannot at the moment provide. Its carrying out of these aims elicits our wholehearted support and gratitude. But this body has no part in the running of the school or in the formulating of its policy: it has no voice to the School Council save the headmaster's voice. At such of its meetings as the headmaster may attend, he will find himself unable to listen in plaints and grievances, nor will he discuss the deplorable decline to young Alfred's Latin proses.

If the latter, then it is certain that no communication will exist at all between the institution and its public; if the former then at least he is admitting that certain communication of grievances is permissible and at least he is defining his objectives —an exercise which could be most helpful to both the administrator and his public.

So far attention has been directed towards the implications of Crane's paper for independent schools in general. It could be useful as well to consider the implications for a particular school, and to do this I should like to present an instance of a major administrative change initiated within the school of which I am headmaster, and endeavour to indicate some examples of failure of communication which led to administrative difficulties that might otherwise have been avoided.

Some time ago it was decided to change from a school day of seven periods of forty minutes to eight periods of forty minutes. The purpose behind this was largely to enable more time to be devoted to activities which, because of the comparatively short day, had been neglected. For instance it was intended to include an extra music period for some forms, an extra period of physical education, a long assembly in which time could be allowed for talks from visiting speakers, a "club" period in which students could indulge in activities of their own choosing, and in general to provide a little more flexibility in a rather tight daily schedule. Because of the importance of this change, a careful strategy should have been devised for presentation to the staff. However partly because of pressure of time, but mainly because of lack of knowledge of staff behaviour, this was not done. The outline of the scheme was discussed first with the Deputy Headmaster who sought permission to discuss it with a few of his colleagues. As might well be expected the upward-mobiles gave it support for the obvious reason that it was seen as a policy desired by the headmaster, the indifferents opposed it, probably on the grounds that the longer day interfered with their established programme (though this was, of course, never openly stated, their stated reasons being that it was "not really necessary"), and as could be expected, the ambivalents expressed no opinion. An administrative mistake made was in trying to explain the situation to a staff meeting of forty-two members in a limited time during a lunch hour, and the result was that considerable discussion, some heated, was evoked but no conclusion was reached. At a subsequent meeting the question was asked whether it was the intention of the headmaster to introduce the scheme, and if so, why he had bothered to spend time in discussing it. Eventually the scheme was introduced, but opposition was such in some quarters that support for the voluntary and non-academic aspects of the new time-table was at best grudgingly given, to the detriment of the whole plan.

As Crane suggests, several questions arise from this exercise in administrative change, such questions as: Would it have helped to have known more of the ways in which individuals adapt to organizational press and in particular which staff members adapt in different ways? Would it have been better to have communicated the proposed suggestion first to a small group who could exercise more influence by horizontal communication? Would it have been better to have presented the staff with the problem first rather than try to convince them of the wisdom of the solution? To what extent were the difficulties of communicating the values of the proposition impeded by the presence of subgroups and pressure groups within the staff itself? Undoubtedly many other questions dealing with the communication problems inherent in this single administrative action could be posed, but sufficient have been raised to indicate the complexities of communication and the relevance of the points made in Crane's paper.

Let me now attempt to sum up the particular implications of this paper by means of a series of questions which occur to the writer as an administrator who has to deal with communication problems each day.

1. How do I know whether vertical communication downwards has been acted upon as I would wish it to be?
2. What administrative action do I take to ensure that policy is carried out at the productive level?
3. How do I interpret vertical communication upwards? Am I aware of the upward-mobile, ambivalent, indifferent, and variously orientated members of my staff?
4. If I am aware of these particular qualities in staff members am I also aware of how this affects communication with them?
5. Have I built up a barrier against criticism of the school by the outside public? How much of what is told to me do I perceive as being affected by the tactics of ingratiation?
6. What methods are best for getting across new ideas to the staff?
   a. Full staff meetings
   b. Smaller subgroups
   c. Task-oriented subcommittees.
7. What administrative style do I employ? Is it autocratic, professional, paternalistic and if so is it the most appropriate style to the situation? Am I able and adventurous enough to try another style?
8. What provisions have I made for the improvement of horizontal communication amongst the staff? Am I aware of any spatial or physical barriers to horizontal communication?

Perhaps finally the crucial question would be for all headmasters to ask themselves whether they feel adequately trained and sufficiently well informed on the task of educational administration to deal with the complicated problems of running a school and particularly with the problems of establishing effective communication within it and outside it. In the light of the problems posed in Crane's paper, who would be foolish enough to answer in the affirmative?

8 The University

A true university, like most successful marriages, is a unity of diversities.

It is a truism that today's universities are complex organizations. Some understanding of their structure, and particularly of the changes taking place in them, is necessary before communications in them can be examined and understood.

Until quite recent times, and for many centuries of university history, university organization was very simple. The classical picture of one is of a student sitting on one end of a log and the teacher on the other. Communication was both direct and horizontal. To this day the official structures of organization and government reflect this simplicity and, in a legal sense, the difference between the teacher on the log and his modern counterpart is not great. It would, however, be a little hard to press this analogy with the student.

Though nomenclature changes and minor variations in organization occur, in the formal organization of universities in the English speaking world three important links with the past remain. Officially all teaching staff have the right and responsibility, either by direct participation or through representation by their peers, to have control over the formulation and implementation of academic policy—and anyone who has worked in a university knows that that word "academic" can, at times, embrace everything from muddy footpaths to the salary of a departmental typist. Through representation on largely administrative committees such as those concerned with finance, buildings, and management, the academic staff can extend their influence over practically every aspect of university life. Finally, as a community of scholars, it is a community of equals. Rank exists, but it is based on the criterion of excellence within a person's chosen discipline. While a lecturer may give due deference to a professor on the grounds of his quality as a scientist or scholar, in all other issues he recognizes him only as an equal. On the various boards and committees, the lecturer's voice is as strong as the professor's, his vote carries equal weight; if he wishes to criticize the professor he is free to do so and, if he is one of the ambivalents referred to in the position paper, he will almost certainly do so.

What are the implications for communication in this official and formal structure? There is every opportunity for communication to be continuous and both vertical and horizontal; channels of communication both for sending and feedback are direct and clear; sender and receiver are on the same wave length; in a community of fellows the purposes of communication are mutually understood and the need for interpretation and decoding minimal. It would indeed be fortunate if this paper could finish at this point. You might also say that it would be miraculous! In spite of the fact that members of universities form an elite body, and an elite in ways which one would expect to have considerable bearing on organization and communication, like other formal organizations they have not been particularly successful in conquering the non-rational elements of organizational behaviour. Universities, while not being hierarchical structures in terms of the criteria of Talcott Parsons or Haberstroh, suffer many of the communication breakdowns common to such structures.

An explanation of this and a key to the understanding of communication in universities is to be found in the concept of structural lag. This, as defined by Ronald G. Corwin, is "an inconsistency throughout the organization due to the fact that subparts change at different rates".[1] The social changes of this century, and particularly in the post-war years, have produced great stress both on and within universities. At the same time the traditions of centuries have acted as a fairly effective counterweight. The resulting pattern is one of great disparity between the formal, official structure referred to above and the actual structure, and a nice point is the way in which universities endeavour to function within the formal, traditional structure while trying to ignore the changes being forced upon them. The result is an interesting study in communication which must be looked at from the standpoint of three crucial developments—the influence of outside agencies on universities, the growth of an administrative section within universities, and the change in role of the academician.

Influence of outside agencies on universities

In today's universities there is no room for the lecturer sitting on a log. He now peers out over a sea of student faces in a large lecture theatre. He uses elaborate and expensive equipment devised and assembled by highly qualified technical staff working in very sophisticated workshops. Lecturers and students work in the equivalent of a large town with all the problems of government and finance that such would have. Support staff—technical, clerical, and maintenance—outnumber the teaching staff and the academic is likely to believe that they outnumber the students as well. Two factors emerge from this change: the entry of a third group, the administrators, to the team of teacher and student; and the obvious need for the financing of this large enterprise.

Universities, as Sir Eric Ashby has indicated, "serve local communities by supplying an international commodity—scholarship, science, technology, medicine—at international standards".[2] While Ashby invokes universities' maintaining their cosmopolitan traditions and international standing, it is well to remember that in this technical and scientific age and time of national rivalries, scholarship is also an important instrument in the national economy and in the development of national prestige. Governments are thus very interested in their universities. At the same time the commodity the university produces is extremely expensive, and the costs are not shared internationally but locally, largely by the government and by the not-too-understanding taxpayers the government represents.

The result is that, as universities lean more and more on governments for support, governments, in the interests of the taxpayers, require more and more accountability for the way in which money has been used—and it is accountability in terms that governments understand, not criteria which necessarily would be used within universities themselves. The upshot has been the growth of a veritable plethora of governmental agencies and instrumentalities dealing with universities. We in this university almost believe that we exist largely to service them. Such development is endemic too in the United Kingdom and the United States where state and regional coordinating and planning committees are well in evidence.

The growth of administration

The demand and interest of governments have contributed largely to the development of a professional administrative core within universities and this has led to a dramatic change in the authority and communication structure. The quantity and kind of information sought by governments and other bodies financing university activity are such as only a centralized administration could supply. Many, for example staff-student ratios, teaching hours, space utilization, were once purely academic matters, but these, together with budgetary matters and cost analysis are now very much at the heart of the administrative exercise. Sophisticated aids such as computers and institutional research units have been brought in to support the administration in its endeavours to satisfy these external pressures. As communication between the outside world and the university is through the central administration, and as the issues are usually vital to the survival and well-being of the institution, the administration has emerged quite suddenly as a powerful member of the triumvirate of teacher, student, and administration.

This development has been strengthened, too, as the administrator has accepted responsibility for the university's public relations. In this country, particularly in recent years, the "public image" of the universities has not been bright. Legislators have tended to regard them as highly expensive ways of training teachers, doctors, and other professional workers. Industrialists and men of commerce, usually self-acknowledged alumni of the "university of hard knocks", criticize them for inefficiency and high cost as well as for the scandalous behaviour of their students and staff. Though we in universities in our fairly extensive reciprocal dealings with these people remain unimpressed by the gloss and superficial efficiency of many industrial firms and with the endless demands by competing government departments for what can often be meaningless records and statistics, the need has been felt to polish up our public image. For better or for worse most universities have succumbed, and to the stable of specialists bolstering the administration has been added the public relations man. The administration, to use Cicourel's analogy,[3] has assumed a new and important function of being the organization's front, of presenting the official line and policy of the university to the public at large.

At this point it is important to identify the "administration", for it is a comparatively small elite group which does not encompass the mass of clerical, technical, and other specialist staff referred to earlier. Odd as it may seem, though the support staff is large in number they appear to play but an insignificant part in the affairs of the university. They seem to have been effectively cut off from the main stream of university activity by the conscious creation and maintenance of two elite groups— the academic staff and the upper echelon of administration. In the main they fit in closely with Presthus' description of indifferents or Griffiths' benefit-oriented, being primarily concerned with employment opportunities. In Australia negotiations with their employers are conducted largely through industrial unions rather than by direct approach. This does not preclude the occasional professor from turning all his technicians into gilded lilies who are over-worked and under-paid by a harsh administration, but apart from such odd exceptions it would be generally agreed that they play no significant role.

The administration core consists of the Vice-Chancellor, the Registrar, and their gate-keepers—graduate and professional staff who, because of their positions, in Selznick's words have "special opportunities for access to communication, for direct contribution to the most vital work of the enterprise, . . . for contact with outside groups" and opportunity to "affect the dependence of different parts of the organization on the good will of other parts as well as their relative ability to influence the evolution of policy".[4] To this group may be added a small number of academic staff who will be discussed later.

Change in the role of the academician

While radical changes have been taking place in the administration of universities, the organization and attitude of academic staff have also undergone change but it is not of the same magnitude nor can it be regarded to any great extent as an outcome of the other. Two forces of a very different order seem to be at work. These relate to the concept of structural lag previously mentioned, and to the degree and kind of participation of academic staff in university government and administration.

A characteristic of the administration in universities has been that as it has diversified its tasks it has brought in specialist labour to carry them out. Budget officers, statisticians, public relations officers, buildings officers, and a string of others support the administrative core. Probably because of the influence of tradition no such functional division of labour has taken place among the teaching staff. Rather has the role of the teacher been re-defined to encompass each new function. As Gross has pointed out, where once the main responsibility of professors was the teaching of undergraduates, now they are expected

to teach graduate and undergraduate courses, carry out research or scholarly enquiries and write them up for publication, provide consultant, advisory or other service functions related to their specialities, as well as advise undergraduate and graduate students, supervise doctoral theses, and serve on departmental, graduate faculty, and university committees.[5]

And, as has been indicated by Gross, in the reward system of universities, it is not the prime function of teaching but research activities and publications which merit most attention. To add to this confused situation, university budgets are geared to teaching rather than to research and members of staff requiring substantial support for research must seek it outside the university. Gross summarized the position as follows:

Caught in this nexus of multiple expectations and demands something must give. The patterns of response to these incompatible expectations are undoubtedly diverse, but my own observations lead me to suspect that the modal pattern for senior professors is to give minimum effort and time to their teaching responsibilities and greater attention to their research obligations and outside activities such as consulting.[6]

Thus, though academic staff talk of their university as being a community of teachers and scholars and at one level of thought believe that the actual and official structures are co-incident, the majority are, in the terminology of Presthus, indifferents in so far as their own university is concerned, or cosmopolitans according to Gouldner's designation. They regard themselves more as self-employed professionals, as members of a world-wide society rather than as employees of a particular state or national institution. Success and satisfaction are gained through recognition by their professional peers in universities throughout the world. They regard administration at times with suspicion but mostly with indifference. The administrators, striving to meet the demands of legislators and an uninformed public, are seen as seeking efficiency in its narrowest and local sense of achieving the greatest results with a given expenditure of resources. To an academic this has no meaning. Universities should be concerned with effectiveness— the degree of success in achieving the institution's objectives. The real outputs of a university meet cosmopolitan standards; they are neither short-term nor measurable but may well be the first casualties of the administrative type of efficiency.

A few, of course, enjoy university politics and in every university will be found a handful of academics who conform with Presthus' upward-mobiles or Gouldner's locals, seeking satisfaction and power within the institution. Thus these few upward-mobile academics join with the administrators to represent the "front end" of the university, being highly concerned about the values it embodies and the responsibilities they have assumed for the maintenance of these values. On the other hand the remaining academics form Cicourel's "back end"[7] of the organization, giving some lip service to the values enunciated, and at times becoming vocal about their rights, but in reality sharing only such goals, as Korten has pointed out, as "relate to maintaining routine functions necessary to maintaining the status quo and making adjustments to it".[8] This also helps in understanding the extreme conservatism in university affairs of men who, in their own field, are constantly seeking to break new grounds.

In relating these observations to communication within universities, one is faced with an interesting paradox. On the one hand there is a formal, legal structure virtually unchallenged by anyone, which gives all power and authority to the academic staff. This staff is a community of equals sharing a common purpose and common values. The actual position is that partly as a result of size but largely because of relations with outside agencies, a new group, the administration, has emerged. Because the administration is the intermediary between the academic staff and these agencies on which the institution depends for its financial and other support, and because the administration presents the university to the public, the academic staff is in many important respects in a state of dependency on the administration. This is not assuaged by the belief of the academics, only too well founded in many instances, that the administration shares the values of the outside groups and tends to be identified with them. At the same time the academic staff itself is suffering the effects of structural lag. This has intensified their ambivalent attitude to their host university.

It would be easy to hypothesize from this situation the development of conflict, or organizational and communication breakdown. Viewed from this point in time this would seem particularly so. The demands by local agencies for closer accountability and for universities to serve special and local needs, the absence of evidence that the public image of universities is improving in terms of what academics value, would not presage any lessening of tension.

Unlike the academic staff, who so far have not been unduly perturbed by the changes taking place around them, the students have reacted and are acutely aware of the need for a review of the present structure. In the traditional idea of a university the student was half of a partnership of teacher and student. Now he finds that he is one of a crowd fighting for the scarce resources of lecturers' time, laboratory and library space. In all probability he quickly learns that his teachers are more interested in personal research than in academic debate. He discovers, too, that he is beset by rules and regulations, that he is coded, punch-carded, and impersonalized by the unseen, unknown men of administration. What power he has is latent. It lies in the size of the student body and its potential influence at time of crisis rather than in direct participation in the daily affairs of the university.

Not content with this, the students have taken matters into their own hands. In Britain, there have been persistent demands, including a petition to the Privy Council, for greater participation on the governing bodies of universities. What students have been seeking is the kind of representation that is common in Australia but which, perhaps not known to them, has not been particularly successful. In the United States, the Berkeley Revolt of 1964 was perhaps the largest and most publicized of student reactions both against the academics who were too preoccupied with research to do teaching and with the administration. "I am a student", read some of the placards at Berkeley, "please do not fold, spindle or mutilate". In Australia and elsewhere the "free university" movements are at once a condemnation of our universities as teaching institutions and a wistful attempt to return to the halcyon days of a lecturer at one end of a log and the student at the other.

Though the cycle might seem to have been completed it is doubtful if flight is the answer to the threat of organization and communication breakdown in present-day universities. The large, complex university is here to stay and remedies for its ills must be found within its structure. Might not part of the solution be found in the very sources of its dis-organization? The difficulties of large universities are largely ones of communication breakdown. This is not to state that the channels for communication are weak. On the contrary the formal structure ensures that there is continuous debate for all who want it. Committees, telephones, all the paraphernalia of an elaborate communication system exist. But what exist also are "information screens" as described by Caplow and McGee[9] which prevent, inhibit, and distort communication between one section of a university and another. At the present time information is seen largely as a source of power. The more information administration gets from and about academic departments, the more control it is likely to gain; the more information a professor or dean can get the more he is likely to use it against his fellows in the battle for scarce money and resources. Administration tends to suppress the flow of information because it upsets the dependence pattern referred to earlier. Heads of departments feel their autonomy is threatened if information is passed down the line too far.

Yet if knowledge is power might it not also be used to the advantage of the institution as a whole? Ironic as it may seem, might not the build-up of total information systems, coupled with the expertise which backs the administration and the sophisticated machinery and techniques of this computer age, be deployed for this purpose? Might not they open the way for each member of staff and each student to be treated in terms of his unique personality and needs? Might they not also enable universities to create a structure which makes possible the goal its members espouse—a universitas, a unified body of men devoted to the cause of learning?

Part OCCUPATIONS, PERSONNEL, AND
Four CAREERS IN EDUCATION

R.O. CARLSON, with J.D. THOMPSON and R.W. AVERY

9 An Overview

Jobs in complex societies can be considered from at least two viewpoints. A *job* is a localized version of an occupation which fixes the practice of that occupation in time and space. A job also is a personalized unit in the career of an individual. It is in the *interaction* of the two aspects of jobs that organizations are able to recruit members and achieve results, as was pointed out by Barnard and elaborated by Simon and March in the "inducements/contributions theory".[1]

Our purpose in this paper is to move a notch ahead by examining what sociologists have been learning about occupations and careers and advancing propositions aimed at relating this to organizational processes of personnel and manpower management, especially in the United States.

Jobs as localized occupations

The problem of matching the individual performer of an occupation with the specific need for it is done largely through the "personnel management" processes of complex organizations. This approach to jobs tends to be in *short-run terms*. What tasks need to be performed? Where? And in what temporal and spatial relationships to other tasks? Jobs, therefore, tend to be defined as they fit here and now into the flow of action—and a technical innovation today calls for job redefinition today.[2]

The techniques most widely used in personnel management— techniques for matching individuals and jobs—are those which measure tasks and the attitudes or abilities to perform them. Whether it is dealing with the initial relationship of member to organization (recruitment, testing, selection, hiring, and placement) or with successive moves within the organization (training, on-the-job education, employee development, transfer, and promotion), personnel management uses as its basic standards techniques which are rooted in views of jobs as localized units of occupations.

Ultimately, an individual in the labour force leaves behind a job history. He traces a *career*. By "career" in this paper we refer to any unfolding sequence of jobs, whether or not consciously planned in advance.

The career-unit approach to jobs tends, therefore, to be in *long-run terms*. What is the future in this job? Where might it lead? And for what other jobs is it a stepping-stone? Jobs tend to be evaluated, from this point of view, as they fit into an unfolding life cycle.

In a dynamic society, few members can rigidly and accurately map out a career in advance. The career results from a series of decisions jointly made by organizations and the individual, and the future holds many uncertainties. But however vague the conception of the future or however pessimistic the anticipation, few members of the labour force in a society such as ours can avoid hearing the emphasis on promotion, security, insurance, hope, and aspiration. Few can take a job without learning quickly from fellow-workers that the job is considered a dead-end or that eventual movement upward is likely to be in one direction rather than another.

Thus some meaning quite extrinsic to the technological utility of the job can be attached to it by the job-holder or candidate, and this meaning can change as the individual proceeds through the life cycle.

Types and bases of careers

The sequence which results in any particular career is not simply a random selection from among millions of jobs but develops out of the possibilities presented after various constraining or channeling factors are accounted for.

The ultimate job history may reveal, for some individuals, a sequence of jobs within a single occupation. In such cases the individual has had an *orderly career*[3] for in each job he has employed skills, knowledge, or experience directly related to the others. Often the orderly career is a progressive one, with each job at equal or higher levels than preceding jobs, but it is possible for an individual to have an orderly career, within a single occupation, involving steps down the progression ladder.

Not all careers are built within a single occupation, however, for a variety of reasons. When an individual's career has involved a switch of occupations we will speak of it as a *disrupted career*, whether it is progressive or regressive on the larger scheme of occupational evaluation.

Bases of careers

Competence is an important factor in shaping the career of an individual but if competence alone were the governing factor, disrupted careers would occur only when (*a*) physical or mental disabilities disqualify an individual for his former occupation, (*b*) the need for the occupation dwindles, or (*c*) extra-job learning via education or hobby has developed competence in a new field.

A second important variable is *aspiration*. The *salience* of aspirations refers to the kinds of achievements the individual feels are important and thus governs the directions in which he will expend effort. The career itself, or a particular occupation or job within it, can be highly salient, but other values, such as family satisfactions, may be of equal or higher priority. The *level* of aspiration has significance for the amount of effort the individual will devote to those things he values and indicates what he considers to be satisfactory levels of achievement.[4] Both salience and level of aspiration may change through various phases of the career.

A third factor important in the shaping of a career is the *structure of opportunities* as perceived by the individual. The actual job market sets limits, of course, but the more significant aspect is the job market as the individual believes it to be. It is those jobs which are visible to him and for which he has sufficient visibility that constitute opportunities for him.

Career prototypes

Most occupations are characterized by a series of more or less well-defined grades or ranks. The craft apprentice knows that application, ability, and "breaks" will lead through a series of clear-cut gradations and ultimately to a journeyman rating.

The clerk learns that the route upward from that position usually eventuates in a position as private secretary. The medical student knows that he can expect to intern and then either enter general practice or a residency leading to a specialized practice.

In these and other examples, progression is not guaranteed to the individual but a *career prototype* is provided and known. Career prototypes evolve for occupations because history has indicated that the experiences, skills, or knowledge acquired at a particular level within an occupation are cumulative with each rank incorporating elements of lower rankings in the same occupation.

Some occupations, such as medicine, provide two or more rather clear-cut prototypes and with known points at which they fork or branch off. One such fork in medicine, for example, is the internship, with those planning to enter general practice taking rotating internship and those planning to specialize seeking the appropriate specialized internship.[5]

Occupations differ in the extent to which their gradations are discrete and clear-cut, and hence they differ in the clarity or ambiguity of the career prototypes they offer. Occupations differ also in the number of recognized prototypes they hold out. But virtually all occupations provide some sort of prototype for progression, some impression of the routes to which a particular occupational position connects. They thus serve frequently to channel and guide aspirations.

Career strategies

Careers develop within channels created by the interplay of aspirations, competencies, and perceived opportunities. These factors reflect not only the past and the present, but also the future as it is imagined or estimated by the individual.

Impact of the future on the present

For the member of the labour force the future may intrude into the present in at least two ways: (1) his estimate of the career possibilities open to him, and (2) his anticipation of needed rewards for various stages of his life cycle.[6]

For most members of the labour force it is possible and

probable to hold some estimate of career possibilities and contingencies inherent in his present occupation or in a potential occupation.

From the time he enters the job market, if not before, it is also possible for the individual to anticipate his need for rewards at various points in his life cycle. If his aspirations include home buying or a college education for his children, for example, he can more or less anticipate the spans within his life cycle at which these costs will be incurred.

Individuals undoubtedly vary tremendously in the extent to which the future impinges on the present, and also in the distance into the future which present thinking carries. For any given individual, moreover, anticipated needs for income, security, prestige, or other types of rewards may fluctuate as contingencies materialize, or as family obligations or the standards set by his reference groups[7] shift during the life cycle.[8]

Despite such variations and fluctuations, the individual's attitude at any given time toward his present occupation and toward his specific job within it seems likely to be influenced by (a) his estimate of its potential for him and (b) his estimate of future needs. However varied the weighting of the future relevant to the present and however imprecise his estimates of the future, we believe that implicitly or explicitly the notion of career or job-history-projected-into-the-future is relevant to most members of the labour force in an industrialized society. It is, therefore, possible to consider various strategies for shaping careers.

Career strategies

A number of empirical studies of complex organizations have in recent years reported various orientations of individuals to their jobs. While each study has given unique labels to the typical orientations found and each has employed somewhat different measures in identifying them, the general convergence is striking. With one exception, these studies appear to determine orientation by identifying the types of reference groups most important to the individuals in jobs. If, for example, the individual is primarily sensitive to the opinions and evaluations of others in his particular organization, he may be classed as having a "local" orientation, in contrast to the individual especially sensitive to the opinions and evaluations of occupational colleagues in other organizations who may be labelled "cosmopolitan".

Carlson's study of school superintendents[9] identifies similar phenomena but finds the orientations associated with career plans. Some individuals, for example, are *place-bound*, seeking to advance within a particular organization, in contrast to others who are *career-bound*, willing and ready to advance occupationally without particular concern for the organizational setting.

Whereas most studies of job orientation have measured this phenomenon at one point in time, Carlson's approach raises the significant question of the influence of the future on job orientations and enables us to suggest that job orientation may shift from time to time as the unfolding career brings new perceptions of opportunities and new estimations of needed rewards.

We can, therefore, hypothesize that there are several possible career strategies for individuals in industrialized societies and that each will be reflected in job orientations. Three of the strategies to be suggested seem to be consistent, at a general level, with available research on job orientations, and we will suggest a fourth which seems to fit with common sense but which has not received systematic attention of researchers.

1. *Heuristic strategy.* Here the criterion of advancement or progression is uppermost, and the individual is committed neither to a particular occupation nor to a specific organization. Rather his commitment is to personal attainment wherever it leads him and successive alternatives are evaluated primarily in terms of progress and the perceived promise they hold. What we term the heuristic strategy seems to have been identified under various labels in studies of job orientation.[10]

2. *Occupational strategy.* Here the individual is sensitive only or primarily to those job alternatives within his occupation and places progression within the occupation above progression within a particular organization. The orientation associated with this strategy also has been identified under various labels.[11]

3. *Organizational strategy*. In this case the individual considers primarily those job alternatives presented by his organization and subordinates to this the question of which occupation he will practise. This strategy also seems to be reflected in various studies under a variety of labels.[12]

4. *Strategy of stability*. In this category we would put individuals for whom the notion of *another job* is irrelevant. The strategy of stability can appear in a variety of situations. For some, this strategy reflects resignation to the status quo because of lack of competence for "better" jobs or lack of perceived opportunity, or both. For others, the strategy of stability signifies that *job* aspirations are satisfied, either because the nature of the work is highly rewarding or because the present job affords those things necessary to pursue aspirations in other life sectors which are highly salient.

In brief, the four strategies have these characteristic orientations:

Heuristic: any occupation, any organization
Organizational: any occupation, present organization
Occupational: present occupation, any organization
Stability: present occupation, present organization.

Some characteristics of strategies

We would expect a career strategy to be fairly stable in the sense that it is likely to be retained over a period of years. The individual is not likely to hold one strategy this week, another next week, and still another next month.

A career strategy need not be deliberately and explicitly formulated by an individual to be effective. He may *take for granted* that because he is comfortably employed by X Corporation his future lies there, and he may, therefore, behave to promote that future. Indeed, such an individual may complete a career without having consciously considered other strategies or he may suddenly become aware of strategy questions when an unsolicited opportunity is thrust before him.

Some jobs provide individuals with opportunity to satisfy the requirements of two career strategies simultaneously over rather long periods, thus deferring the time of choosing. So long as the individual enjoys this best of two worlds he can avoid committing himself to either strategy. Until that time, he may reflect the heuristic strategy.

While career strategies are fairly stable and enduring, we would expect most members of the labour force to employ a sequence of career strategies determined in part by (a) the life cycle and in part by (b) competences, aspirations, and the structure of opportunities. The life cycle is common to all, but competences, aspirations, and opportunities are patterned by types of occupations and we turn now to an examination of these.

Social structure of occupations

There are a great many occupations in a modern society and if we are to discover generalized patterns we must find ways of distinguishing *types of occupations*. For this purpose, we will construct a typology based on two variables which we find reflected in the sociological literature of occupations.

Source of occupational role definition[13]

Who determines—and how—what behaviour is appropriate, permissible, or mandatory for individuals in a particular occupation?

In a great many occupations, the behaviour content expected and rewarded is defined by the individual or individuals who pay the performer. Domestic workers, for example, may clean, wash, iron, or cook at times and in fashion outlined by the employer; restrictions on the employer's ability to dictate behaviour are established by negotiation within a legal framework when the contract is established. Many industrial and clerical occupations, such as selling, machine operations, secretarial work, and executive or managerial positions are of this type. There may indeed be restrictions on the freedom of the employer to define occupational roles—as in the case of union-sponsored rules or legal restrictions—but within the legal and contractual framework, the employer defines the occupational role. These are occupations which emerge because large numbers of similar jobs are being created more or less simultaneously. These are occupations composed of jobs invented by employing organizations, usually on the basis of technological requirements. We will speak of such occupations as *enterprise-defined*.

While a large number of occupations are enterprise-defined, there are others in which such is not the case and there is reason to believe that an increasing proportion of the American labour force is engaged in occupations for which the definition of appropriate, permissible, or mandatory behaviour is in the hands of *colleagues*.

Organized medicine and law, for example, define what is legitimate or sound practice for wide varieties of medical or legal situations. The collegial source of occupational role definition is characteristic of the established professions, but it is found as well in many craft occupations, originally as they were organized into guilds and more recently in craft unions.

While there are many differences between the professions and the craft trades, the fact that colleagues are the source of occupational role definition results in both types of occupations controlling (*a*) initial recruitment or admission into training for the occupation, (*b*) the nature of that training, (*c*) the speed with which training and experience can be acquired, and often (*d*) the power to deny one of their members the right to remain in the occupation.[14]

These are occupations which emerge out of the process of assembling and applying or extending knowledge, and technological requirements or organizations are secondary considerations. Organizations thus adapt such occupations into their job structure, rather than creating them.[15] We will speak of such occupations as collegially-defined.

The structure of occupational progression

An important question perhaps even more significant is the rapidity with which pinnacles or *ceilings* are reached by those who progress at normal rates, and this varies widely from occupation to occupation.[16]

The machine operator with "normal" abilities and energy

can expect to reach the highly skilled category early in his career and to remain in that category for years. If he is to ascend in the larger occupational hierarchy, he must break out of the machine occupation and enter another—such as becoming a manager or a self-employed entrepreneur.

The public school teacher likewise learns, during training if not before, that there is a sequence of occupational categories through which she may pass until she becomes a tenured teacher and that if she aspires beyond that she will have to change occupations to become an administrator or leave the teaching field entirely. Moreover, she knows that with "normal" progression, she can reach the top of the teaching ranks early in her career. We will speak of such occupations as containing early ceilings.

Not all occupations contain early ceilings. There may be biological, psychological, or political factors which impede a particular junior manager but there is nothing in the occupational structure which places an early ceiling on his occupation. Each job in his career presumably provides an opportunity to learn preparatory to the next job. Eventually he or others in his category may reach top management—and rather late in the life cycle. The professor likewise faces a late ceiling. Subject to biological, psychological, or political constraints, he may learn in each job preparatory to the next one until, toward the end of his career, he may achieve a "distinguished professorship". We will speak of these and similar occupations, for which prototypes of progression describe possibilities for advancement into the later stages of the career, as containing *late ceilings*.

A typology of occupations

It should be noted that the following typology is independent of particular individuals and of particular jobs in organizations. These variables deal with the structural characteristics of occupations rather than with the individuals in them or with the job structure of specific organizations.

By combining the two variables, and dealing only with their extremes for the moment, we have four types of occupations:

Source of occupational role definition

		Collegially-defined	Enterprise-defined
Structure of occupational progression	Late-ceiling		
	Early-ceiling		

It should be noted that the typology is not limited to occupations typically found in large-scale organizations where personnel management is a distinct specialty. The typology encompasses occupations ranging from those carried out in independent, free-lance, or private practice to those carried out by wage or salary employees. As occupations which traditionally have been "free" become salaried, the free tradition may colour the attitudes and expectations of those who practise them; to understand the salaried professions in organizational contexts, it may help to understand the parallel free professions.[17]

Characteristics of occupational types

Quite apart from the abilities, energies, and aspirations of individuals or from the local ground rules of particular organizations, each type of occupation has distinctive characteristics which are shaped by social, economic, and technical processes.

Enterprise-defined/early-ceiling occupations[18]

Preparation for entry into this type occupation is minimal and available to the bulk of the population. Skill classifications and pay rates are standardized so that individuals of a given skill classification are considered interchangeable.

The individual has little basis for differentiating himself from competitors of equal rank in the job market. Negative distinction —as unreliable or as a trouble-maker—may travel farther and faster than a positive evaluation. Beyond basic skill classifications, performance in these occupations tends to be judged on non-occupational factors, such as union activity, personal relations, cooperativeness, schooling, or ethnic, racial, or religious characteristics.

For all of these reasons—local availability, standardization, and uniformity—and because occupations of this type are found in a wide variety of organizations and locations, the job markets are confined to local areas. Geographic movement is further discouraged by family or friendship ties or non-occupational investments such as home.[19] Inter-organizational movement within the occupation, even locally, is discouraged. The individual not only lacks a basis for bargaining power because he cannot establish distinction, but he also is rewarded for remaining in the organization by seniority benefits provided under union contracts, civil service rules, or similar arrangements.[20]

The dominant *career prototype* for an *orderly career* in occupations of this sort, then, we suggest, calls for the following sequence of career strategies:

1. A heuristic strategy during which the individual "shops" among jobs, organizations, and even occupations.[21] As he gradually acquires an investment in an occupation and mobility into other organizations is reduced, the heuristic strategy gives way to:

2. An organization strategy, during which the individual seeks to progress on terms offered by the organization and tries to break out of the occupation into an open-ceiling occupation within the same organization (or to escape the organization by becoming an independent businessman).[22] For the majority in these occupations, progress within the organization is unlikely,[23] and the organizational strategy quickly gives way[24] to:

3. A strategy of stability, oriented to job security and viewing the job as a means to other aspirations. Occupational aspirations tend to be projected into the careers of the children,[25] and the individual may seek to meet mounting needs for income and non-occupational achievement through collective action;

i.e. he may attempt to gain through contract renegotiations the increased rewards that can be transformed into non-occupational achievement. If he cannot personally advance occupationally but is subjected to increased needs, his best bet is to seek to elevate the occupation.[26]

Enterprise-defined/late-ceiling occupations

Preparation for entry into these occupations generally occurs at the college level, hence, under present conditions, is not available or acquired by a majority of the population. In most cases these occupations call for skills, knowledge, or aptitudes stated only in general terms and measured imprecisely if at all. The specific content of that educational preparation is less significant than is the diploma certifying that the individual has been exposed to the values believed by the organization to be appropriate. A case in point is the great variation existing in the training of school administrators.

Skill requirements are not highly standardized nor is performance easily measured and there are, therefore, no uniform classifications which are widely recognized. Nevertheless, individuals in these occupations are evaluated by those around them on some basis and, since this is not routinized, it becomes important for the individual to become visible;[27] i.e. to perform in such a way that his contributions are recognized. Not only ability and industry but also the knack of managing relationships thus become bases for differentiating himself from competitors of equal rank.

At the entry level the job market is regional or national since most candidates are in colleges and these are visited regularly by personnel recruiters. Once launched, the individual may find the employing organization itself to be the most readily available job market since he is more likely to be visible there than elsewhere and since much of the competence he is building rests on knowledge of the particular organization and its environment.[28] Some jobs in this category call for external relations which permit the individual to gain visibility outside his employing organization. But it appears that except for the unusually able or unusually visible individual, the American job market tapers off at approximately age 40. Progression after that age is quite possible, but the opportunities tend to be within the organization.

The dominant *career prototype* for an *orderly career* in occupations of this sort, then, seems to call for the following *sequence of career strategies*:

1. A heuristic strategy during which the individual shops among occupations and organizations. Gradually he gains knowledge about a particular organization and visibility within it and finds that both are marketable and he, therefore, adopts:

2. An organizational strategy which calls for an aggressive search for more useful knowledge about the particular organization and/or its environment. To the extent that his search is successful and that he manages to make his competence known properly, he can progress within the organization and frequently can do so by crossing occupational lines.[29] Ultimately, however, a personal ceiling is reached or his aspirations call for the investment of energies outside the career and he adopts:

3. A strategy of stability preparatory to retirement. Because this occurs late in the career and after the usual peak of economic demands on the individual, collective action does not take place in jobs of this sort.

Collegially-defined/early-ceiling occupations[30]

Preparation for entry into occupations of this type comes through acquisition of specialized knowledge or skill which is not available to the population at large. Agencies of the occupation control recruitment or access to the occupation and govern the preparation process through accrediting programmes or an apprentice system.

Experience within a specific organization is of secondary importance in determining the competence of the individual. Skill classifications are standardized and the ranking of the individual on such classifications is governed by the tradition that merit can be evaluated only by colleagues or by those in the relevant senior occupation (e.g. nurses by physicians; teachers by administrators; electronic technicians by electrical engineers; etc.).

Because level of competence is judged by the occupational group rather than the enterprise, the individual's rank and prestige tend to be transferable from one organization or locality to another.[31] Thus job movement is possible but, because occupational rankings are standardized and reach an early ceiling, job mobility tends to be a means to more challenging cases or more satisfactory living conditions rather than a means of occupational progression.[32]

The dominant *career prototype* for an *orderly career* in occupations of this sort, then, calls for the following *sequence of career strategies*:

1. An occupational strategy with the employing enterprise viewed as a place to practise the occupation and with an eye always open for opportunities elsewhere to practise that occupation under more rewarding circumstances. On a normal schedule, the individual passes through a series of ranks and reaches a ceiling rather early in the career and switches to:

2. A strategy of stability. Since this strategy usually develops before the peak of economic demands on the individual, collective action to improve the position of the occupation (and thus of the individual) relative to others tends to result. In the crafts this is expressed through unions but in those occupations related to the professions unionism is considered inappropriate and the "professional association" usually is called upon as the vehicle for collective action to gain economic and prestige advantages for the occupation.

Collegially-defined/late-ceiling occupations

These occupations are entered only by long training, usually prescribed by the collegiate group, which carries with it a set of attitudes and controls, a professional conscience.[33] While minimum skill levels are explicitly stated and evaluated before certification of the individual, gradations in skill above these minima are vast. Once the individual has been accepted, moreover, there is no guarantee that he will maintain his skills at entry standards or that he will increase his skills consistent with the growth of the knowledge underlying his occupation. Thus the collegial group contains members of many degrees of competence. This affords an opportunity for the individual to differentiate himself from competitors in the market, depending not only on his actual ability and performance but also on his ability to manage a reputation, to manage his visibility.[34]

Local markets tend to be quite limited for these occupations; they are highly specialized and usually are employed in small numbers in a particular organization or locality. Individuals seeking new opportunities therefore must cast a wide net just as job-seeking candidates must,[35] and job markets tend to be regional or national. To maintain his market potential, the individual must so manage his reputation as to remain visible to colleagues in the network. Publication or its equivalent and professional society activities are therefore important. Readiness to move is also necessary.[36]

Competence in occupations of this type is governed by the opportunity to practise the occupation, and enterprise aspects of the job are of incidental consideration. Perceived opportunities within a particular enterprise are likely to be very limited and the aspiring individual, therefore, is more likely to look elsewhere for opportunities to progress within his occupation. Aspirations may continue to centre on occupational achievement so long as the individual's reputation is growing.

The dominant *career prototype* for an orderly career in occupations of this sort, we suggest, calls for the following *sequence of career strategies*:

1. An occupational strategy with the individual practising the occupation in any setting which affords an opportunity to gain experience and increase his competence and at the same time to make that increased competence known to colleagues elsewhere. Eventually, aspirations are satisfied or visibility fades and the individual adopts:

2. A strategy of stability which comes rather late in the career if the individual has been "successful". If, however, his professional practice has been founded on service to non-professions, as in social work and general medical practice, his professional visibility is with laymen rather than colleagues, and the strategy of stability may come fairly early in the career.

Patterns of disrupted careers

Disrupted careers may result from a variety of factors, many of which appear from this level of abstraction to be idiosyncratic although upon closer analysis of the individual and his situation they may indeed be understandable. In a dynamic society the tasks to be attempted change and with this come changes in the occupational structure of society and in the career opportunities for individuals. Some occupations are discontinued or are reduced in strength and importance; others emerge. Moreover, new combinations of occupations in new or revised technologies also encourage disrupted careers.

When such disruptions occur frequently enough to be recognized as patterned, additional *disrupted career prototypes* have emerged—and raise additional problems of career strategies for individuals.

From collegial to enterprise occupations

Those who enter the labour force through collegially-defined occupations are expected to have formed a loyalty to the occupation and to have internalized a sense of dedication. As indicated earlier, the dominant career prototype calls for progression within that occupation and job movement from one locale to another as occupational progression demands or allows.

The mobility requirement can be negated easily, especially by factors in the larger life cycle rather than by occupational factors per se. Climate and health problems or family ties can circumscribe mobility opportunities. Vested economic interests perhaps are the more frequent source of limitation on mobility, however. Organizations often provide retirement plans and fringe benefits which force the individual to make substantial forfeits if he leaves.[37] The longer the individual remains in such an organization, the greater his investment in it—and the closer he has moved to retirement.

Moreover, when collegially-defined occupations are practised in organizations, individuals incidentally or deliberately can absorb considerable knowledge about the organization itself and thereby become candidates for enterprise-defined jobs which remove them from actual practice of the collegially-defined occupation.

The nurse[38] or teacher, for example, fairly early in the career may face the choice of a strategy of stability with little hope of progression or of adopting an enterprise strategy, moving out of the original occupation and into a new one where collegial credentials are of less direct importance. In both of the examples cited, the most frequent path is into administration, whereby the individual exchanges an early ceiling for a later one—but also gives up the collegiate definition for one controlled by the enterprise.[39]

The temptation to make this switch is likely to be strong under the following conditions:

1. When the collegially-defined occupation has an early ceiling and the individuals in it are the primary income producers for the family. Where the individuals frequently are wives, as in nursing, teaching, technicians in medicine and dentistry, economic progression may be of secondary concern and, since job location usually is determined by that of the primary income producer in the family, investment in occupational standing may provide more future opportunities than would investment in knowing the ins and outs of a particular organization.

2. When the practice of the collegially-defined occupation lies mainly in dispensing services to and for laymen. This can occur for the general practice physician[40] or the independent lawyer; e.g. who must conform to the expectations and cater to the demands of those who cannot evaluate his performance according to the norms of the profession. It can also occur when the individual practises a collegially-defined occupation in an organization for which the job is auxiliary; e.g. the lone teacher or physician on a ship expedition or the nurse in an industrial plant.

3. When the individual lacks confidence in his ability to maintain occupational standards or visibility.

4. When non-occupational demands on the individual, such as family needs or aspirations, call for greater rewards than can be anticipated from what the individual believes his occupation will yield.[41]

The disruption of a career which starts in collegially-defined occupation is likely to pose problems for the individual, especially if he entered the labour force with a commitment to the occupation. The occupational strategy requires that the collegial group be an important reference group for the individual and leaving that occupation requires a rearrangement of reference groups. The relinquishing of old standards and reference groups would seem to be especially difficult when the individual continues to interact with those of his former occupation—such as the teacher becoming an administrator or the surgeon becoming a hospital administrator—for two reasons: (*a*) he continues to be exposed to conversations in which the old standards are reinforced, and (*b*) he knows that the reference group he has discarded frowns on leaving the professions and questions his reasons.[42]

The switch may, therefore, be easier emotionally for the individual who has earned indisputable distinction in his profession than for the one who is only partly established; it may be easier late in the career rather than midway.

For occupations specialized in dispensing occupational knowledge and skill to laymen, as in nursing and teaching, the lay groups may be important reference groups, for many in such occupations find intrinsic satisfactions in the appreciation expressed by their clients. Movement into administration divorces the individual from direct contact with the client and calls for the development of a new reference group as the source of standards and of recognition.

From enterprise to collegial occupations

It would appear at first glance that those experienced in enterprise-defined types of occupations would not be able to switch to collegially-defined occupations, for by definition the latter control entrance and preparation channels. We are adding to our original formulation of occupational types the complicating factor of the "professionalization of an occupation".[43]

Collegially-defined occupations do not suddenly emerge, full-blown, in the occupational structure of a complex society. Many individual careers may thus intersect with jobs in occupations which are in the *process* of becoming collegially-defined. Casual observation would suggest that various phases of accounting are in the process now, following the public branch of that occupation. Public relations, having grown out of the press agent phase, seems also to be in the professionalization process. Social work, likewise, appears to be in the process of professionalization.[44]

Participation and perhaps leadership in the professionalization movement may be motivated by the fact that staff specialists, whose climb has been gained within a particular occupation *and* enterprise, eventually see a ceiling which can be circumvented only by (*a*) moving into general management or "line" jobs, or (*b*) gaining visibility outside the organization and thus becoming candidates for similar, but larger, jobs of the same type in other organizations. The professionalization movement would appear to be a most likely way to achieve the necessary visibility.

The late heuristic strategy

Career prototypes provide individuals with patterns or channels for aspirations. At the same time, career prototypes provide organizations with realistic guides as to where to recruit.

But a complex society inevitably creates certain leadership positions which do not appear to be anchored in or at the apex of any career prototype and for which there is no established, automatic recruitment pattern. Here organizations look for capable individuals wherever they appear and often the appointment goes to someone outside the enterprise. Thus, the university may appoint one of its members as president, but it may import its president from another college, or it may seek a retired general, diplomat, or business executive. The government may staff its cabinet and its embassies with "career personnel", but it is also likely to select a lawyer prominent in private practice, a former governor or business executive, a banker, or a foundation president.

In such examples, the recruitment appears to be patternless and, from the standpoint of occupations, this may indeed be true, for the skills and knowledge required in such jobs are not normal results of the practice of any particular occupation. The criteria employed in recruiting are many and varied and often rather vague and elusive, but the lists from which nominees are drawn are usually made up of highly visible individuals whose visibility extends beyond a particular occupation and a particular oganization.

For such visibility to be achieved, usually, an individual must have gained prominence via the occupational strategy in an occupation or via the organization strategy in an organization or perhaps by a sequence involving both strategies. Once the necessary visibility is achieved, however, the heuristic strategy is appropriate. Often it is advisable; the business executive who resigns to become a cabinet member cannot expect to remain in the new position more than a few years and even if he can return to his old job, this may not be appealing.

Implications for personnel management

The preceding remarks have attempted to take a long-range view and have focused on jobs as units in a career. The remarks have necessarily had a hypothetical quality based as they were on *ex post* analysis. At this point we would like to suggest several additional propositions which are more oriented toward jobs as localized occupations and take the "short-run" perspective necessitated by the problems of personnel management.

Proposition One: As an occupation, personnel management is itself in a state of ambiguity. In the decade prior to World War II, the occupation of personnel management was ascending in importance in complex organizations, but its emphasis on short-run, psycho-physical variables ill equipped the occupation for the realities of more complicated occupational structures resulting from larger social forces. The individual, psychological base, for example, could not comprehend the socio-political unionization movement, and industrial relations management emerged as a rather separate and distinct occupation. The techniques of personnel management have not been appropriate for collegially-defined occupations and as they have been incorporated in complex organizations recruitment, selection, and promotion have been the responsibilities of "line" officials. Thus the personnel "function" in present-day organizations has expanded far beyond personnel "management" as a recognized occupation.

Proposition Two: Important managerial positions tend to be occupied by those who have found the organization strategy personally rewarding and who find it difficult to understand behaviour guided by other strategies.[45] Especially as organizations recruit those whose skills are collegially-defined and guarded, traditional management procedures and assumptions are subject to strain. The more deeply ingrained the occupational strategy, the less the individual is ready to respond in opportunistic ways to the whims of the organization. When personnel policies are established and controlled by those deeply committed to the enterprise, the social forces of the occupational structure tend to be overlooked and those with occupational strategies are likely to be judged "uncooperative".[46]

Proposition Three: Organizations which select professionals for their readiness to conform to organizational customs are likely to recruit professionals whose commitment to the colleague group is weak and whose professional education is incomplete. This type of recruitment policy may contribute to harmony within the organization but at the expense of the full impact of the professional occupation. Especially if the occupation in question is a dynamic one, the organization may find that the lack of professional reference groups results in the individual becoming technically obsolete rather rapidly.

Proposition Four: An individual's switch of strategies is likely to be accompanied by anxiety, tension, and low morale.[47] The career strategy provides a set of ground rules for the individual in his "career game" and when he finds it necessary to change ground rules he is likely to be uneasy about it; his self-perceptions are called into question. The uneasiness is likely to be extreme for the individual switching from an occupational to an organizational strategy and especially in the late-ceiling category. In this case the long professional training has provided a basis for guilt feelings when the individual leaves the profession. When upward mobility in terms of income rather clearly requires that he leave the profession in order to climb, anxieties may build up several years before the choice is made and may continue for several years afterward while the individual feels he might still rectify his "possible mistake".

Proposition Five: Because switches of career strategy do not occur in only one sequence but depend on the occupational entry point and the individual's perception of his opportunities and future needs, there is no one-to-one correspondence between career anxiety and either age or hierarchical level.

Proposition Six: The anxieties, frustrations, and satisfactions which individuals experience in jobs are only in part responses to the actions of those organizations. Both in collegially-defined occupations and in those which are undergoing professionalization, the gains and losses of one occupation relative to others may have significance for the individual regardless of what his organization may do. The splintering and fragmentation of occupations likewise has its impact on the individual,[48] just as technological redefinitions of occupations may impinge on the individual in an enterprise-defined occupation.[49] As occupations change, career prototypes also change, not only for those entering the labour force but for those already well along in the process of building careers.

Proposition Seven: The personnel management activity takes on especially dynamic qualities in the rapidly developing nations. The hypotheses advanced in this paper have been based on the analysis of occupations and careers in a highly industrialized society in which family, occupation, and community have been recognized as distinct spheres of activity, in which occupational careers are considered to be necessary, and in which multiple career prototypes are available. When complex organizations are introduced in societies which do not present these conditions, the recruitment, assignment, and promotion of individuals must take place simultaneously with the incorporation into the social structure of new occupations, new definitions of career, and new understanding of career prototypes.

I.F. VACCHINI

10 The Government School

In this paper an attempt has been made to relate the theory and data presented in the previous chapter by Carlson, Thompson, and Avery to the New South Wales public service and the Department of Education in general, and to the teachers in the secondary education system in particular.

Some general comments are made on the work of Professor Carlson, on the position in theory and research which constitutes the basis for his present paper, and on the material presented in the paper. Then follows a consideration of each aspect of the paper, drawing attention to the application of concepts to the New South Wales system. It will be seen that while some concepts apply directly, others stimulate comparison. It is hoped that this application to a local system will highlight some problems of administration in terms of the career patterns of personnel and give indications for further discussion and possible research. This paper asks some questions. It does not attempt to provide the answers.

Throughout this paper, chapter 9 by Carlson, Thompson, and Avery is referred to as the position paper.

* * *

Carlson, as part of his work in educational administration, has made valuable contributions to the categorizing of organizations, of their personnel, of administrative functions and in examining the characteristics of each of these. Most will be familiar with Carlson's work recorded in the 1964 *Yearbook of the National Society for the Study of Education*,[1] in which he proposed categories of service organizations—the "wild" and the "domestic"—in terms of client control and organizational control of participation. In that work, and again in the position paper in his definition and classification of career types and career strategies, Carlson implicitly draws our attention to two things: first, that administration and the organizations and personnel it is concerned with are open to systematic clasisfication, and that "experience" and "common sense", however important they may be in administration, can be complemented by theory and objective research. Secondly, in his work on organizations and their members, Professor Carlson reminds us that educational administration is not unique. There are some features of educational administration which are not shared with other forms of administration but we certainly do not work in a closed compartment. As the position paper reminds us, behaviour patterns and types of situations may be common to organizations widely differing in nature.

The propounding of theory without subsequent evaluation of propositions is of little value in application to administration (however popular deduction from "principles" has been in educational administration in the past). Much of Carlson's valuable work has been in the area of research, in objective testing of his own propositions and those of others, as, for example, in his investigations into the adoption of educational innovations.[2] In developing this position paper Carlson and his co-authors use as one basic concept that of "cosmopolitans" and "locals" as professional types. These terms, originally adopted by Merton,[3] were used by Gouldner[4] in a systematic study of the conflict between professional and organizational commitment. Carlson developed from these his theory of "place-bound" and "career-bound" individuals and tested it by research involving school superintendents in Oregon.[5]

It will be noted that the standpoint of Carlson and his co-authors in the position paper is that theoretical consideration has been given to the interaction of the role of the individual in his job (as he sees it in terms of his own viewpoint) with the role of the organization which provides the job in order to fulfil some technical requirement. In addition, studies have been carried out to provide measurements of this interaction. The authors move from this standpoint, which they regard as established in a static (one point in time) sense, to present a theory designed to account for interaction in a more dynamic (extended time) concept. The theory has been formulated in terms of previously established data as well as in terms of indications of probable patterns from the work of sociologists. Most important, the paper recognizes that it is theory that has been put forward, that the remarks made have "a hypothetical quality based . . . on *ex post* analysis".[6]

Accordingly the position paper, in addition to the value of its content, illustrates one stage in the development of the orderly body of knowledge which is the "science" component of administration. From this point, further research (as objective as possible) will most likely be carried out to validate (or otherwise) the statements concerning jobs as career units as well as the propositions concerning jobs as localized occupations.

As far as I am aware, there are no published results of research in Australia on the relationship between the individual's view of his job and the organization's view of it. Indeed, very little research appears to have been done in this country[7] on job "orientation" at all. The only work that I know of in the educational field is a study by Professor Walker of the job attitudes of teachers one year and then five years after they had left Armidale Teachers' College. The results of this investigation have now been published.[8]

Not only does this mean that there is opportunity for research in this field as applied to Australian conditions or to the conditions in one system: it means also that the person "reacting" to the position paper can draw on no local research in his reaction. The remarks that follow are thus limited in two ways: first, by the limitations of the writer's contact with systems, and secondly, and more importantly, by their being based entirely on impressions with no research or even survey backing.

Bearing these limitations in mind we might now look at the implications of the paper for local conditions, beginning with the dual definition of a job.

Jobs and careers

We might agree that a job can be seen in two ways, both as a localized version of an occupation and as a personalized unit in the career of an individual. There will be some, however, who may query the applicability of the word "job" to teaching as we know it, or the clarity of the distinction between the two viewpoints of a job as applied to teaching. There must be many teachers (especially, but not exclusively, in church teaching orders) for whom teaching is scarcely a "job" but rather a "vocation". Even in cases where there is little dedication one never hears the Australian expression, "It's just a job", applied to teaching. The nature of teaching is such that even where enthusiasm is lacking, a degree of involvement seems inevitable, preventing the teacher from seeing his or her work as just a job, as just a means of earning income. This is not to deny that teaching is technically a job (in terms of the paper's definition) but rather to point out that this characteristic of teaching modifies the view of it as a "job" from the standpoint of both organization and individual.

Do we, for example, as employers of teachers, recruit persons in "short-run" terms? Are we looking for an individual to perform a set task, i.e. to teach science? Is there more to the selection, recruitment, training, and promotion of teachers than fitting a person to a set task, or is it merely that the task is more complex than tasks in many occupations and not clearly defined in many of its aspects? What would we include in the job specification for a teacher if we had to spell out his role more precisely than "teaching" a subject or "teaching" pupils? At the conclusion of the position paper seven propositions oriented towards jobs as localized occupations are presented and it may be well to bear the above questions in mind when we consider them later.

Similar considerations present themselves when we examine the "job" of teaching as a career unit. Perhaps the entrant to the teaching service might ask, "What is the future in this job?" and answer himself in terms of job satisfaction, salary, security, and so on. How many also ask themselves "Where might the job lead?" or "For what other jobs is it a stepping stone?" The limited relevance of these questions to the member of a teaching order is obvious but one has the impression that for many teachers in public and independent schools also these questions are of less importance than they are to entrants to most other occupations. While the by-products of teaching (salary, security, and so on) must remain significant for most, the intrinsic values would appear to constitute a more important factor in the decision to take up teaching as an occupation.

It is partly for this reason that teaching, as we know it in Australia, gives most commonly an orderly career. Despite publicity about shortage of teachers, loss of teachers to other occupations (and to teaching elsewhere), the teaching division of the New South Wales public service has a lower staff turnover rate than any other division of the service. This is so even though there is a high proportion of women employees, both single and married, with their respective characteristics tending to produce "disrupted careers". There are records of this phenomenon in the public service and while I have no evidence about other occupations my impression is that teaching would rank high in "orderly careers" in the community. If this is so, then an area for investigation presents itself. Is teaching in Australia an occupation with characteristically orderly career patterns because of its intrinsic values or because of the way the occupation is organized in this country? We might go further and try to determine the advantages and disadvantages of a self-contained system.

Bases of careers

We must agree that competence is an important factor in shaping the careers of teachers in New South Wales, although, in public service teaching, career progression is by a rather curious mixture of competence and seniority. In primary, secondary, and technical education, apart from initial competence (judged largely on "qualifications"), the teacher must be deemed to have achieved levels of competence (by largely subjective assessment) and then to defer to seniority at each level. Presumably in independent school systems competence is a more important factor because seniority need play no part.

Both salience and level of aspiration are also recognizable factors in the career patterns of teachers, but there are, here, some differences between teaching and many other occupations. For many, teaching gives a degree of satisfaction unrelated to salary or prestige. It is seen as a worthwhile and rewarding occupation within itself, so that while teachers frequently feel that they would gain greater financial returns from jobs outside teaching (largely a myth, some say) they see the intrinsic rewards of teaching as compensating somewhat. At the same time, factors such as security, superannuation, and long vacations are obviously determinants in the salience of aspirations. Similarly, it appears that, because classroom teaching is regarded as rewarding in itself, the level of aspiration is lower for many teachers than it is for some other teachers or for many persons in other occupations.

The structure of opportunities as seen by the entrant to teaching is an important factor also. While today the job market seems very open in terms of opportunities there are many teachers of some years' standing whose choice of occupation was far more restricted when they commenced. There are others for whom there was virtually no choice, for economic or other reasons, when teaching offered free training with a living allowance during the training period. Administrators today might ask the question, "Are we getting only two classes of entrant to the teaching service today—those who are 'dedicated' and those who fail to make the grade for more attractive occupations?" The markedly evident trend in New South Wales towards a higher and higher proportion of women teachers in primary schools presumably reflects the more open job market for young men. Classroom teaching in the primary school, formerly regarded as an honourable level of aspiration for men, is in this state becoming more and more the province of women. Will we reach the stage where the writer on Australian education need use only the pronoun "she" to refer to the primary teacher, as Carlson has in referring to the elementary school teacher in the United States? If we do, what are the implications of this for the administrator?

The structure of opportunity within the occupation is of equal importance. An interesting phenomenon has occurred in the secondary education system in New South Wales. Today, for a number of reasons, promotion to each level is being achieved at ages ten to fifteen years younger than was the case a decade or more ago. This is resulting in younger administrators in the schools, but it does not appear to have reduced dissatisfaction amongst teachers anxious for promotion. Young teachers are coming to expect promotion as soon as they are eligible in terms of seniority, often without regard to competence. We might say that the prototype has shifted somewhat. There are problems from the administrator's point of view in this changed structure of opportunities. Even greater problems will probably occur in another decade or so when it seems likely that the age levels of promotion will rise again.

Career prototypes

What are the career prototypes of teaching in Australia and how important are they to individual and to organization? Does the would-be public school teacher in New South Wales see the prototype as college student: probationary teacher: certificated teacher with progression through a salary scale based on years of service? Or does he see it as student: teacher: master of department: deputy principal: principal? Does he ever see it as teacher: school administrator: inspector: system administrator? I would suggest that very few at the time of entry to the service see beyond the first prototype. I would further suggest that while, for many, the prototype shifts in later years to the second or third mentioned, many others do not ever see beyond the first prototype. I have no evidence to support this impression—readers of this paper may have evidence to the contrary and disagree strongly.

Because a high proportion of teachers are women it might be well to consider also the particular prototypes teaching presents to them. If we take the majority of career patterns, the prototype will be student: assistant teacher: marriage: parenthood—a disrupted career. Does such a prototype affect the quality of teaching? Is there a significant difference between the teaching by women in New South Wales who see the emerging fork in the prototype, student: assistant teacher: marriage (permanent status and equal opportunity in teaching preserved): continued teaching: promotion, and the teaching by women in some other systems where marriage brings loss of occupational opportunities? What are the implications of any differences for the administrator? Has the policy of equal pay and equal opportunity for women, whether single or married, changed the male teacher's perception of the structure of opportunities?

Career strategies

Impact of the future. How important is "the notion of career or job-history-projected-into-the-future" for teachers? As noted above, there would appear to be many teachers who do not see their careers projected beyond classroom teaching. They have, to use Carlson's term, adopted the "strategy of stability", but not necessarily with dissatisfaction. What is the relative importance for the teacher of "(*a*) his estimate of [teaching's] potential for him and (*b*) his estimate of [his] future needs", on the one hand and the present rewards (intrinsic and extrinsic) from his work on the other? Is the teacher, in the terms used by Presthus,[9] an upward-mobile, an indifferent, or an ambivalent, or does he sometimes belong to a fourth category, satisfied with his job levels as in the "indifferent" but retaining satisfaction from the intrinsic values of his job. Does this type of teacher have all the characteristics of those who have adopted a strategy of stability?

Carlson's distinction in job orientation between *career-bound* and *place-bound* is of considerable significance when applied to teaching as an occupation in Australia. How many teachers or educational administrators in Australia are career-bound? With our centralized state systems and public service inducements, very few are tempted to pursue their careers outside the state educational organization once they enter it. Some teachers in independent schools may be career-bound, but even here, for a number of reasons, careers are frequently confined to one school. In teaching orders in church schools the place-bound orientation is, for particular reasons, almost universal.

What are the implications of this extensive place-bound orientation? What results when a person is educated in primary and secondary schools of the state system, trained in a teachers' college which belongs to the state system and where all the staff have come from the teaching ranks of the same organization, works as a teacher and eventually becomes a principal or administrator in the same system? How much conservatism does this "inbreeding" produce—how difficult is it to achieve innovation? Are change or development slow to come because there is no cross-fertilization of ideas or are they achieved easily by handing down from above to a centralized system receptive to direction, and conformity?

The effects of place-bound orientation would appear, in Australia, to be aggravated by the high incidence of orderly careers. Are our teachers who mostly keep to one occupation and one organization as unaware of life "outside" as critics claim? On the other hand is the orderly career norm a disadvantage from the administrator's point of view? Does it not give a relatively stable staff comprising teachers who are freed from the concern about security and are able to devote more time and energy to their teaching?

Even a change of occupation may occur in an organization as large as the New South Wales state system. The teacher may become a college lecturer, a research officer, a guidance officer, an inspector, an editor, an aids officer, an administrator "divorced from the classroom"—all without ever leaving the one organization.

We must not confuse *place-bound*, in Carlson's sense of orientation to one organization, with lack of geographical mobility. There is in New South Wales and, as far as I know, in other states, a high degree of geographical mobility among teachers. Early in the teacher's career this movement from place to place within the organization is most frequently determined by decision of the centralized authority of the organization. Later in the career there is much movement by decision of the individual in quest of promotion or favoured living area. Mobility of the second type is a feature of the structure of opportunities, and willingness to move or not depends often on the salience and level of aspiration. There is the teacher who is prepared to "go bush" to gain promotion as soon as possible. There is also the teacher for whom stability of home and family, or residence in a favoured locality, is more important. These factors produce interesting results and some problems for the administrator where certain favoured country and metropolitan areas tend to have teaching staffs who have almost all adopted the strategy of stability in an extreme form.

Career strategy types and characteristics

The four types of strategy described in the position paper can all be recognized among Australian teachers but, as already indicated, the heuristic strategy is rare and the occupational strategy unusual. In the New South Wales public school system the organizational strategy is quite commonly found (especially if we regard the change from teacher to non-teaching principal, inspector, or administrator as an occupation change). It is the strategy of stability which perhaps is most common. The notion of another job is irrelevant for some teachers because of lack of competence for "better" jobs or lack of perceived opportunity. In other cases, as the position paper points out, the strategy indicates that *job* aspirations are satisfied because of intrinsic or extrinsic factors.

The characteristics of strategies noted also appear to apply locally. Strategies do tend to be retained over a long period by teachers. Very often strategies would not be deliberately and explicitly formulated. At times two career strategies are adopted concurrently.

Social structure of occupations

While career strategies may be recognized quite clearly in Australian school systems, occupational role definition and the structure of occupational progression are not as easily determined. As Carlson points out in introducing his typology of occupations, the four types described represent combinations of the extremes of the two variables, definition and ceiling. Some reflection on teaching and related occupations in Australian systems will show that the distinctions are not clear cut. Teaching has elements of "free" occupations and although it is almost entirely a salaried occupation, the "free" elements colour the attitudes and expectations of the teacher.

Occupational role definition

"Who determines . . . what behaviour is appropriate, permissible or mandatory" for teachers in New South Wales? Is it a Department of Education backed by a Public Service Board or a school council or a religious order? Is it the statutory boards of studies to any extent? Clearly all of these influence the teacher's role in some way through policy, laws, regulations, curricula, and so on. Does this mean that teaching in this state is an enterprise-defined occupation? On the other hand occupational preparation in universities and in New South Wales teachers' colleges is determined by colleagues without enterprise interference. Primary and secondary curricula and syllabuses are determined by boards of teachers and former teachers. Departmental policies and regulations are devised by administrators who, in the New South Wales system, have all been teachers at some stage. Further, much of the teacher's role is determined by influences within his school and especially by collegially-defined values gained in the staff room situation. In terms of the above, teaching in New South Wales may well be regarded as a collegially-defined occupation. In large systems it is perhaps best considered as a collegially-defined occupation which has been adapted into the job structure of an organization. What significance does the relative weight of collegial and enterprise definition have? What indications are there in this for administrative behaviour?

The structure of occupational progression

It is clear from the examples used[10] in the position paper that Carlson and his co-authors regard teaching as an early-ceiling occupation. If we accept the concept that teaching as an occupation remains in the classroom then it is true of New South Wales teachers that theirs is an early-ceiling occupation. But acceptance of this concept involves defining school administration as a *separate* occupation. While this fits the most common patterns of school administration in the United States, where administration is usually more clearly separated from classroom teaching, it is a concept that is not really appropriate to the Australian situation.

Administration in Australian schools by school principals, deputies, and so on is seen as a job in which the individual employs skills, knowledge, and experience directly related to classroom teaching. Thus, by the position paper's definition[11] the Australian teacher who becomes a school principal is following an orderly career in a single occupation. The modes of progression in the various state teaching services add weight to this argument. In the New South Wales secondary system, for example, the teacher who becomes a subject master does not relinquish teaching. Nor does he become merely a faculty chairman, with curriculum responsibilities only, as is the case of many systems in the United States. He is given at the same time a role in the general administration of the school. The deputy principal's position carries the individual a stage further into administration but he or she retains a classroom teaching "load"—about half that of the classroom teacher.

My contention here is that while for many teachers (those who see their career prototype as not leading beyond the classroom) teaching is an early-ceiling occupation, for many others (those interested in promotion of any kind) the prototype is one of a late-ceiling occupation. If this view is correct then there are implications for the administrator. For many of the teachers who early adopt the strategy of stability there will be satisfaction in the rewards of classroom teaching. For many others, those who seek promotion, there will be a sustained organizational strategy for the greater part of their careers. In New South Wales, administrators from the lowest level up can and do utilize this situation to advantage.

It must be remembered, of course, that there are teachers who adopt a strategy of stability, not through any intrinsic interest in their work but because they are resigned to a lack of progression or because an extrinsic purpose of their teaching, a supplementary income, as in the case of some married women teachers, is adequately achieved. With these individuals the educational administrator often faces problems of conservatism and lack of motivation for the improvement of teaching.

Characteristics of occupational types

Each of the four occupational types described in the position paper can be readily illustrated by jobs in the Australian community but, as noted earlier in this paper, no one type matches the Australian teaching situation exactly. For most teachers and administrators in New South Wales the orderly career prototype has the sequence of career strategies suggested for the collegially-defined, early-ceiling occupation or the enterprise-defined, late-ceiling occupation or a combination of both.

Because of the "inbreeding" in state systems and because of their large size and centralized nature, the occupational strategy is frequently inhibited or absent altogether, teachers very early adopting an organizational strategy or a strategy of stability. Other factors inhibiting the occupational strategy in New South Wales include the vested economic interest that a teacher progressively acquires in his own system, through superannuation, long service leave, sick leave, salary increments based on service, and so on. Movement to teaching positions in other states or overseas involves not only the obvious large distances and expense but penalties imposed on return to the local organization. In New South Wales it has been policy to re-employ a teacher who has had, say, two years' teaching overseas, at a salary lower than that he received before going overseas. In theory, the policy is to prevent staff losses and preserve the interests of those who remain with the organization. In practice the policy gives the appearance of a belief that a teacher who broadens his experience in another organization is a poorer teacher. It is not suprising then that the occupational strategy is exceptional in New South Wales and, presumably, in other state systems. For those who adopt the organizational strategy in a state system, "visibility" and organizational knowledge do, as the position paper indicates, become very important while industrial action is less in evidence.

For those who early adopt the strategy of stability, industrial action may become important but need not do so. The strong teachers' union in New South Wales and its success in industrial matters are due, *inter alia*, to the presence of teachers who have adopted a strategy of stability and directed energies to union activities. As we might expect from the analysis in the position paper, industrial action is most strongly supported by, and is most directed to the interests of, the classroom teacher. There is less support by and less interest in those who have adopted an organizational strategy and succeeded in gaining promotion. There are, of course, many exceptions amongst those in promotion positions, partly due to the nature of Australian state systems, but at the same time there are many teachers who are dedicated, enthusiastic about their work, involved in the intrinsic values of teaching and with relatively little interest in collective action or individual promotion.

Patterns of disrupted careers

While contending that disrupted careers are not a feature of teaching services in New South Wales, I would agree that those entering teaching from other occupations or leaving for other occupations do so when the conditions outlined in the position paper are in evidence.

That more men than women are interested in promotion is most likely due to the fact that men are usually the primary income producers for the family. But again this leads most to adopt an organizational strategy and follow a prototype within the occupation, not change to another occupation or even to another organization in the same occupation.

We have all heard of the loss of Australian teachers to positions in Canada. Presumably if they are still teaching their career has not been disrupted, but might we take this as an indication of a growth in occupational orientation rather than organizational. I feel that we should not place this interpretation on the phenomenon. Certainly the higher salaries offered are attractive but the impression one gains is that most of those leaving for Canada are doing so for reasons quite outside occupation or career at all. Most appear to be younger teachers taking a relatively secure means of seeing the rest of the world, as is the fashion these days. After all, the United States, Britain, and Europe are much closer to Canada. I do not wish to imply that the teacher who wishes to travel overseas is to be blamed or discouraged. Rather, I would hope that, despite the staff problems it gives to administrators, the trend will continue. My point is that it appears, and I have no objective evidence of this, that they are leaving for reasons unrelated to occupation, organization, or career and, I suspect, most will return to Australia in time.

The late heuristic strategy, another basis of disrupted careers discussed in the position paper, calls for some comment. In the Australian political-economic-social system some such disruption occurs and it does occur even to teachers and those in related occupations. Some teachers have become politicians, union leaders, members of statutory boards by a "late heuristic strategy", but these are quite exceptional. In the Australian political systems, unlike those of the United States, cabinet members must be elected members of legislatures, and public service heads of departments are "permanent heads", almost invariably appointed at the peak of an orderly occupational and/or organizational career. The quite unusual appointment to the principalship of an independent school of a person from a non-teaching occupation would be our closest equivalent to a late heuristic career disruption.

Before concluding this reaction to the position paper comment might be made on some of the additional propositions more oriented towards jobs as localized occupations.

Implications for personnel management

1. School systems of all types in New South Wales illustrate well the contention that personnel management in large organizations incorporating collegially-defined occupations such as classroom teaching tends to be the function of "line" not "staff" officials. Is there a place for the "personnel manager" in an educational system of the Australian type?

2. This proposition is consistent with the earlier observation in this paper, that the organizational strategy is the one most frequently adopted by those desiring promotion in the system. Does this aggravate the effects of "inbreeding"? Does it greatly increase the difficulty of innovation?

3. Do we select professionals for their readiness to conform to organizational customs? As we recruit most teachers from departmental teachers' colleges and in a sense directly from school, it might be claimed that we do. Certainly many would claim that by recruiting non-graduates, especially when they are destined for secondary teaching, we are recruiting professionals whose professional education is incomplete. On the other hand it is unlikely that there is any conscious policy of recruitment for organizational harmony. In practice in New South Wales, we recruit non-graduates for secondary teaching because we cannot get enough graduates. We recruit as many graduates as we can and these are less likely to have a commitment to the organization.

4 and 5. Anxiety, tension, and low morale do not generally appear to accompany a switch of strategies in the New South Wales state system at least. Perhaps this is due to the lack of

clear distinction between occupational and organizational strategies in a large centralized system comprising mostly locals and very few cosmopolitans.

6. While we must agree that anxieties, frustrations, and satisfactions that individuals experience in jobs are only in part due to the actions of organizations, the relative stability of the occupation of teaching means that these experiences have not been due to occupational relativity, splintering, or re-definition.

The position paper prepared by Carlson, Thompson, and Avery gives us a structured view of some relationships between careers and organizations. It gives us a measure, based on all occupations, to apply to the patterns in our own systems. This application I have tried to make, looking in very general terms at New South Wales and relying almost entirely on impressions. The position paper gives us a series of hypotheses as a basis for proceeding further by controlled research in our own systems.

Even without this, where observation and impressions alone indicate career patterns in our systems which appear unique or unusual, we might be stimulated to question them. If so many features of teaching as an occupation are collegially-defined, is it desirable or even healthy to have an organizational-oriented teaching staff? What are the advantages and disadvantages of a teaching staff which has little mobility between occupations and even little mobility between organizations within the same occupation? If I am correct in my contention that administrative positions (within schools at least) are seen in New South Wales as jobs in the same occupation as teaching, do we need to re-think our concept of school administrator? Traditionally in New South Wales, and, I suspect, in other states, the teacher becomes an administrator by building on to a sound teaching career by experience, by trial and error, by rule of thumb and "common sense". Is this enough? Do our principals and other administrators need training in "administration" as it applies to all occupations?

The position paper prompts me to ask questions such as these. I have not attempted to answer them. To be able to do this with any confidence we will need to apply administrative theory and research to the local scene.

G.W. BASSETT

11 The University

This is an exercise in contrapuntal writing. The major paper has been written by Americans; this comment is made by an Australian. The theme of the position paper is theoretical and deals in a broad way with occupations, personnel, and careers; that of the reaction paper is practical, and deals with the particular occupation and careers of university teachers, and of those who learn from them. It is to be hoped, however, that some harmony is apparent.

In following the definitions, psycho-sociological analyses, and hypothetic inferences proposed in the major paper, and using the university as a reference point, one is tempted to vacillate in attention on the one hand between university teaching as a job with its associated features and issues, and on the other, the many kinds of jobs for which the university prepares its students, and the form this preparation takes, particularly with regard to the occupational value system which makes role definition and protection by colleagues possible.

Both are of great interest in the Australian university scene; both can be profitably explored in terms of the ideas presented in the paper. The number and complexity of issues however that might be brought up are likely to outrun the scope of a "reaction" paper. The main paper was content with the rather modest objective of moving "a notch ahead" in understanding about occupations and careers, and it is presumptuous perhaps for a minor paper to attempt more. The only justification for this is an introduction to discussion. For this purpose wider implications may be raised, and more numerous problems identified within them than can comprehensively be explored and resolved within the paper. It is defensible to bite off more than one can chew, if there are others to help with the chewing, even though this is a rather nauseating metaphor.

First, then, to a number of questions concerned with the university teacher.

The characteristics of the university teacher

It will be helpful before raising personnel questions, such as recruitment, promotion, training, etc., to try to see more clearly what kind of person we are dealing with.

With Carlson's typology in mind we could say, I suppose, that university teaching is collegially-defined and has a late ceiling, that is, that the definition of appropriate, permissible, or mandatory behaviour is in the hands of colleagues, and that top positions are reached rather late in one's career. I say "I suppose", because it fits this position in the two-by-two scheme proposed better than others. Actually the professor is specifically cited in the paper as one who faces a late ceiling, achieving a "distinguished professorship" towards the end of his career. This kind of statement does not ring quite so true in the Australian setting. Certainly some professors are more distinguished than others, but appointment to a chair in this country may be regarded as reaching the ceiling, and this is achieved at a moderate age, if not early in the successful person's career. In the University of Queensland, for example, in 1967 19 per cent of the professors were under 45, and 56 per cent were under 50. Since the retiring age in this university is 65, and may be extended on an annual basis until 70, 45 or 50 must be regarded as being reasonably young. If actual ages on appointment were taken, the averages would be lower.

Without the incentive to move for greater financial rewards, this group of university teachers tends to remain in the position where their appointment occurs, and to become increasingly organizationally-minded. Many of them accept greater administrative responsibilities along with their occupational duties, and some switch mainly to administrative tasks, perhaps in some cases with the accompaniment of the "anxiety, tension, and low morale" referred to by Carlson *et al*. This moderately early age for the appointment of professors sets corresponding ceilings for lower ranks of staff. A person who at 45 can see clearly that he will not become a professor has a difficult career problem. He is less able than the professor to switch to administration, and the main academic route is impeded if not blocked. In more diversified occupations, for example in a large school service, a person with the academic qualifications of the kind needed for appointment to a university (for example, the possession of a doctorate) would almost certainly have more promotion avenues open to him.

The second major characteristic, that the main features of the profession are defined by the occupational group itself rather than by the enterprise, is of more central importance, and to this I now turn.

University teaching seems a clear enough case of a collegially-defined occupation. The views of the members are represented on the governing body of the university by staff membership of this body, and by the fact that lay members themselves are often university people who understand the objectives of university education, and appreciate its spirit. Further, academics have a large say in forming policy, directly on academic matters, and less directly on financial ones. They have a virtually determining voice in recruiting new staff, in training them, and in promoting them. They have a virtually determining voice in deciding the courses that are offered, the way they are taught, and in the standards applied to them. To many in other occupations, even in the established professions, the university person appears to be unusually free in determining the pattern and rhythm of his day-to-day work. Yet there are contradictions and ambiguities that appear on closer examination.

First, there appears to be an increasing disposition in Australian society to control the activities of academics, and to apply to them the usual tests of bureaucratic and professional efficiency. Carlson claims that an increasing proportion of the American labour force is engaged in occupations for which the definition of appropriate, permissible, or mandatory behaviour is in the hands of colleagues. I find it hard to see that this applies to Australia. I would have thought that the opposite was true; but perhaps there are grounds for different interpretations of what is involved in the role definition of occupations by colleagues. So far as the university is concerned, there appears to be an increasing tendency towards "domestication" (to use a graphic metaphor of Carlson's from an earlier work)[1] as it becomes more dependent on public money and political support, as it becomes increasingly coordinated with other institutions of the same kind, and with other tertiary institutions, and as pressures on it to serve socially useful purposes in its research and teaching become clearer and more insistent. Whatever grounds there may be for the diversification of tertiary education, it is clear that one of the possible effects of alternative institutions is the form of social control that they will exercise on the universities. To me it appears that the universities are entering a period when, to an increasing degree, the appropriate occupational behaviour of academics will be influenced if not wholly defined by people outside the colleague group, and when role ambiguity and conflict are likely to increase.

Second, within the academic fold itself, there is great diversity. We sometimes talk as if academic behaviour as defined by academics is clear, explicit, and agreed on. But this is not so. Academics are a varied lot, with affinities to professional groups outside the university often closer than across departments and faculties to one another. It is not easy to see what they have in common, and to define it in unequivocal terms that make them easily recognizable to each other (outside the common room and the meeting room), and that give a clear public image. If academic behaviour is defined for a person by his colleagues, as it is the common stereotype to believe, the definition is given in a minor key; or to change the figure, one has to read between the lines to see what is intended.

Is teaching a unifying activity, in terms of which their differences as historians, chemists, architects, dentists, and the like are transcended? Most do teach, but this is not usually regarded as a significant area in which role definition should be concentrated.

Is research a unifying activity? Most do undertake research, or keep abreast of the research of others in their field. This is a widely respected activity, and undoubtedly is a major cohesive factor among university teachers.

How are university teachers to be distinguished from other teachers, particularly other tertiary teachers? Are they different from teachers' college lecturers, and from those being recruited to staff the colleges of advanced education? Are they separate but similar, just as the institutions are supposed to be separate but equal? If there are differences at present, for example in the lesser weight placed on research and publication for non-university tertiary staff, will these differences tend to be reduced as these other institutions are developed?

Perhaps in saying that university teaching is an occupation for which the definition of appropriate behaviour is in the hands of colleagues, it should be added that this definition is rather taken for granted than made explicit. In view of the importance of the nature of the job in determining a wide range of administrative acts and processes, it is suggested that a clarification of the role of the university teacher is needed. While not attempting to do this in any extended way in this paper, a brief indication of one way in which it might reasonably be approached is given.

The teaching role in the university, it is suggested, is what needs sophisticated examination. It is this that can give the most mature interpretation of the nature of the profession, and can effectively bridge other expected differences within the occupational group.

The present approach to teaching by university staff is usually unsophisticated. It makes an artificial separation between teaching methods, the material being taught, research, and the intellectual tradition with which the staff identifies itself, even though this identification is sometimes only vaguely recognized. As is expected, when only a common sense approach to teaching method is used, formality and conservatism are common. An excessive use of formal lectures, presented in stilted form as the reading of a paper, often results. If modern aids such as television are used, these are likely to be handled in such a way that the same formality is apparent, reproduced on a larger scale.

Yet the lecturer may have priceless assets as a teacher. His level of scholarship, his contribution to knowledge through research, his close contact with the work of other scholars in his field, and his commitment to an intellectual tradition, if seen as elements of his *teaching*, could bring great vitality to his work.

The separation of teaching and research has been particularly harmful. There are a few people with a talent for research, but with little for teaching, and less interest in it. Such people should concentrate on research, although there is no special reason why they should be in a university. Research is a powerful form of teaching when undertaken in association with students. It makes clear the scope and limitations of knowledge, the methods by which new knowledge is sought, as well as conveying many of the essential attitudes of the scholar, the respect for rigour, and the excitement of discovery. In teaching at university level, research should never be far away.

At the school level great changes are presently being made through curriculum development. This movement embodies the somewhat novel idea (at least for Australians) that the material of a course of study, the educational objectives sought, the methods by which it can be most appropriately learnt and taught, and the kind of evaluation necessary, *together* constitute the curriculum. Many of the newer curriculum schemes developed in America and England have made notable contributions to educational innovation because of the system of inherent relationships which has been possible when the structure of subjects (the terms used by them, their grammar, major concepts, and methodology) are put into functional sequence in accordance with some explicit appreciation of the behavioural objectives sought, and an appropriate appeal to cognitive and affective learning processes.

It is this kind of effort at the university level that would put teaching into proper focus, and would bridge the present unproductive distinction between scholarship and research on the one hand (which are highly prized), and the communication of this scholarship on the other (which is much less highly prized). It would also have a beneficial effect on examining because objectives would be much more functionally expressed.

Snyder in a paper, "The Preparation of Educational Administrators",[2] gives a good example of curriculum development in a university. The strategy followed was to work backward from stated objectives. This strategy, he states,[3]

has the distinct advantage of compelling us to relate explicitly everything which is allotted time and resources in the formal educational process to the acquisition of those intellectual capabilities deemed necessary for future use.

Space does not permit a full description of the programme that resulted. It could however be stated that it involved a novel arrangement of courses and non-course kinds of learning experiences, an inter-disciplinary approach, team teaching for the course "Foundations of Administration", and a new form of evaluation departing from the familiar hours of credit.

A more sophisticated approach to curriculum development in the universities would increase the common ground between staff members divided by disciplines, and between the different elements of the university teachers' work. It would also have obviously beneficial results for the students and the community generally.

The career strategy of the university teacher

I find the concept of a dominant *career prototype*, embracing a sequence of *career strategies*, understandable, but rather distasteful. I take perhaps a minority old-fashioned, and perhaps even romantic, view that a person should to a substantial degree carry out a job like this for the sake of his students, or for the development of his subject, or to put it in even more idealistic terms, in the pursuit of truth. The idea of a person self-consciously assessing the future and manipulating the present to bring some career pattern about repels me, at least if put forward as a typical pattern or prototype. In existential terms, as a literary man might create a character, I find it fascinating; in conceptual terms as a behavioural scientist brings forth an idea, I find it depressing.

Yet in the Australian setting, as well perhaps as in the American one, the type is common enough, and the description apt. Listen to the relevant section from Carlson's paper:[4] he talks about the opportunity for the individual to differentiate himself from competitors in the market, depending not only on his actual ability and performance, but also on his ability to manage a reputation, to manage his visibility.

Individuals seeking new opportunities must cast a wide net just as job-seeking candidates must, and job markets tend to be regional or national. To maintain his market potential, the individual must so manage his reputation as to remain visible to colleagues in the network. Publication or its equivalent and professional society activities are therefore important. Readiness to move is also necessary.

Thus the strategy that leads to success is an occupational one, with the individual practising the occupation in any setting which gives opportunity for experience and increase in competence, and to make this increased competence known to colleagues elsewhere.

This exploitive strategy (the phrase is not Carlson's) gives way to one of stability which is oriented more to job security, viewing the job rather as a means to other aspirations.

Carlson makes the interesting observation that if professional practice is founded on service to non-professions, as in social work and general medical practice, that is, if the person's professional visibility is with laymen rather than colleagues, the switch from occupational orientation to stability may come fairly early in the career.

In the case of university teachers the main laymen concerned may be assumed to be students; and the moral of this is that visibility with students does not give advancement in the same way as does visibility with colleagues or other professionals who have influence. The university teacher who devotes himself to teaching may give up his occupational strategy, and substitute a concern for the organization and for the more stable rewards of the job.

If, as was proposed earlier, a new definition of the work of the university teacher were to give greater prominence to the teaching function, not only would it be necessary to place greater value on it, but also opportunities for making it more visible to colleagues would have to be made. Books, articles, conference speeches are public performances. Teaching is less so. Even when there is a disposition to reward good teaching, it is not easy to know that it is occurring. The relevance of this for any promotion scheme for university teachers is obvious.

Implications for personnel management

No doubt there are many more implications for the management of university teachers that arise from a consideration of the nature of university teaching than will be raised here. The most obvious ones are those that occur in connection with recruiting, training, and promoting staff, and in the more personal aspects of management such as the exercise of authority, and assisting in the achievement of job satisfaction.

Carlson's paper does not deal with all of these. Of the seven propositions given, one (No. 3) deals with recruitment, three (Nos. 4, 5, and 6) take a psychiatric line and deal with the person's adjustment to his occupation under conditions of career change or disruption, one (No. 2) deals with the relatively few cases (among university people) who become full-time administrators, and two (Nos. 1 and 7) with more general aspects of the personnel function itself.

Use will be made in the brief commentary that follows of No. 1 which concerns the general nature of personnel management and of No. 3 which deals with recruitment.

The issues of personnel management in the university are treated here as being closely related to the central question already raised about the nature of the university position. How this position is defined determines in large measure the selection, training, and promotion criteria, and the appropriate part to be played by members of staff in academic policy making, and university government generally.

Personnel management, as is pointed out, is itself in a state of ambiguity, and its techniques have never been quite appropriate for collegially-defined occupations of a professional kind. University staff particularly are usually fairly individualistic in their outlook, and do not take too kindly to being managed. The academic air in Australia is still faintly ringing with the clamour set off in 1961 by Hartwell[5] and O'Neil[6] by their criticism of university administration. In the catalogue of oligarchic abuses advanced by them and various other critics who joined the fray, the god-king conception of the professor came in for a major share of the attack. Hartwell[7] wrote about them as follows:

Until the absurd power of the professors is drastically reduced, morale in most university departments will remain bad, with too much time devoted to worrying about salaries and to criticising the professor and the administration . . . Australian university government is like that of an army, completely authoritarian, and, as such, bitterly resented by all below professorial rank. People as intelligent as university teachers like to, and should, have some say in the determination of policies that determine their work-life.

Since then the number of professors has been increased, and the more common arrangement of multiple chairs within departments has altered their previous monolithic structure.

The question of the government of universities is a many-sided and complex one, far broader than the management of personnel. In the management of staff it is suggested that genuinely democratic procedures which allow them adequate scope for expression are essential, and that a wide range of individual differences should be accepted. Whether the notion of an educative community fits as a special case into the more general case of fruitful administrative relationships within organizations is perhaps debatable. But certainly it appears to me to be unanswerable that an educational institution (and particularly a university) is best served by cooperative relation-ships that encourage individual participation in policy making, and which help to release and develop the individual's powers. This is *not* the same as accepting a laissez-faire situation in which individual differences are egocentrically expressed, competitively or exploitively. This situation is likely to be less productive academically, and to generate hostile attitudes. The most effective staff is one that is strongly task-oriented, and this is most likely to occur if the position of university teaching is interpreted in a way that gives unity to the variety of activities that presently are included in it.

Recruitment

Carlson's proposition 3 deals with a recruitment procedure that stresses the conformity of the recruit to organizational customs. It asserts that such a procedure is likely to lead to the appointment of people whose commitment to the occupation is weak, and whose potential for professional development is unpromising.

The proposition does not seem to fit the university situation closely, unless the reproduction of academic qualifications similar to those held by the recruiting staff of the institution may be interpreted as being in line with organizational customs.

The type of recruit called for in a typical advertisement is one who has done well in meeting the university's academic requirements, and who has carried his studies to the point where he has undertaken some significant research, or made some contribution through publication. In a minority of cases he is expected to be a successful practitioner. In very few cases is any training in teaching expected, and where a candidate's potential as a teacher is considered at all, the methods of assessment of it in interview are rather inadequate. Nor is the candidate's concern with university teaching, with its objectives, its relationship to research, and with the measurement of student achievement seriously probed.

In the main the recruitment procedure tends to perpetuate the main features of the occupational group, and does little to call them into question in any way.

It may be countered by some that the emphasis being placed on teaching is likely to result in an even closer kind of conformity among recruits. Certainly this is not intended; it is the conservative approach of most recruits to university teaching that is being criticized. A serious concern for the teaching function, and an informed insight into it, are likely to lead to great variety and experimentation rather than to routine practices. It is worth repeating that formal methods of teaching tend to occur most frequently among the untrained.

Training

Nor do the training experiences after appointment do much to alter the expectations of the recruits. In few universities is in-service training taken very seriously. The newcomer learns the mores through an unplanned induction procedure, and quickly takes on the protective colouration of the rest.

There are, however, straws in the wind, research units which study the institution's procedures and assess its success and failure, advisory units and training courses for lecturers, induction seminars on teaching and examining. In the University of Queensland, for example, new members of staff of the rank of demonstrator or tutor and above meet with a large number of the staff to discuss questions like the aims of university teaching, lecturing, the conduct of tutorials, and examining. The induction seminar lasts only for a few days, but it is a promise of a growing recognition of the need to try to make a reality of a definition by colleagues of university teaching. The value of conferences such as these is not that they tell new members of staff "how to teach", thereby confirming their suspicion that teaching does consist of nothing more than a few pedagogic routines. It leads them to a better appreciation of the significance of the teaching function, and a respect for its complexity. It helps them to make better sense of their own position.

Promotion

According to Stenhouse,[8] under the present system the quality of one's teaching is irrelevant (providing classroom riots are reasonably infrequent and that one's failure rates are reasonably near the standard 30 per cent). "One is well advised, from the promotional point of view, to devote maximum energy and time to the production of published research papers." Such advice might well be echoed round the Australian universities.

It does not necessarily derive from an attitude of unconcern about the importance of teaching, although this is involved, but from a genuine perplexity both about the criteria for evaluating good teaching, and also the practical measures needed to evaluate it. Undoubtedly these constitute serious difficulties. At the school level there are wide differences of opinion about the nature of good teaching, and equally different views about its assessment. It is only in recent years that some precision is being introduced in judgments of this kind by a more detailed statement of objectives, by a closer examination of the kind of learning experiences likely to lead to the achievement of these objectives, and of the actual behaviour of teachers in classrooms, and by a more efficient form of evaluation. It is this kind of study that is needed among university teachers in their own subject. Progress along these lines would make it more likely that teaching and examining would count for promotion; it would also make it fairer for them to do so.

The vocational role of the university

As vital to the idea of a university (and to the administrative processes that flow from it) as a clear appraisal of the role of the university teachers, is a clear appreciation of the role of the various professionals being trained there. This also requires a sophisticated understanding of the teaching function of the university.

The vocational role of the university appears to be well accepted in Australian society. The usefulness of the universities is perhaps the major fact that reconciles the Australian public to them. This fact is supported by Philp's study of Sydney University[9] in which he reports that 74 per cent of undergraduates and 66 per cent of graduates stated that their chief reason for attending the university was training for a profession.

Below are set out a number of influential opinions on the same point.

Partridge of the Australian National University writes:[10]

The majority of students now enter a university in order to get as efficiently, as speedily, as economically as possible the training they must have in order to pursue some learned or highly skilled profession.

The Martin Report[11] recognizes the vocational role and states that Australian universities are likely to expand their traditional function of training for the professions:

As additional occupations are based on solid foundations of academic disciplines, and offer scope for basic research, they may justifiably be included as university studies.

R.G. Menzies, speaking as Prime Minister of Australia at Sydney University, 1959:

Slighting references used to be made about the academic mind as if a university degree . . . detached its possessor from the realities of everyday life. Relatively few graduates reached administrative posts and comparatively few entered parliament.
Now great organizations are eagerly looking for graduates. In my own ministry there were no less than twelve ministers including myself who had university degrees.

An earlier Prime Minister of Australia, Mr. J.B. Chifley, is also worth quoting. A.P. Rowe,[12] a former Vice-Chancellor of Adelaide University, had approached him regarding the financial state of the universities, and urged him to ensure that they were producing enough scientists to meet the needs of Australia. Chifley sat back puffing at his ever-glowing pipe, and said, "I don't mind helping the universities to produce more scientists, more engineers, and more doctors, but I don't want any more bloody lawyers."

Finally, may I quote Rowe's[13] own views on vocationalism in universities.

The general public and most students would say that universities exist to produce professional men and women, and would find it hard to think of any other function for them. This is of course a primary task of a university, and what a gigantic task it is!

Considered as a factory, a university receives schoolboys and schoolgirls as raw material, and after a few years turns them into doctors and dentists on whom the public is dependent for its health; into lawyers who administer and safeguard the laws of the land and to whom are entrusted funds and knowledge of intimate family affairs; into scientists and engineers on whose knowledge, wisdom and adaptability the very existence of an industrial and agricultural country depends; into secondary school teachers with their vital role in a community, and into senior civil servants and economists, who through the advice they give may lead a nation from or into disaster.

As the professions for which the university prepares are presumably *collegially-defined* also, the function of the university in assisting in this task of role definition is an important element in its teaching responsibility.

The appropriateness of the university as an institution for undertaking professional teaching is based on the level of scholarship and research in studies on which the profession rests, and in the academic and liberal spirit in which the theory and practice of the profession are approached. Professional studies are usually undertaken in collaboration with the profession itself.

The function of the university as the interpreter and defender of liberal values has long been acknowledged, but with the expansion of its role in vocational training, and with the shift towards scientifically based professional studies, older ideas of this liberal tradition have changed. Newman's words[14] " . . . giving enlargement and sobriety to the ideas of the age, facilitating the exercise of political power, and refining the intercourse of private life" now have an old-fashioned ring about them. Yet its historic function in defining and defending liberal values may still be its most distinctive, and the exercise of this function in professional training its most challenging present task.

Professional practice, whether in the established professions which have been shaped largely within the context of private practice, or in the newer professions which have grown up mainly on a salaried basis, is now commonly carried out in an organizational setting. Particularly in government, with its extensions into many fields of welfare, and with its large stake in scientific enterprises in agriculture, industry, defence, and the like, there is an increasing use of professionals within bureaucratic organizations. These modern professionals find that behaviour as defined by the profession is not always easy to reconcile with the demands of the enterprise, and that the exercise of professional judgment based on knowledge and competence is not always compatible with the exercise of authority based on position.

The preservation of a professional spirit is a task for which the university tradition is well suited. The adherence to principles, and the open-mindedness and self-criticism on which both professional integrity and progress depend, are akin to the academic spirit, the humane element which should permeate professional activity is akin to the liberal spirit. Mitchell and Passmore,[15] writing of the humanities in Australian education, express this humane element in these terms.

Whether a man is a humanist who has acquired some understanding of science and technology, or whether he is a technologist who has acquired some understanding of human subjects might be regarded as a matter of degree. The fact remains that his point of view as an executive must be humanistic, not technological; he must treat human beings as potentially creative, not as mere cogs in an organization. Otherwise our society will collapse into some form of totalitarianism, however benevolent.

Suffusing professional training with a liberal spirit may well be one of the major contributions of the university to modern society.

Again it could be said, as *was* said when discussing the role descriptions of the university teacher, that the roles of the various professionals with whom the university deals are not explicitly expressed, nor usually does the professional training programme include an effective blend of academic, liberal, and practical elements. Academic and practical requirements, professional knowledge and professional values, are often disconnected or even antagonistic. The major contribution referred to will occur only when the professional programmes are imaginatively planned and effectively carried out.

The question of the other institutions in the emerging tertiary education system in Australia again obtrudes. On what basis are the differentiations between professional training programmes to be made, particularly with occupations such as engineering or teaching which will be carried on both in universities and other tertiary institutions? Does Carlson's concept of being collegially-defined point in the direction of a solution, or merely emphasize the point that it needs to be solved?

Concluding comment

A job, as is stated in Carlson's paper, is a localized version of an occupation which fixes the practice of that occupation in time and space.

It is the main contention of this paper that the version of the occupation university teaching, current in Australia in the latter part of the twentieth century, would benefit greatly from careful re-examination, and explicit re-statement. A great deal of research is done by university teachers on problems within their sphere of interest; it is high time that a similar effort be turned back onto the occupation itself, and that studies of university teaching be undertaken with the same degree of sophistication as is applied in these other studies.

| Part | THE PREPARATION OF EDUCATIONAL |
| Five | ADMINISTRATORS |

G.W. MUIR

12 An Overview

The title of this paper provokes a number of questions. First, are there such beings as "educational administrators" or are they part of the larger group "administrators"? Secondly, can such people be prepared for their task? Thirdly, if preparation is possible, how should it be carried out?

Culbertson[1] claims that the view that administrative processes are similar, even though they take place in diverse organizations, has been widely accepted. This would accord with the quoted view of Sir John Crawford, that "the only thing unique about educational administration is that it is concerned with children".[2] On the other hand, it is to be inferred from Halpin's statement that because "the educational administrator needs to continuously examine the purpose of his organization as it attempts to serve its unique role in our society and to make recommendations for re-shaping the organization as well as operating it",[3] there is a unique quality about educational administration which differs greatly from business, military, hospital, and other varieties of administration. This argument stems from the uniqueness of the educator's task and, presumably, from the uniqueness of the organizations which it is necessary for him to administer.

Bassett[4] takes the view that within an individual school and system of schools, there are many tasks that are not educational at all; that those which directly establish and maintain a particular kind of educational activity within schools are the primary concern of educational administration. This peculiarity would make educational administration unique and since it presupposes a degree of autonomy for individual teachers, it becomes an extension of the teacher's initial preparation and thus should be taught.

Cunningham and Radford[5] examine the changes which are taking place in education and raise the issue as to whether a professional educator or a general administrator would be preferable or more capable in the administrative problem areas he selects.

The concept of universal education raises problems of a social and sociological nature which demand, according to Cunningham and Radford, a kind of competence and interest "which arises out of special training and a particular kind of experience", and which would need a "properly trained educational administrator".

The fact that, unlike many human tasks, education cannot be standardized into uniform mechanical processes makes the task of the administrator one of *not* insisting on or even encouraging "uniformity in the classroom". It is rather to ensure the professional development of the teacher so that he will have a clearer grasp of his goals and of the most efficient way of attaining them in relation to the potentialities of his pupils. In this Cunningham and Radford think the general administrator would be inadequate.

The expansion of educational objectives is a matter for the community, and though the professional educator may help to gather information and advice, the final decision is a community one. Cunningham and Radford think a well-educated general administrator would be as effective as a professional educator in establishing such goals. They hold similar views about the role of the administrator in the school's task of preserving the social and ethical values of the society. Cunningham and Radford see that one of the most important of the school's tasks is the development in each learner of the capacity to think for himself—"to avoid hasty or biased conclusions, to distinguish between genuine argument and specious propaganda". For this a *professional* educator is required. On balance they consider it essential that educational administrators receive some professional training in educational administration.

Snyder[6] takes the view that while formal preparation is necessary, a generalist approach would be more fruitful in the establishment of a graduate school of administration. He considers that there are many reasons for the powerful centrifugal forces which would call for a unified approach. The fact that governmental, educational, and business-industrial leaders find it difficult to communicate may make it reasonable to suppose that identical or parallel preparation will establish bases for enhanced communication. Furthermore, the possible need to rethink organizational leadership or the nature of the organizations themselves would make it imperative that the administrator of the future be not tied to the conceptual framework of a particular organization or even to a particular kind of institutional form. Snyder feels that foreseeable major changes in the curriculum and government of schools in the United States indicate that school administrators will need a formal preparation different from that of their predecessors.

In an organizational society, where most of an individual's time is spent in organization,[7] educational institutions are among the most prominent of formal organizations. Crane,[8] following Parsons[9] and Haberstroh,[10] sees four levels of performance in a formal organization. At the top of the hierarchy, the entrepreneurial level (Parson's institutional level) is the one where the organization makes the greatest contact with other organizations and the community at large. Directors-General of state departments and Vice-Chancellors are examples. The second level, the managerial level (Haberstroh's organization level) is the one in which the administrator is responsible under a delegated authority for the running of the organization. Into this category Crane would put state inspectors and headmasters. His third level, Parson's technical level or Haberstroh's operation level, where the actual tasks of the organization are carried out, consists of a technical level, where decisions rely on the professional knowledge and skill of the organizer, and a production level where these decisions are carried out. In the nature of the school and of schooling it is sometimes difficult to check whether technical decisions, say a staff decision made with the guidance of the principal in his managerial role, are carried into the classroom. Further, it is difficult to check whether failure, if any, is due to lack of skill or to a rejection of the decision.

Given that some preparation of educational administrators is necessary, the level at which such administrators operate will affect their needs for formal or informal preparation. These levels may also reflect the history of trends in thinking about administration. The earlier approach, with its emphasis on job performance, began with the work of Frederick Taylor[11] and translated into educational terms by Cubberley[12] was aimed at the operational level.

The human relations approach followed Mayo's[13] Hawthorne experiments. These started out to study the effects of environmental conditions, including illumination, on performance; they ended by stressing human relations because performance could not be explained in other terms.[14] This approach is perhaps of more significance for the managerial level, though today it permeates programmes for preparing government, business, and educational administrators alike.

It was followed by the scientific movement, which probably dates from Simon's *Administrative Behavior*[15] and received tremendous impetus in the 1950's with the publication of books like Halpin's *Administrative Theory in Education*[16] and Griffiths' *Administrative Theory*.[17]

With an emphasis on what *is* rather than what *ought* to be and an emphasis on empiricism and a high premium on rigorous logical thinking,[18] this movement highlights the shift of emphasis from an economic perspective on administration and organization to one which concentrates more on the psycho-sociological aspects of these phenomena. More recently the writings of scholars like Presthus,[19] to whose work both Crane and Walker have referred, have added a considerable body of theory about the nature of organizations. All of these have implications for administrators—and for the people who take courses in administration.

One would rarely see in a course in administration one of Presthus' indifferents unless he were paid to come. The vast majority of students would be upward-mobiles who, having learned to live in an organization, seek to know more about it and its operation. The difficulty of the ambivalent is ever present and his is, as Griffiths says, "a miserable lot in the modern large organization". The teacher, unable to resist the appeal of power and unable to play the role necessary to achieve it, who enrols in a course in educational administration in order to establish a new claim to preferment, is among the most difficult and frustrated of students.

In another way Gouldner's[20] locals, who have derived their skill and experience in one organization, are often less satisfied with courses than the cosmopolitans whose values and standards are derived from experience outside the organization in which the students work at present.

These implications could be extended by examining the theories of Etzioni, whose typology of organizations Walker has described above, but sufficient has been said to indicate that these theories have implications not only for the *content* of courses in educational administration but also for their *design*.

The contribution of Griffiths,[21] in developing a paradigm for the development of a theory, points to two problems in the study of educational administration. The first problem arises out of the observation stage. Little has been done to produce a taxonomy of terms in educational administration and one result is that descriptions are often ambiguous. What is said of biology in the quotation below may be equally applicable to administration.

It is hard to see how biological science would have entered a properly dynamic period except for the continual gathering of more descriptive natural history. The great botanist Linnaeus will serve as an example. For Linnaeus, species and genera were fixed Aristotelian forms rather than signposts for the process of evolution but it was on the basis of a thoroughly Linnaean description that any cogent case could ever be made for evolution.[22]

One of the end products of any course in administration, then, is that all administrators should be familiar with the process of developing a theory.

Let us now turn to the task of the administrator. Lazarsfeld[23] has argued that all administrators are confronted with four major tasks and that these tasks vary little, other than in emphasis, from organization to organization. These tasks are:

1. The administrator must fulfil the goals of the organization.
2. The administrator must make use of other people in fulfilling these goals, not as if they were machines, but rather in such a way as to release their initiative and creativity.
3. The administrator must also face the humanitarian aspects of his job. He wants the people who work for him to be happy. This is morale—the idea that under suitable

conditions people will do better work than they will under unsuitable conditions.

4. The administrator must try to build into his organization provisions for innovation, change, and development. In a changing world people and organizations must adjust to varying conditions. Conditions for growth must be incorporated into the organization so that there may be a steady process of development rather than a series of sudden disruptive innovations.

If these are the tasks of the administrator (and obviously there are arguments of an ethical-political nature which could be raised about the above statements), then what are the implications for the preparation of such a person for his task?

First, the administrator must be able to perceive, delineate, and help achieve the goals of his organization. These will be different according to the level of his administrative responsibilities. The works manager of a motor manufacturing firm might properly see his goal as the production of as many cars as possible. The managing director of the firm might see his goal as the making of the largest amount of profit possible. A hospital administrator may be a medical man, a matron, or a secretary. Each may see the goal of his hospital but lack the technical skill to achieve it in full. No hospital secretary would diagnose or prescribe, no medico would be able to attend to nursing, and no matron would be able to carry out the organizational and procurement tasks of the secretary. A teacher may see his goal as the maximum achievement of each individual in his class; a state director may see his as the provision of educational facilities for all children. This, then, raises the question of his being able to fulfil the goals he perceives.

Is such a division possible in an educational organization or does the nature of the task require a direct line of technical skill from top to bottom? Whatever may be the answer, the fact remains that the educational administrator must catch or be taught the processes whereby developments in the profession may be applied to the achievement of the goals of his organization. The ability to separate the real from the spurious is one which all administrators need, but educational administrators most of all.

The administrator, then, needs to be prepared to understand his organization and the technical skills required to run it. This reveals one of the choices which must be made. I would think that Australian school men would agree with Griffiths'[24] opinion that courses in educational administration are too "theoretical". The confusion which arises when "theoretical" is taken to mean "impractical" or even just "poor" is one which bedevils designers of courses for educational administrators as for any other educators.

The false view described by Griffiths, that a theory is a well-developed set of values, that is, a set of "oughts" which are rules telling one how to administer, is one which also appears in the group needs which students wish to satisfy by attendance at courses. Recently the University of New England, for example, re-organized its courses in the Diploma in Educational Administration in order, in part, to meet the criticism of students who claimed that the first year courses had insufficient to do with administration.

If one accepts Fiegl's[25] definition of theory as "a set of assumptions from which can be derived by purely logico-mathematical procedures a larger set of empirical laws", then obviously theory provides the raw material for decision making—but not the decisions themselves. If it can be established that, if an administrator acts in one way the outcome will be X, or in another the outcome will be Y, the decision still remains as to whether X or Y is the better, and this rests on an interpretation of a set of value judgments related to the goals of the organization.

Second, reverting to Lazarsfeld, the administrator must use people to achieve the goals of his organization. This implies some understanding of the behaviour of people as individuals, as members of groups and as members of organizations. A number of theories have been proposed and March and Simon[26] have categorized these as follows:

1. Theories of conflict. I.e. role conflict where the role expectations of an individual are mutually exclusive or incompatible, or personality conflict, or role personality conflict. The now famous Getzels[27] model of a social system is an example of such a theory.

2. Theories of motivation. The Barnard-Simon theory of organizational equilibrium which discusses the inducements for, and contributions by, individuals in organizations, is an example.
3. Theories of decision making. Griffiths' theory of decision making is an example of these.

Griffiths adds two more:

4. Organizational theories such as those of Presthus or Etzioni.
5. System theories such as that presented by Griffiths where a system is described as a complex of elements in mutual interaction and is designed to look at social organization as a whole.

To these might be added:

6. The philosophical mathematical theories which lie behind the use of computers in and for social organizations.

Third, the administrator must be concerned with morale and the creation of conditions in which people do better work. This is related to organizational climate and stems from the same sorts of argument as does the first premise. Once again, it is a matter of the theory-practice dichotomy in the preparation of administrators and the development of theory rather than recipes.

Fourth, the preparation of administrators must include preparation for building into the organization "provision for innovations, change, and development". This is an area where there has been a neglect of organization theory and system theory in writing about educational innovation. The fact that the educational administrator will be operating in a formal organizational framework needs a great deal of examination before courses in administration deal satisfactorily with this aspect of the administrator's task.

Culbertson, in an unpublished address at the University of New England, claimed that an academic discipline needed to satisfy the following criteria: there must be a body of knowledge; there must be ways of adding to that knowledge; there must be a felt need for its study; there must be ways of transmitting it.

Whether or not educational administration is unique or merely a subsection of general administration, the first three criteria seem to be met. Let us turn to the particular qualities of the teaching of administration. These seem to form a continuum of sophistication from the on-the-job sink-or-swim method of personal training to a sophisticated pre-service training of people whose first job aspiration is administration.

We have glanced at educational theory and its development and it is clear that there is no academic reason why this discipline should not be amenable to the scholarly techniques of the social sciences and the humanities. The false dichotomy of theory and practice, however, raises the question of the application of what is taught to practice. The "reality" of the preparation is backed by the same need for perceived relevance to the practice of the profession which is at the root of the criticism of many professional courses in education. Since administration, like medicine, is a process dealing with people, it is wasteful, to say the least, to allow a practitioner to make his inexperienced mistakes on his clients, though this is done and no doubt will continue to be done. For this reason the development of the simulated situation has been vigorously followed. I will mention but a few of these; the case study, the management game, the in-basket, and the computer-programmed learning approach.

The case study is a well-known technique in medicine and law, and involves presenting the student with an open-ended problem in which all the information for a solution is presented. Walker's [28] collection of Australian examples will be known to you. From a case a management game may be developed in which solutions are ranked in order of "correctness" and a "winner" determined. The in-basket is a technique involving the use of a number of items about which the would-be administrator must make decisions—notes, letters, memoranda, calls, records of visits, etc. About these he makes decisions in the light of his training and against the background of a thoroughgoing description of a school and its environment. It is, of course, possible to adapt any or all of these techniques to the so-called teaching machines and the tremendous capacity of the computer for storing and relating facts makes it ideal for presenting simulated situations. The link trainer for the practice of airline pilots is a well-known and sophisticated simulator— undoubtedly the educational hardware can be adapted to the problems of administration and perhaps even to the selection of administrators on the basis of their reaction to simulated situations.

There are two forms of realism, both involving participation in real situations—one as an observer in much the same way as a student counsellor observes through a one-way screen and the other is controlled participation or internship where the candidate spends his time making decisions and executing them under experienced guidance.

One problem in the preparation of administrators has remained unstated—the problem of when it should be done. In Australia two approaches seem evident: one selects the administrator and trains him on the job; the other selects an experienced person and prepares him for a proposed job—the latter being the approach of the University of New England.

We have not discussed the pre-service preparation of administrators, though it is done elsewhere. Whether this would be a valid development takes us back to the argument with which we began: is educational administration unique and do its practitioners require to have successful knowledge of practice in educational institutions? When it is accepted that an educational tyro can administer a school, then pre-service preparation becomes possible. Perhaps the immense social and educational developments in the next half century will make it not only possible but necessary.

The preparation of educational administration requires, it would appear:

1. Courses which introduce the students to current theories of society and its organization and which prepare the administrator to be not only sensitive to new movements but capable of assessing them
2. Courses which describe the structure of the educational organization, its articulation with the community and the internal and external modes of communication
3. Courses which prepare the student to understand the behaviour of people in an organization and the development of an appropriate organizational climate
4. Courses which bring up to date the administrator's understanding of the goals and expertise of education and which provide him with a frame of reference and the methods of acquiring and evaluating new ideas

5. Experiences in the development and application of theory to his task
6. Experiences which bring reality to his learning by placing him in real or simulated situations requiring the application of his learning
7. Opportunities to examine the particular specialities of particular kinds of administrators, e.g. the political-economic decisions of a director, the disposal procurement functions of a manager, or the technical functions of a foreman
8. Opportunities to advance thought about administration and education generally.

This is obviously not a how-to-do-it process, in my view, but a horizon-lifting one. The real test of the success of such a course is that its product will have continued learning at a rate which will allow him to cope with a problem five, ten, or fifteen years hence.

13 The Victorian Government School

My task is to follow up Muir's general survey by referring in particular to the preparation of administrators in state departments. Muir's clear and logical framework has made my task much easier.

I do not propose to comment on his opening question as to whether educational administration differs sufficiently from business, hospital, military, and other forms of administration to be a complete, independent study in its own right. My reason for not pursuing this topic is that I believe educational authorities are so convinced of its unique quality, and of the inadequacy of other forms for their purpose, that they would be unlikely to send educators to other-purpose schools, except perhaps occasionally an experienced person involved in teaching educational administration. Such a person could benefit by change of perspective on his own work, and possibly by the sparking of a new idea, or by observing some new item of equipment or method of presentation. However, such schools and courses are likely to be quite appropriate for the clerical staff of education departments, and my own Department has sent senior clerical officers to such courses. Other clerical officers have studied public administration in universities or technical colleges.

We come next to a consideration of levels of performance in the practice of educational administration and the type of preparation specially appropriate to each level of performance. How far from the actual into the anticipated level we should go is a matter of opinion. I do not believe that every private carries a field marshal's baton in his knapsack, or wants to do so. Nor do I believe that every teacher would wish to wear on his breast the clipped wings of a Director-General, symbolic of plans cut back by parliamentary budgets.

Nor shall I comment on the four levels of performance as

attributed to Crane. I do not agree with them entirely, but the disagreement is not vital to the main discussion. Let us accept the fact that in a state department there are different levels of experience and activity for which we must plan appropriate courses in educational administration. I find it convenient to think in terms of teachers, potential administrators, administrators, and top-level administrators—the last-named ranging from Assistant-Directors to Directors-General. What formal preparation should be available to each of these groups?

For the front-line teacher I would be content with simply a cultural or communication level, sufficient for him to be able to understand and contribute to the aims and methods of the organization, and appreciate the problems and difficulties of those to whom he must give loyalty. My impression from Muir's paper is that he would go further at this stage. Some preliminary thought could be given to such aspects during pre-service training to be followed up later through in-service courses. The title of such a course could be "The Role of the Teacher in Educational Administration".[1]

I believe that the first level at which we must give serious attention to the formal preparation of administrators is at the potential administrator (potential principal or potential inspector) stage. This formal training may be given as in-service education or as university training or preferably both. In any case the numbers involved are extremely formidable. In the Victorian state system alone the number of teachers whom the department already regards as potential administrators or actual administrators would probably amount to at least 3,000. And no doubt at least double that number would regard themselves as potential administrators, and have a good case for admission to courses.

Under present conditions it is difficult to see such numbers, which must increase each year, being given adequate courses either as in-service or university education. This leads us to the position that selection for courses in educational administration will continue to be a major problem for a number of years to come. Criteria for selection must therefore be carefully studied by both state and university authorities. It also stresses the need for sound evaluation techniques. Much harm could come if precious places in university schools of educational administration were filled by people who are not potentially either administrators or university staff (teaching or research) in educational administration, and if such people were given the hallmark of the university for future key appointments.

A special problem arises at this point. In Victoria there are a great many potential administrators (at Principal level) who have not matriculated and have not university degrees, but who have qualified by training and experience for their principalships. This suggests that the University of New England and any other university which may have substantial courses in educational administration should try to maintain flexibility regarding entrance qualifications. Generous recognition of non-university teacher-training courses and of experience in responsible administrative positions could give entry to substantial courses. This may be the ultimate role of the Diploma of Educational Administration, leaving the Bachelor's and higher degrees for graduate students. Otherwise, the only alternative for such teachers appears to be in-service courses conducted by their own state departments or by non-state teachers' colleges.

It has certainly been found by experience that very useful groundwork can be covered in evening courses and short residential seminars. I have here details of an evening course of twenty-four sessions of two and a half hours duration which has been conducted over each of the past two years for potential administrators in the Victorian Education Department. The course has been planned and directed by Mr. T. J. Moore, Assistant Director of Secondary Education, who took his degree of Master of Education at the University of Alberta.

Moore's combination of advanced study and high level administrative experience make the structure and content of this course worthy of careful examination by those responsible for such training in any Australian state. Among the topics studied are: The use of simulated material, (i) the case study, (ii) in-basket material; the school as a social system; task areas of educational administration; situational factors in educational administration; skills of an effective administrator; job analysis; leadership (four weeks' study); communication; evaluation; finance; human relations; public relations; curriculum development and planning; experimentation; decision making; staff development; the initiation of change; new practices; current issues; management.

Moore's appetite was whetted for the study of educational administration through the National Seminar for Inspectors held biennially, initially under the direction of Professor J.J. Pratt, and always including a top level overseas consultant. In a fortnight's concentrated residential seminar the participants, mostly brilliant young inspectors with about three or four years' experience, wrestle fiercely with topics such as these: The inspector's role in the administrative system; human relations; the professional development of teachers; supervision; evaluation; teacher assessment; recent research and trends in (*a*) education, (*b*) educational administration; learning theory and the classroom; teacher education; education and the adolescent; the inspector and the curriculum; the initiation of change in education; the inspector as leader.

The participants then become discussion leaders for annual residential seminars of about four days' duration where one of the topics of the National Seminar is dealt with by all district inspectors.

Now if we were to consider the time factor, even in Moore's twenty-four week evening course, it adds up to less than one term of full-time university study; so that it is obvious that such courses and seminars although very valuable are not to be regarded as a substitute for full-time university study. In the course of time—because there could be a problem of devaluing hard-won qualifications—I could imagine the Diploma of Educational Administration being awarded to non-graduate teachers on the basis of, say, two summer schools and a significant essay or piece of research done in the period between the summer schools. This would enable non-graduate principals and potential principals to gain valuable insights into their role, and establish guidelines for continued self-improvement through reading and research.

For graduates whose chosen area of service is the principalship I believe that there should be opportunities here in Australia to take a Bachelor's degree in educational administration. This could include the Diploma work mentioned above, plus an academic year of full-time residential study. This should mean a very valuable and thorough grounding as a basis for a principalship or inspectorship.

The Master's degree I would see as requiring two years of full-time study which should give an experienced man a reasonably good preparation for any administrative post in a state system.

Doctoral and post-doctoral study I would visualize as being designed for university teaching staff or research workers although many practising administrators will no doubt also proceed to such studies. I think it highly desirable that a considerable proportion of such personnel should be drawn from the state teaching service including the administrative positions so that the coursework done may retain close contact with the realities of the school, college, and central office situation.

There is no need for me to comment on the historical outline of trends in administrative theory given in Muir's paper. However, I shall add just a little about recent developments. I shall begin with a heart-stopping statement made by Daniel Griffiths at the U.C.E.A. conference which some of us attended in October 1966. As you know, he has been for more than a decade a dominant figure in the development of theory in educational administration, and is now Dean of the School of Education in New York University. However, he qualified as the fourth "Gloomy Dean" when he declared to the conference that theory building in America had virtually come to a halt in the 1960's. He declared that the writings of Graff,[2] Saunders,[3] and Halpin[4] published in 1966 had failed to produce anything new, in spite of the fact that their titles suggested otherwise.

We had expected the mighty Daniel to bring forth a lion but instead he appeared to have delivered a mouse. However, it was "a mouse that roared", as he went on to say that there had been a lot of what he called "theorizing"—that is, answering fundamental questions which in due course could result in theory building. Perhaps I should recall here Griffiths' own definition of theory as "a set of principles on which action may be predicted".

Among the significant contributions to theory over the past two years are a number by political scientists. Iannaccone,[5] Lutz,[5] and Azzarelli[5] have made important contributions to the study of relations between education and government, particularly state government.

Carlson[6] of Oregon has done important work in the study of innovation and change. Griffiths[7] himself has included in two of his own books a section on budgeting and an account of some aspects of research in classification or taxonomy.[8] I should mention that this research produced 142 categories of organizational behaviour.

I believe that we should not accept too hastily Griffiths' quick brush-off of Graff's *Philosophic Theory and Practice in Educational Administration*, which must interest those who believe that some systematic consideration of values should have a place in the preparation of administrators. Graff and the southern school of thought consider that progress without values is rudderless, and likely to lead to undesirable destinations or to an advance in a retrograde direction. Griffiths and the northern school of thought appear to believe that values must emerge incidentally from sociology and anthropology, or, with more cynicism, from economics and political science. However, all schools stress the importance of establishing goals, and it is difficult to establish educational goals without philosophical values.

I must confess to being quite unimpressed by Lazarsfeld's four major tasks of all administrators as set out in Muir's paper and I would not regard them as an adequate basis for administrator preparation, although they may be no better nor worse than half a dozen other lists of major tasks.

If my memory is correct the American Association of School Administrators had by 1956 managed to get the aims of education to an all-time high of seventy-two! Five years later education writer Paul Woodring found widespread support when he reduced these to one. But when he went on to explain his one aim it became clear that you can either have seventy-two aims or one aim with seventy-two clauses.

So the Lazarsfeld Task No. 1, to fulfil the goals of the organization, can be made to include all tasks and all skills. You name them, we write them in. It is as though we said one of the four major tasks of a boxer is to win his fights. Unless you amplify them to take in the old scientific management skills of Fayol and Taylor as refined and up-dated by Gulick, Gregg,

Campbell, and others over the past fifty years, and unless you add some additional tasks and skills to these, your administrator will be more ill-equipped than Don Quixote.

The other three tasks attributed to Lazarsfeld are useful enough: development of staff initiative; consideration of staff conditions; provision for change without instability; and Muir has performed valiantly in trying to put some substance into the Lazarsfeld theory. However, this theory is not the kind of stimulus to arouse the lethargic or the unimaginative from their slumbers, nor to inspire the enthusiastic or the creative to new heights.

What we need is a list of tasks or processes or functions which will do just that. I would like to see a list which an administrator might read on 31 January each year and say, "Good heavens! did I neglect all those?" and again on 1 February and say, "Well, schools open in a week's time—we'll give it a fly". I am now of course obliged to submit to you a list which I think might do this.

My list is, if I may misquote, "a poor thing sirs, and not even my own" and I merely say in a more serious misquotation "Go thou and do better". I gladly acknowledge a line of descent from Taylor[11] and Fayol of half a century ago, through Gulick[12] 1937, Gregg[13] 1957, Campbell, Corbally, and Ramseyer[14] 1962, and will show the descent (or ascent) in Table 1.

Having considered various opinions regarding the major tasks of the administrative process we now come to the question of courses designed to prepare administrators for their major tasks. Most of the studies which I suggest as basic would be treated with increasing depth and sophistication at all levels from the in-service seminar to the Master's degree, although some could be treated once only at the early levels.

I am in complete agreement with Muir regarding the inclusion of the courses which he proposes. However, I am disposed to make some additions and some sub-divisions. This additional detail should at least give more kindling for the fire of discussion. It will be noticed that although I agree with Muir that we should not adopt a "how to do it" approach I have included a section entitled Administration Practice. It is my belief that with theory and practice each illuminates, illustrates, and tests the other. The old saying, "It is all right in theory

TABLE 1 Major Tasks in the Administrative Process

1968 Russell	1962 Campbell, Corbally, and Ramseyer	1957 Gregg	1937 Gulick	1916 Fayol
Planning establishing goals forming policies solving problems making decisions	Decision making	* also Decision making	* also Budgeting	*
Leadership initiating involving stimulating implementing changes professional development showing consideration values	Stimulating	Influencing	Directing	Commanding
Communication information understanding sharing cooperation enthusiasm		*	Reporting	
Training initial inservice re-training training for change training in administration				
Human Relations staff students parents community press government				
Organizing allocation of duties responsibilities resources	Programming	*	*	*
Supervision of operations staff methods effects				
Coordinating smooth flow staff use maintenance of supplies and equipment	*	*	*	*
Evaluating determining effects and efficiency for re-planning control and feedback	Appraising	*		Controlling

* means included under the same title

but it is no good in practice", is now rarely heard, because it is generally realized that if a thing is no good in practice it is not sound theory.

Course requirements for administrator preparation as they seem to me are as follows:

1. *Personal skills and insights*
   (*a*) *Communication.*
   (*b*) *Leadership.* Skills have been variously described by:
   Reeves:[15] technical managerial; technical educational; human relations; speculative creative.
   Halpin:[16] initiating structure; consideration.
   The L.B.D.Q. research team: initiating structure; consideration; production emphasis; sensitivity.
   (If the humanities are to convert their toehold to a firm footing it may well be here, since the education of leadership depends on values, ethics, character, and motives.)
   (*c*) *Decision making.* This includes or results from: planning; goal setting; problem seeking (Simon's "intelligence"); problem solving.
   (*d*) *Conceptual.* What Katz described as "seeing the enterprise as a whole". This is the mainspring for what Downey[17] called "statesmanship" in education: the vision which gives the necessary energy and courage.
   (*e*) Insights from the behavioural sciences.
   (*f*) Insights from the social sciences.

2. *Administration theory*
   (*a*) Organization theory—including the school as an organization
   (*b*) Systems theory
   (*c*) Power and responsibility
   (*d*) Innovation and change
   (*e*) Learning theory
   (*f*) Conflict theory
   (*g*) Curriculum making
   (*h*) Needs and motivation
   (*i*) Interpretation of research

3. *Administration practice*
   (*a*) Supervision—art, purposes, effects
   (*b*) Evaluation—programme, pupils, innovations, ideas, staff, school, system

(*c*) Professional development of teachers and supporting personnel

(*d*) Organization—groups, staff, curriculum, materials, space, technology, experiment, research, establishing the environment

(*e*) Office management—records, management and disposal, office personnel and equipment

(*f*) Buildings and equipment—school architecture and its effect, material resource centres, libraries, audio visual including TV maintenance and replacement

(*g*) Supplies—procurement, distribution, costing, quality and quantity checks

(*h*) Legal and constitutional—teacher and the law, supervision of children, injuries, compensation, insurance, rights, public comment, conduct—pupils, teachers

(*i*) Negotiation—teacher organizations

(*j*) Simulation of practice—case studies, in-basket exercises, computer programmed exercises

4. *Financial administration*
Cost analysis, return for cost, budgeting, accounting, controls, fund raising, economics of education

5. *Comparative studies*
Centralized and de-centralized systems, role of federal and state governments in different states and countries, power and responsibility, roles of individuals and groups, professional freedom, involvement in decision making, teacher training, supply of teachers to less favoured areas, primary, secondary, tertiary, vocational, continuing education, grading or non-grading, transition

6. *Provision for fostering and developing individual interests and ideas of students*
Research design, research methods, research interpretation, areas of challenge or doubt, mutual criticism, data interpretation, statistics

7. *Essay, dissertation or other written contribution*
(Essential at all levels of training.)
Eliminates "levitation" and miasmic thinking. Indicates

capacity of students for clear thinking, planning, and research. Stimulates individual and group thought. Choice and development of subject helps with evaluation of student's capacity.

It need scarcely be said that some very great administrators past and present had no university training in administration. For them the necessary behaviour was either innate or a result of environment, and the skills were acquired by intelligence acting on experience. But for such the sun will have set within a decade.

What is needed is a tremendous cooperative effort between universities, teachers' colleges, and practising administrators to make available for all who need them continually improving courses in educational administration.

D.A. BUCHANAN

14 The New South Wales Government School

Muir, in his penetrating paper, raises issues which have significant implications for those of us who are interested in educating future and present administrators in large school systems.

The suggestion that administrative processes are similar in all organizations, and the inference that educational administration requires no special expertise, come at a time when it appears there is a shift in emphasis from a school-centred to a community-centred approach. Whether the schools exist to pass on the culture of the community or whether they exist to influence that culture is a sociological question beyond the scope of this paper, yet there is an acute awareness by many educators that all must face the political and legal realities of living and working in dynamic, democratic communities. It is this broad-based frame of reference within which our schools work which may have prompted some writers to suggest that educational administrators require no special skills beyond those afforded by an understanding of administrative processes in general. However, schools exist solely for learners, who are ends in themselves rather than means, and a tendency to forget this sometimes results in the view that schools can function effectively using operational techniques which are borrowed from management in industry and commerce, etc. But learning is not a mechanistic process, nor are learners mechanical.

No doubt there is common ground on which all administrators may with benefit tread, yet the educational administrator has a unique task in that he is concerned with total human development, be it for the benefit of the individual or the community. Others also may be concerned with human beings, but they are seldom involved with the *whole person*, although medical and legal men may deny this.

If Sir Graham Balfour[1] is correct in claiming that learning and teaching are the first and chief acts of education, then the educational administrator, except at the higher levels, needs to be first and foremost an effective classroom teacher. He will need a body of knowledge and skills not expected of administrators in other fields. When Simon[2] points to the administrator's involvement in decisions about an organization's structure and the broader decisions as to the content of the organization's work, there is cause to reflect on every organization's unique expectations, which demand specialized administration if they are to be met, the expectations in educational institutions being no less important than in others. In some non-departmental schools are to be found outstanding administrators whose skills may not have been grounded in educational theory and practice, yet we wonder if they might have been even more effective had such knowledge complemented their general administrative ability. In emphasizing the need for educational administrators to place their foundation skills firmly in the classroom, Bassett points to one of the major competencies which should distinguish the *educational* administrator from the general administrator.

No matter what favouring experience a headmaster may have, or how efficient he is as an organiser or manager, if he has not a proper understanding of educational objectives, or if he is ignorant of modern materials and methods, his administration is to that extent limited.[3]

Whilst an administrator at Crane's[4] *managerial* level would have diverse concerns and abilities not directly connected with educational practices in the classroom, a clear understanding of the organization's educational objectives and their foundations would be needed if his decisions were to be in the best interests of the learner. Professional technical competence along the entire line organization would inspire confidence among teachers and permit a readier identification and understanding, at all levels, of the organization's common goals. At the *entrepreneurial* level, an administrator without specific educational knowledge and skill may be both effective and acceptable, yet it is pertinent to note that the Directors-General and their senior executives in each of the Australian states' educational departments are respected for, among other skills, their professional knowledge of educational theory and practice. Observation reveals that at the managerial level, the professional knowledge and technical skill of the administrator is of some importance in teacher morale, and the extent to which teachers will respond favourably to supportive guidance.

If an educational administrator is identifiable as such by the uniqueness of his responsibilities, then expertise must come from preparation with programmes rooted in the context of educational theory, because it has an a priori strategic relevance to the improvement of educational practice. Yet, if the administrator is to ensure excellence in education, preserve the social and moral values, and maintain an equality of learning opportunities he must somehow combine the consuming task of teaching, with a knowledge of the *real* world, with all the aspects of human nature demonstrated in the affairs of men in other fields of endeavour. The facility with which older entrants to the school systems, such as ex-servicemen and those transferring from other jobs, fit their comprehensive roles, points to the value of such knowledge, though obviously training courses, properly structured, can go part of the way to meeting this need. Since most of those at present in school systems usually have had training in only the content of teaching, it is essential that existing courses, and especially those for high administrative posts, be broadened into the general field of the social sciences and the humanities.

With the further development of Barnard's[5] thesis that psycho-social factors are an indispensable part of administration, and the shift in emphasis from a value-centred concept to scientific exploration of the processes of administration, it appears there is still a distinct need for an interdisciplinary approach which would involve philosophy in the preparation of administrators. Whilst a study of sociology and psychology is considered essential, the inclusion of philosophy would aid the student in overcoming the inevitable moral dilemmas which he must face. Culbertson goes to the crux of the matter when he notes that " . . . administrators, in making decisions as leaders, must rely ultimately upon basic human values".[6]

Even assuming that preparation programmes could provide the student with a satisfactory accumulation of empirical data, there is still the need for the development of a taxonomy of educational administrative terms, existing theories, and objectives which would aid comprehensiveness, communicability, stimulate thought about administrative problems, and aid both student and practising administrators in formulating hypotheses. At the same time those in the field could benefit from a dissemination of ideas which could be readily understood and applied to ordinary school problems. Possibly, this would be a fertile field for research by a university with a specialized educational administration programme.

Though not condemning the pragmatic approach which could result in accomplishment and achievement, a preparation programme which orientates its courses towards the explication of sound theory will aid administrators to transform the already extensive body of empirical data into a useful framework as a basis for decision making. The distrust of practical men for theory is legend in our schools, yet all successful administrators theorize, in some way, about their experiences and those of others in the field. This distrust possibly has its foundation in a misunderstanding between what Homans[7] refers to as *analytical* and *clinical* science. Probably the analytical approach appears too aseptic for administrators dealing with the ethical dimensions of human behaviour. When the administrator in the school realizes that he is at one and the same time an analyst who generalizes and a clinician who makes decisions so that action proceeds, he will resolve the almost universal dichotomy of theory and practice which is, as Walker notes, "founded on an untenable assumption that it is possible to take action quite independently of our motives".[8]

Whilst no theory can be *the* theory, *a* theory is a good one when "there has been established a set of principles upon which action may be predicted".[9]

The administrator who can understand the function of theory in the conduct of practice will find himself in a more exciting role, since the less adequate his theory, the more he must depend on his experience alone, and the more he is limited by it. Yet, even in the process of developing and understanding a theory for the purpose of problem solving and decision making he is still confronted with the problem of the validity of the data obtained from observation of human behaviour in the school setting, since this will change in response to many variables, thus limiting the degree of objectivity at which the formulation of theory aimed. Nevertheless, it is more important for the administrator to base his habits on the theories of his foundation disciplines than to imitate practices which he sees succeed in an empirical way. Skill acquired from non-rational observation of other administrative practices, rather than theory, denies the administrator the chance of the semantic accuracy and simplicity to which his deliberations should at all times be directed.

Whilst an explicit concern for theorizing about human behaviour is necessary to, and has patent values for, successful practice, administrative skill cannot be gained by theoretical courses alone. It requires continuing study in the light of experience. Yet Culbertson points to the special demands made upon decision makers when he suggests that "administrators must be able to generalize perceptively about problems which are characterized by complexity and which involve tangled and even chaotic relationships".[10]

If we accept Fiegl's[11] definition of a theory, and Getzels' theory of organizational behaviour as: "a social process in which behaviour is conceived as a function of both the nomothetic and idiographic dimensions of a social system",[12] we can appreciate the difficulty of preparation course planning which must cater for personnel with diverse attitudes, from large organizations such as school systems, departmental or non-departmental, each of whom supposedly fits into one of Presthus'[13] three discrete patterns of personal accommodation. Even assuming that an *indifferent* administrator would attend a preparation course if he were paid to do so, it would not necessarily follow that an improvement in his administrative practices would occur. Assuming that attendance at courses remains voluntary those at the university level, graduate or undergraduate, would still cater for the needs of the graduate upward-mobiles who would comprise most of the students; less intensive, non-graduate courses, using simulated materials, could assist the non-graduate upward-mobile, inspire the indifferent, and possibly go some way to achieving a congruence between the institutional expectations and the individual need dispositions of the ambivalent.

If Lazarsfeld's administrative tasks[14] are valid for all school systems, it would seem that the administrator, in concerning himself with the relationship between personal and organizational needs, would require a preparation course founded on a broadly based liberal education, a study of the social sciences in depth, administration as an applied science, and what is difficult for a general course, a study of the technologies of the organization to which the student belongs. As Blocker observes:

> Vicarious experiences with and intellectual understanding of human behavior are not enough for the administrator. His responsibilities lie at the exact intersection of the academic disciplines and clinical application.[15]

It is towards guidance in such responsibilities that the University of New England's Diploma in Educational Administration course, and others which I mention later, direct themselves, yet the problem of structuring a preparation course to involve the technologies and goals of many school systems in the one general course still remains as a limiting factor. However, their contributions in providing the academic discipline and *general* clinical situations are of considerable significance when they form a firm foundation for later in-service preparation within a school system.

If reactions to authority constitute the most critical variable in organizational accommodation,[16] any preparation course, whether pre-service or in-service, should involve an intense study of morale. Whilst the building and maintenance of morale are necessary for the cooperative attainment of goals, such a course needs to emphasize the worth of the individual in an organization. At the same time an administrator needs to be a realist with respect to his legitimate authority and influence while he plays his role in the position which he temporarily occupies.

In overcoming the false dichotomy of theory and practice, courses should be developed in such a way that the integration of theory, knowledge, and various types of actual administrative experience become possible. It is in this latter aspect that the case method and other simulated materials become of such importance in preparation. Realism can be controlled so that it results in a better understanding of theories for attacking and solving educational problems. Though very useful at all levels of preparation, experience suggests that it is within the in-service training structure in particular school systems that such material is most valuable. However, let me introduce a note of caution. It is wise to use such material only with personnel who have had some administrative experience. Since principles are abstracted from situations made up of technologies, personalities, and traditions, experience is needed for an awareness of all the implications, in addition to an intellectual grasp of the concepts to which the simulation approach is directed. Exaggerated cases must be avoided, and at the same time details should be based on operational problems as close as possible to the positional level of the students. The ideas are more easily retained when they are related to an actual problem, rather than to a hypothetical future situation for absorption and storage "just in case".

With its acknowledged success in medicine and law, the case method could well be used as the basic pattern for the improvement of research, for training, and the continued professional development of the educational administrator. Whatever teaching technique is used, the courses should involve intellectual vigour, a Socratic spirit of enquiry and the development of those behaviours which are appropriate for dealing with the major processes of educational administration.

In Australia there is still much scepticism about the value of training for educational administration, mainly because emphasis has been placed on the view that administrative skill can be caught as one proceeds through the school system. This view stems from the fact that our state school systems, and to some extent their "independent" counterparts are large centralized organizations which draw on their own personnel for administrative positions as they evince merit and reveal administrative potential in each role they occupy. The exception to this arrangement is one church school system which appoints its administrators for schools from the teacher ranks, on a rotational basis, for a given period. This is held to be "democratic", but provides little scope for the development and continuity of administrative skills. Since few administrative personnel are recruited from "outside" the respective school systems, the need for specific training for educational administration is not seen as one requiring special courses which are not arranged within the system itself, to meet its own specific needs. Whilst there is some validity in the common argument that this arrangement produces a degree of in-breeding, it is pertinent to note that in many states these "internal" courses, especially those for inspectors, do involve some general administrativet opics, given by lecturers drawn from the school systems, industry, commerce, the armed services, and senior administrative personnel from other government departments.

Pre-service administrative training in the sense of training a *career* educational administrator has not been seriously considered by Australian school systems, since the present arrangement which tends to select people for intensive training after they have proved themselves in junior executive positions in the field is considered preferable. At the same time, each positional level of class teacher, headmaster, inspector, and higher administrator has special needs which it appears no single course, pre-service or in-service, may be able to meet.

Although the provision of specific training for the educational administrator is still in its infancy, there are two types of training facilities available in Australia. There is the larger group of courses for training in public administration, whatever the government service, for the armed services, the medical field and in management for business and commerce. Whilst there are over one hundred and fifty of these courses,[17] many of which are open to educators, they are of short duration, often only two–three days or three–four weeks long. On the other hand some of those in universities are of one or more years' duration, and in technical colleges they may span a number of years on a part-time basis. Perhaps one of the most useful general courses for administrators from any field, permitting senior administrators to disseminate their ideas in a residential setting, is the three-month course conducted by the Australian Administrative Staff College in Victoria. This course draws some senior administrators from at least three state education departments.

The second and much smaller group of courses are for the educational administrator as such, and are held at universities and other educational institutions. Schools of education in most state universities provide courses in educational administration as electives towards general degrees. Examples of other facilities include the school of education in the University of Queensland which conducts an annual three-day conference on school administration, involving the latest administrative theories and practices, attuned to the needs of practising school administrators.

As part of an extensive programme of in-service training, the South Australian Department of Education instituted in 1967 a non-graduate course on school administration,[18] for teachers from government and independent schools, with weekly lectures extending over a full academic year and open to teachers with Teachers' Certificate qualifications. Satisfactory completion of the course is counted as a post-Diploma in Teaching unit, and is aimed at teachers who aspire to become heads of schools. The course is conducted at the South Australian Institute of Technology and Adelaide Teachers' College. This particular type of course is of considerable significance in training school administrators, in that it is extensive in scope, with a substantial theoretical background, and perhaps more importantly, caters for the majority of personnel without graduate status, who could reach positions of administrative responsibility in the schools, especially primary schools.

Despite increasing decentralization of administration in education, especially in New South Wales, the sheer geographic size of the country reduces the practicability of establishing further courses in educational administration where personal attendance is required. There is perhaps scope for an extension of correspondence-type courses to ensure equal opportunity for all, for as Bassett points out:

Heads of schools in the various state systems of Australia are only now approaching that degree of autonomy which makes a concern with administration meaningful for them. Both they and the heads of independent schools must tackle together, and from a not very different starting point, the task of making principles of educational administration more explicit.[19]

Quite the most comprehensive of Australian courses offered in the specific field of educational administration is that conducted by the Department of Education at the University of New England. The course is a postgraduate one, extending over one year full-time, and two–three years part-time study, leading to a Diploma in Educational Administration. The course aims at the explication of sound theory, aided by a penetrating use of empirical data and simulated materials. The student is introduced to factual information about the education administrative system in Australia, combined with instruction in the psychology of group management, leadership, and communication. It is aimed at helping both those who are administering and those who hope to administer in education and ranges over problems such as the administrative structure, evaluation techniques such as examinations and statistics and the more subtle qualities of evaluation of a teacher's competence and the effectiveness of a school, while a considerable portion of the course is devoted to information about comparative educational administration and systems of other countries.

Whilst it does not aim to present a blueprint for budding administrators, experience suggests that it does sharpen the student's perceptive ability in appraising administrative problems with more discernment. At the same time the course topics are sufficiently comprehensive to lay a suitable factual foundation on which students may draw when they assume decision-making responsibilities in any school or school system in Australia.

Considering the purposes for which the course was intended, and the diversity of school systems from which it draws its students, it has been well designed. The claim that the course is only a correspondence one is not entirely valid, since attendance at University residential seminars is prescribed; yet, in presenting its course partly through correspondence, the University is meeting the needs of many interested administrators in Australia, who would, for geographic reasons alone, be precluded from undertaking such a comprehensive course. It is pertinent to note that all intending students must have foundation teaching skills and be in some administrative position or have a likelihood of being so placed; the heterogeneous nature of the usual student body which is drawn from every school system in Australia, the armed services, government departments, and administrators from overseas, points to its wide appeal. With modifications in the course to include philosophical considerations, and an extension of the present section on sociology, it would further meet the needs of those administrators in Australia who, with a background of resourcefulness and adaptability, would wish only the raw material for their decision making. Such a course educates but does not *train*, and as such is appealing to those who realize that the ultimate administrative decisions are made for a special educational problem in a single school situation, by an individual administrator using his own mind. As Dr. A. Lawrence Lowell suggests:

> There is only one thing that will train the human mind and this is the voluntary use of the mind by the man himself. You may aid him, you may guide him, you may suggest to him, and above all you may inspire him; but the only thing worth having is that which he gets by his own exertions.[20]

For the institution to which I belong, the New South Wales Department of Education, departmental courses in educational administration are varied in length, scope, and level to meet the needs of administrators at all stages of their careers. At present our schools are passing from the stage of rigid methods and tight discipline to the stage where an awareness of individual differences is reflected in flexible curricula and understanding, though unfortunately traditional examination techniques and their attendant stresses still remain. To cope with the more enlightened approach to education generally, many progressive principals and teachers are undertaking a great variety of courses to keep abreast of modern developments.

Participation in such courses is voluntary, and it is our constant hope that those with the greatest need will "come to the well", yet despite the virtually unlimited facilities which are provided and some heartening attendance trends, we have yet to attract the majority of those who would benefit most. However, as mentioned previously, participation does not necessarily bestow administrative skill, though observation in the field points to the aroused interest and increased competency of many who undertake courses appropriate to their particular responsibilities. Since the successful completion of any course in educational administration does not directly affect promotion or salary in our department, interest is usually confined to those who view continuing self-improvement as a professional commitment. Facilities are available for those who, because of relative geographic isolation, are unable to avail themselves of the established courses provided in the cities. Correspondence courses on some aspects are available, whilst many courses which require personal attendance are conducted during periods when schools are closed.

Whilst control of the main avenues for training remains with the central In-service Training Branch, considerable use is also made of university and teachers' college facilities for training in all categories.

For the administrator with graduate qualifications, the universities still provide the most comprehensive courses with theoretical foundations, and this situation should remain in the years ahead. Seminar courses in educational administration, as part of the Master of Education programme, are conducted at the University of Sydney, and it is pertinent to note that the lecturers include the Director-General of Education and his Deputy. The University of New South Wales provides through its Master of Education programme much the same type of course, but labelled Educational Planning and Administration, whilst I have mentioned previously the comprehensive course leading to the Diploma in Educational Administration at the University of New England which attracts personnel from the level of assistant to inspector, both from here and overseas. In encouraging the pursuit of such studies, the department does, under certain circumstances, pay all lecture fees and subsidize travel and textbook costs.

The teachers' colleges make a considerable contribution to training generally, with a wide range of courses conducted annually, at Wagga, Newcastle, Sydney, Wollongong, and Armidale. At each college a course is usually available on some topic in administration. Armidale Teachers' College pioneered courses in educational administration, and has for many years, with the aid of specialist staff, offered courses which have considerable depth, and employ the latest teaching techniques. These courses are usually attended by non-graduate, practising administrators.

Beyond the universities and teachers' colleges, the organization and supervision of in-service training courses are handled by the special branch mentioned previously. Not only are courses in any district arranged at the request of principals and inspectors throughout the school year, but annual three-day seminars are conducted for all personnel in administrative positions at North Sydney, Glenfield, and Narrabeen, the latter two schools being residential and designed for those in senior positions. At each seminar, lectures are given and discussions arranged by senior departmental administrators. At the inspectorate level, seminars in administration are conducted for principals and infants' mistresses by inspectors, whilst the latter give appropriate advice during normal visits to schools. In one inspectorate, an Educational Resource Centre has been established. To this centre go administrators from the infants', primary, and secondary fields to peruse up-to-date material and disseminate ideas amongst their colleagues.

For the inspector, administrative training commences on appointment with an induction course at head office, followed by seminars at directorate level, and conferences with other inspectors and more senior administrators at sporadic intervals during the period of appointment. An excellent reading service provided by the department's library ensures that each inspector is kept informed of current trends. As early as possible following appointment, and at various stages throughout his career, he undergoes a course in educational administration at Basser College, University of New South Wales. The course, held every two years, is conducted by senior departmental administrators with lecturers drawn from their own ranks, senior administrators from commerce, the universities, other government departments, and members of the New South Wales Public Service Board. Study leave for short periods is available for selected applicants, many of whom pursue further studies abroad.

However, the effective running of our department depends not solely on educationists, but also on a large body of other officers whose training is the responsibility of the Public Service Board, which body encourages self-improvement through "programmed" training, liberal study arrangements for all officers, and nomination for courses in administration at the Institute of Management in the University of New South Wales.

It will be seen that facilities for training administrators are diverse and readily available, yet several problems arise within our service. Existing courses do much to aid the school administrator in meeting his obligations to support and stimulate the teacher, yet some administrators experience uncertainty in situations where the exercise of legitimate authority is demonstrable, and where critical decisions have to be made. With increased autonomy has come enhanced status, and as a natural consequence a higher degree of responsibility. Whilst school administrators are encouraged to use their own judgments in dealing with all questions on which specific instructions are not issued under departmental regulations, there is still some residual hesitancy, which points to the continuing need for preparation course content to involve an intense study of the exercise of authority, especially of the kind Weber[21] refers to as *rational* authority. In effect, we would hope that every school administrator would use his mandate to the limit and constantly test his organization to see where the parameters of his legitimate authority may lie.

The use of management games, cases, and in-basket material would be ideal to aid this process, though they may not always entirely promote the audacity and creativity to which Walker refers.[22] Such preparation techniques, either in preservice or in-service courses, would however help the administrator reach satisfactory decisions without the need for constant advice or referral to higher authority.

It is possible that the dualism in New South Wales administrative organization which involves the principle of accountability to administrative officers higher up the line for non-educationists, and the principle of relative self-determination for educationists, may account, in part, for the latters' tardiness in seeing the need for formal preparation as administrators. As in other branches of the public service, perhaps selection for administrative posts in the schools could depend, in part, on the successful completion of accredited courses in educational administration endorsed by examination. However, to maintain the element of professionalism, highly prized in medicine and law, participation in courses should remain voluntary.

Problems do arise from the fact that school administrators are not selected and trained before commencing work in particular positions. Many who are currently holding positions have not had extended preparation and are confronted with many problems they are not prepared to meet. Hence there is a need to concentrate as much on training those already in positions as those who may rise to administrative posts. When considering our present method of selecting school administrators, the answer to our problem may lie in a combination of both pre-service and in-service training. For the graduate such courses as the one offered at the University of New England whilst for the non-graduate the type of extended course offered by the South Australian Education Department, could meet our needs in the foreseeable future.

The whole question of in-service training in New South Wales is under continuous review. Problems concerned with duplication, fragmentation, and course content to meet specific needs are being considered, in the hope that a greater cohesion among existing courses and the rationalization of resources will result.

The problem of when to conduct courses, and under what circumstances, is a persistent one. At the present time, courses in administration for two–three days are conducted at various departmental centres, during school vacations or weekends. Perhaps a two-week intensive course, during one vacation period each year, at a residential centre with an adequate library and other resources would be a useful supplement to existing arrangements. Such courses, extending over a period of five–ten years, would permit follow-up training so that courses could be built up, each of which would be more rigorous, illuminating, and pertinent as a man progresses in responsibility. As Cunningham and Radford[23] suggest, those at the earlier levels of responsibility could work in homogeneous groups, but as one moves up to higher levels of responsibility, contact with administrators from other fields would become more and more important.

Educational *leadership* being a constant aim in our service, it seems that we may more easily achieve this through *specific* training and experience, following selection of administrators with the highest *personal* qualifications, for as Chase observes: "The priceless ingredient of school administrators is (1) a vision as to what education can and should be, and (2) an ability to develop creative potential in others."[24]

15 The Independent School

Educational administration as a field of study is still, regrettably, suspect in some quarters. Is this due to its own adolescence, public ignorance, apathy or opposition, or its uncertainty of purpose?

Muir, in answer to his first question, concludes modestly that educational administration should be regarded as a separate discipline. This sounds harmless: just a new field of study to be acquainted with, another adjunct to successful management. On the contrary, it has earth-shaking consequences.

Consider his remarks near the end of his paper: "When it is accepted that an educational tyro can administer a school, then pre-service preparation becomes possible. Perhaps the immense social and educational developments in the next half century will make it not only possible but necessary."

That forecast, spelt out, means that educational administration would cease to be what it appears at present to be, viz. an adjunct to education, a specialist field of study desirable for those experienced teachers destined or eager to administer. It would involve, ultimately, the creation of a special class of educational administrators to whom all principalships, inspectorships, and directorships would logically go.

This is careerism not just in educational administration, but rather in educational leadership. Administration ceases to be the handmaid and becomes the master.

There are examples of this and, of course, long-standing parallels for this sort of leadership training in the armed services, with their officer class, and in big firms with their cadetship systems. Is education destined to join these and carry an executive class—a class which has not been through the teaching mill? What will they have that we, who have reached administrative status, have not got?

The preparation for administration which we and our "untrained" colleagues have had is reflected in the methods of selection used. Simply, it seems to have been on the basis of presumed merit, as judged by job performance and estimated potential. Much value has been put on junior administrative experience; little or none on formal administrative training.

The pattern of "promotion", of selection for administrative tasks in government secondary schools, has been somewhat like this:

Teacher → Subject Master → Deputy Principal →
Principal → Inspector →
Senior Administrative Position

The pattern reveals a fairly set line of vertical promotion, much lateral movement representing advancement within a grade, and some diagonal leaps into teachers' college or elsewhere. Three characteristics of this pattern are: the operation of seniority up to a certain point; after that, selection on ability; the use of advertisement outside the state service for certain positions.

The practice in Roman Catholic schools is complicated by the policies of different teaching orders. Apart from having a line of appointment to increasing responsibility given by selection, it has in some schools limited tenure—three or six years as a head—after which transfer occurs sideways, upwards, or even downwards. There is one feature which this system (or some of it) shares with the state department: shortness of tenure, or, if you like, high mobility.

In the other independent schools, the procedure for selection of a headmaster or headmistress is by advertisement and the candidate usually comes, often at an early stage, from outside this school. There is no set line of promotion at all. One feature of heads is low mobility and long tenure, which gives a proprietary interest, a personal stake in their enterprise.

The preparation of the majority of heads is such as is provided by the promotional pattern within each system, viz. on-the-job post-appointment experience, occasionally supplemented, individually, by courses or tours of various types.

What are the requirements for preparation as head of an independent school?

In an independent, largely boarding, school of small size, the headmaster's task, as I see it, includes:

1. Objectives — setting and formulating into policy
2. Staffing — appointment, conditions, salary scale, load, control, direction, structure, organization, non-teaching staff, unions
3. Finance — budgeting (running expenses and capital expenditure), allocations, fees, fund raising
4. Buildings — development plan, design and execution with architect, site management, maintenance priorities
5. Curriculum — supervision, planning (within state limits), innovations, reports and records, time-tabling, examinations, choice of subjects, religious teaching and observance
6. Extra-Curricular Activities — choice, time allocations, supervision
7. Internal Organization — rules, regulations, discipline, routine, paper work, delegation
8. Pupil Care — academic, pastoral, medical, etc.; eight hour, twenty-four hour control, guiding prefects, knowing boys, promoting proper attitudes, preventing problems
9. Headmaster's Teaching and Activities — load, area of attack (usually VI Form), coaching of sport, attendance expectations
10. Public Relations — parents, parent education, Old Boys' Union, Parents and Friends' Association
11. Social, Community, and Professional Duties
12. Personal and Professional Refreshment.

Looking at these, you will see that his most important tasks depend on a broad "horizon-lifting" background; *he must know where he is going.* Much again depends on an ability to make concordant decisions, and these decisions are often intuitive; *he must know what he is doing.* And for swift efficiency he will require a knowledge of techniques; *he must know how to do it.*

A headmaster's first task is to set his objectives. From these he will formulate policy. Objectives are ideal; policy is the practical manifestation of these objectives. It takes into account the existing climate of the school, the material provisions (grounds, rooms, equipment), finance, organizational requirements, and parental reaction.

Policy questions might include: Should we give our boarders sex education? Should Latin and French give way to Asian languages? Will we widen our definition of sport to include sailing, surf lifesaving, and hiking? Should the new classroom block provide for team teaching?

The next stage let us call *procedure*—policy processes into action. At this stage, we frequently get pressing problems which require quick decisions. For example, consider the implications of the following case:

Objective: Spiritual training
Policy: Regular religious instruction and observance
Procedure: Morning chapel daily, two Sunday services, and one Divinity period per week for all . . .
Problem: Well-argued conscientious objection from formerly good observer now in Form VI
Decision: To enforce religious observance or not to enforce such observance.

I was asked to examine the implication of Muir's paper for an independent school. This I have found very difficult to do, and so I set out the Objectives-Policy-Procedure pattern above. This pattern requires different sorts of knowledge, skills, and approaches at the three stages. I cannot articulate these properly but they seem to embrace philosophy, leadership, and management, three words which I do not recall reading in Muir's paper, banished perhaps by the new vocabulary of administrative theorists. I am sure that he has adequately covered philosophy and management, but I need to be convinced that leadership is equivalent to an understanding of organization, communication, and behaviour. (This may be because I belong to a microcosm or mini-organization.)

Leadership is concerned with my policy stage and with procedure to a certain extent. It involves imagination to implement the objectives, personality to get others to follow enthusiastically, the power to convince by argument, authority to command obedience, the sense to avoid the futility of regular compromise, and so on. Consequently, while I acknowledge enthusiastically that good organization will solve many of the problems that occur, Muir's paper reveals a bias toward organization studies which (perhaps in my ignorance) seem to be interpretative rather than directive.

Two tail pieces I would like to have seen in the Muir programme:

1. After objectives have been set and policy and procedures developed, there should be an in-built system of evaluation to see whether the objectives are being fulfilled.

2. The development of a healthy school (pupil) climate is quite an art. The relationship of the headmaster with boys—individually, in groups, or en masse—with regard to development, guidance, instruction in leadership, creation of opinion, etc., needs careful attention in a school.

To conclude, I must compliment Muir on his perceptive paper. He has been logical, comprehensive, and virtually armour-plated. It is difficult to avoid the conclusion that we would all be better headmasters if we had experienced training of the sort he describes.

APPENDIX ONE

The Governance of Education: Policy Making and Local Education Authorities in England

G. BARON

My purpose in this paper is to throw some light on the consequences for policy making in education in England of our
having all-purpose authorities charged with providing the
means of education in their areas.

This will involve me not only in tracing briefly the sequence
of the decision-making process in one or two chosen cases, but
also in indicating the part played by the various actors involved:
councillors and their political parties, education officers and
their staffs, heads of schools and teacher associations, parents
and citizen groups, expert opinion and, of course, the press.
Closely and intricately involved in all major issues there is the
central authority, the Department of Education and Science,
working against the backcloth of government policy.

First, however, I must recall to your minds the total context
within which local education authorities operate. England is an
extremely densely populated country, but with much variety
in its population distribution. There exist side by side great
industrial cities and conurbations, county areas dotted with
villages and small towns of long traditions, ancient cities and
rapidly growing new towns of very recent birth. For a mixture
of reasons, therefore, historical, geographical, political, and
economic, local authorities responsible for education range in
size from cities of over half-a-million inhabitants to towns of
less than one-tenth of their size; and from counties of over a
million acres to others of less than one hundred thousand. The
basic pattern of administration is the same throughout, of
course, since education in England is essentially a national
system, though in most respects one that is locally administered.
But there are substantial variations as between area and area
in respect, for example, of the nature of the control exercised

by local authorities over their schools, of the means by which children are selected for the various forms of secondary education existing at the present time, of the proportions of children staying at school beyond the statutory school-leaving age, and of the use made of the school meals service and other welfare services.

The position of the local education authority as a political and administrative institution can be summarized as follows:

1. Both the central authority, that is, the Secretary of State for Education and Science, and the local education authorities derive their rights and duties from laws made by Parliament, and neither can act save within the provisions of these laws. In important cases of dispute, rulings must be sought in a court of law.[1]

2. The finance of education is ultimately a national concern. Local authorities contribute from rates (that is, a local property tax) towards all their services, but most of their expenditure (nearly 80 per cent in the case of some poor authorities) is derived from the block grant paid to them by the central government. School building, like other local authority building, depends upon loan sanction being granted at national level.

3. It is the major all-purpose county and county borough councils that constitute the local education authorities. They are required to appoint an education committee from among their members and can delegate to that committee their powers in respect of education, save that of raising a rate. What must be borne in mind is that an education committee (and here it differs from a school board) consists of men and women who have been elected to serve local government generally and not only education. But to this I should add that they can coopt other people to help them, by reason of their specialist knowledge.

4. Education is, then, very much a part of the general politics of local government and also, in its party rivalries, a reflection of national politics. Party divisions are transmitted from council to education committee and subcommittees and, in many

cases, to the individual managing and governing bodies of schools and colleges.

5. Local government officers are, of course, like civil servants, non-political appointees. Senior officers serving the education committee, because they are invariably ex-teachers, form a distinctive professional group.

6. As thus presented, it might appear that policy making is confined to political institutions at national and local levels and to the officers of the Department of Education and Science and of the local education authorities at other levels. This is misleading, because at very many points in the structure a place in the policy-making process is assured, for example, to voluntary religious associations, teachers' associations, professional associations and, in respect of major examinations, the universities.[2] At the level of the school very substantial powers rest with the head teacher.

I should like to stress the words I have used are "a place in the policy-making process". I do not want to suggest more than that, because the major conditioning element is, of course, national policy, as laid down by the government and as promoted by the Secretary of State for Education and Science through the Department of Education and Science.

At the national level, again, decision making is carried on within a network of consultation and negotiation, whether it is a matter of teachers' salary scales, the general shape of the structure of higher and further education, or university entrance requirements.

Secondary school reorganization

At this point, however, I think that I should move from discussing structure to analysing policy-making elements at the local level, as they operate in respect of secondary school reorganization, the key issue at the present time.

The background is that the Secretary of State is charged, under the Education Act, 1944, with promoting the education of the people of England and Wales and with securing the effective execution, by local authorities, of national policy to that end. But it is the local authorities that actually plan and provide the school systems they operate.

What does this statement mean in practice? Who makes the decisions involved in planning and providing schools? Is it the elected representatives sitting in council and in the education committee? Or is it the members of the political party in power? Or is it the education officer and his staff? Or is it, because of the ultimate controls exercised by the Department of Education and Science, the party in power in Westminster or the civil servants in Curzon Street? What part is played by teachers and their associations and what part by parents and local community? Furthermore, *how* are formal or informal powers exercised by all or any of these elements?

Two short studies made recently throw some light on these questions. One deals with the involved and interesting case of Croydon,[3] a commercial and industrial centre some twenty miles from London, which is characterized by having a number of independent and direct grant schools of high status and also a vigorous and ambitious middle class population determined to secure the best education for their children.

In 1954 the need for more grammar school places was urged in the council and the education committee was requested to report. The chief education officer, who had recently taken up his appointment, rapidly produced a plan designed to make better provision for senior work in secondary schools by concentrating it in a sixth form college. The contents of the plan were made public prematurely in the local press, probably by accident, and aroused the immediate opposition of the authority's grammar schools which were to be "decapitated". At the suggestion of the education officer a well-known educationist, the Director of the University of Oxford Institute of Education, was called in to advise on the plan. He expressed substantial objections on educational grounds, namely that continuity was of vital importance at the secondary school stage, and the authority did not proceed further with the plan as it stood.

In 1961 the issue was reopened, this time as a result of the spreading national as well as local dissatisfaction with the "eleven-plus" selection process. Here again outside experts were called in, this time the Director of the National Foundation for

Educational Research and the Director of the University of London Institute of Education. Their verdict was favourable to the revised plan put forward. Primary school heads favoured the ending of the eleven-plus, heads of non-selective secondary schools favoured the plan as opening the way for some of their pupils to go forward to a sixth form college, but grammar school heads still held out for the retention of the seven-year course pattern of their own schools. A new factor now entered. The heads of the two boys' schools of Public School rank in the town, although they were not involved in the scheme, took a hand. They condemned the proposed "decapitation" of the grammar schools and urged the importance of early selection, if able children were to be allowed to develop their full potential. Despite their being outside the formal structure of local policy making their influence was considerable. Theirs were schools at which a substantial number of influential local people had been educated and which, for many others, represented the highest standards in education.[4] At this point the authority discussed their plans with senior officials of the ministry, which made some further criticisms and pointed out that it would be wise to await the then pending reorganization of local government in the Greater London area.

In Croydon the disputed plan had been initiated by the education officer. In another area,[5] this time one of the new towns, Corby in Northamptonshire, the first move seems to have come from an incidental expression of dissatisfaction with the eleven-plus. The sequence of events was that a councillor asked the council to consider its abolition and to institute a school system giving a greater measure of educational opportunity. This does not appear to have been a move inspired by the councillor's own party but was in line with general left-wing opinion. The upshot was that the education officer was asked to look into the matter and especially to examine the possibility of establishing a plan similar to that of a neighbouring county, Leicestershire. This he did and the Director of Education for Leicestershire was invited to speak to the governors and heads of the schools concerned. Local interest was now aroused and an Association for Comprehensive Education was set up. Then there followed a series of meetings, organized by the authority, at which teachers and parents and teacher associations were invited to formulate their views. At one the heads of Corby's secondary schools put forward criticisms of the Leicestershire plan and at another, this time organized by the National Union of Teachers, five teachers from Leicestershire spoke from their experience of the plan in action. Yet another meeting was addressed by a professor of education from the University of Leicester, a strong supporter of comprehensive education.

The headmaster of the grammar school in Corby now criticized the Leicestershire plan at a school speech day and there followed vigorous discussion in the columns of the local newspaper. Local opinion and especially teacher opinion was much divided but the committee decided on a scheme of reorganization on the lines of the Leicestershire plan. This move stimulated still further opposition but a teacher representative on the education committee who was also the county secretary of the National Union of Teachers succeeded in forming an *ad hoc* committee of teachers[6] which arrived at an agreed solution. This was discussed with the education officer and his deputy and put to the committee. It was accepted, despite the continuing opposition of the Association for Comprehensive Education.

I do not, for one moment, wish to suggest that one can adduce general principles from two cases: but they serve to identify some, though by no means all, of the elements that are involved in policy making.

In neither of the cases are issues presented in overt party-political terms and this tallies with much though not all experience elsewhere. Policies advocated by the two main political parties are not necessarily accepted in all respects at national level and there is considerable flexibility in their interpretation. Some Labour councils have been very slow to move towards the concept of comprehensive secondary education, and some conservative councils have shown less reluctance to reconstruct their school systems on non-selective lines than might have been expected from the statements of prominent party spokesmen. Moreover, the expression of public opinion is not limited to the political parties as such. It can also become the concern of left-wing groups in favour of sweeping changes, of bodies of parents seeking to defend individual schools, and of local associations campaigning for improved educational provision.

There are two other elements to which attention should be drawn. The first is the "church interest". The essential point is that the existence and, under certain circumstances, the expansion of church schools, whether Anglican or Roman Catholic, is guaranteed by law. Reorganization by a local education authority of its school system is thus circumscribed by the need to devise a plan that takes into account the place and possible development of church schools in its area. The second element is the part played by independent schools. In some cases these, as indeed in Croydon, are highly important in forming the general climate of opinion; in others, and this is especially true in the London area, they also cream off a substantial proportion of intelligent middle class children who would otherwise strengthen the upper forms of the authority's own schools.

Within the setting described it is clear that the role of the chief education officer is decisive in that it is he who is finally responsible for working out a policy that is both practicable and acceptable. Moreover, such a policy, as has been seen, is more than a matter for his committee alone: it is inevitably part of the general national policy for education and must take into account church and independent school systems. At crucial points, therefore, the role of the chief education officer can be diplomatic rather than administrative and all can depend on his sense of timing and on his success in fostering workable relationships between the groups with which he is in contact. It is he, too, who is the channel for contacts with professional opinion in the universities and elsewhere.

The power and influence exercised by teachers varies considerably as does also the use they make of it. In most authorities teacher representatives hold places on the education committee and sit on consultative committees concerned with matters affecting both the schools and their own conditions of service. In addition, they are among the most active members of local political parties[7] and in some areas, gain added support through their links with the trade union movement.[8] This has not resulted in such areas in greater reforming activity: indeed, teacher opinion and action has, on the whole, been conservative in respect of changes in the school structure. It could be hypothesized that teachers, and especially head teachers, can exert an influence, within and through the local authority structure, that would be difficult for them otherwise through other means.

The "mobilizing" of consent[9]

The relative strengths and significance of the elements discussed clearly must vary from area to area and from time to time. Certainly it would appear that two events that followed the incidents at Croydon and Corby, the step taken by the Labour Government in 1965 towards abolishing selection at eleven-plus and the swing against Labour in the local elections in 1967, have changed the balance of forces. Local councils that had drawn up plans in accordance with the government's request are now, under different party control, looking at them again; and those who were hostile or lukewarm in their attitude to the policy of comprehensivization are dragging their feet. One result is that still more importance is being attached to local opinion and local pressure groups. Indeed, the need for this was recognized in the circular that announced government policy. It stressed strongly the need for gaining the cooperation of teachers and the support and confidence of parents and proclaimed that "to secure these there must be a process of consultation and explanation before any scheme is approved by an authority for submission to the Secretary of State".[10] The care with which this advice has been followed is shown in the description of the procedure followed by the chief education officer for Gloucestershire. He writes:

In each area the normal procedure has been for initial exploratory discussions to be held between the chairman and vice-chairman of the education committee, the chief education officer and the local county councillors, the chairmen of governors and heads of the schools concerned. As soon as any positive ideas emerge, governors and staff are informed, and given time for their observations. Meetings with them are held if required. Primary schools are also informed. Preliminary proposals are then considered by the schools sub-committee of the education committee and a public meeting or meetings held in the area before any firm recommendations are put forward to the education committee.

He continues:

The most important lesson we have learnt is that when proposals are first put before governors, teachers or parents, they should be suggestions only; that they have not been finally approved by the Authority and are genuinely open to re-examination.[11]

This passage illustrates the extent to which officials accept that policy making is an activity that, though it is focused on the institutions of representative government, is increasingly a matter also for community interests and pressure groups.

School building programmes

So far attention has been paid to aspects of policy making within local authorities. In all major matters, however, the most important and decisive governing factor is what the Department of Education and Science will actually agree to. Local education authorities do have considerable freedom to plan their own systems,[12] but their planning must now be in general line with the move towards comprehensive education. If not, they must face the possibility that any part of their scheme may be disallowed by the Secretary of State when it comes to the consideration of building plans.

The part played by the department in policy making at the local level can be relatively remote as long as the formulation of general plans is all that is concerned; it is decisive when the time comes to spend money, since the Treasury controls the overall national sum available for capital investment in school buildings. This sum is always far less than the total requested by all local authorities combined and therefore allocations have to be arrived at in each case. Each year, then, every education officer has to face the task of drawing up a building programme. But, as Griffith points out, there are many other interested parties.

Others, besides education officers, are likely to make their views known about future development. Her Majesty's Inspectors, concerned primarily with what is taught and how it is taught, are inevitably interested in the physical environment in which teachers and pupils seek to work. The teachers themselves, both individually and through their organizations, exert their own pressures. And if the pupils do not yet, in this country, complain collectively about their conditions of work, they may not be silent in their homes. And so parents, again either individually or through parent-teacher associations, may complain. So also, in the case of existing schools, governors or managers will make their representations about overcrowding and substandard conditions to the appropriate authorities.[13]

The task of the education officer, then, is one of deciding from among a potentially very substantial number of claims and the composition of the list of projects his committee sends forward to the department may depend on the persuasiveness of an individual councillor or the degree of pressure that the Anglican or Roman Catholic authorities can bring to bear on councillors or officers or both.

Pressure for more school building is such that few local education authorities do not demand considerably more than they can possibly hope to get in the way of loan sanctions. Thus their programmes always contain more items than the department is expected to approve in the year concerned.

This, it can be argued, is not entirely a bad thing: it at least gives the department an overall view. What is important, however, is that the local education authority should indicate its priorities and that these should be a matter of professional judgment. But this does not always happen. There are cases of education officers being instructed by their committees or, as Griffith points out, by the party caucus behind the committee.[14] If the programme insisted upon is one that runs counter to the officer's professional judgment, the result is a clash of loyalties. Relations between department and local officials are sometimes close and cases have been known in which, as Dent has said:

... the Ministry has been advised by a Chief Education Officer over the telephone not to approve something which his authority has formally proposed; and vice versa when an officer of the Ministry has suggested to a local authority ways of circumventing some Ministerial pronouncement which appeared to bar a favoured project.[15]

Proposals when submitted to the department are considered

by the responsible officer not only in terms of the written evidence produced, but in the light of his own knowledge of the authorities in his region and the information he may gain from district Inspectors. There may be face to face discussion, too, with officers of an authority. What should be noted is that the department's decision is by no means limited to settling how much an authority may spend: it extends to deciding on individual projects, which are judged in terms of national as well as local priorities. Finally, when a project has been approved the local authority must work within detailed stipulations laid down by the department in building regulations and in cost standards.

Other areas of decision making

Time has been spent in discussing secondary school reorganization and school building because of the extent to which, in these areas, individual local education authorities are concerned in the making of policy. School systems and the schools themselves must vary from area to area and do vary greatly, not only for obvious reasons of geography and population density, but because of sharply diverging patterns of attitudes towards the local control of education.

The situation is different when one turns to the staffing of the schools and to decisions relating to the curriculum. In these areas we have to change the axis of our thinking: we have to concern ourselves, not with local issues or with the relationship of individual authorities with central government, but with a secondary or infrastructure of joint responsibility and cooperation among all local authorities. This is expressed through nation-wide associations of county councils and municipal corporations and, in the case of education, through the Association of Education Committees.

These associations are an extremely important outgrowth of the local authority system and no consideration of it is in any sense complete which does not take some account of what they add to it. At their level decisions are taken in matters of concern to all authorities in their functional interactions with teachers and other interest groups: it is through them that national salaries scales are negotiated, tenure agreements formulated, and understandings arrived at as regards action in such disputes as those associated at the present time with school meals supervision. At their level also arrangements are made for pooling expenditure for such activities of common concern as teacher training and some forms of further education. Moreover, these associations constitute a non party-political intermediate stratum between the necessarily political national and local levels. This is because they are composed of authorities of different and changing political complexion. Therefore, they constitute a neutral ground where many issues can be settled away from the clash of parties. Since their executives are composed of both council members *and* officers, they also constitute meeting places for the two elements in the administrative structure. The existence of a local government interest complex as such, different facets of which are represented through their own organized pressure groups, is of very great importance in giving both stability and flexibility to the whole structure. It is also a phenomenon to which too little attention has been paid.

Some matters relating to teachers are, however, very much a matter for individual authorities. Procedure regarding teacher qualification, probation, and dismissal follows a nationally agreed pattern, but their appointment and promotion is still very much a local matter. In some authorities headships and senior posts are almost invariably filled from within the authority; in others, and these form the majority, such posts are filled by advertisement and are open to teachers from other authorities. But any attempts by an authority to improve its teaching force are limited by national agreements of the kind already mentioned. It cannot, of course, institute its own salary scales, nor can it engage more full-time teachers than the "quota" allowed it under a scheme agreed by all authorities and operated by the Department of Education and Science. It can, however, if hard-pressed to fill its "quota", organize publicity and advertising campaigns and offer suitable candidates help in finding houses or other living accommodation. It also has considerable freedom in determining what advantages its teachers shall enjoy in respect of in-service training. In all this area of teacher supply and recruitment it is important to appreciate that, in a situation in which the finance of education is largely national in character, a major restraining factor operating on all individual local authorities is the common interest of their fellows in ensuring a fair and equal distribution of the resources available.

Local education authorities and the schools

A hundred years ago the Public Schools Commission that confirmed the national status of a small number of distinguished schools that now form the hub of the "Public School system" assigned to the headmaster of a secondary school responsibility for the internal organization of his school.[16] This is now, though erroneously, interpreted as including responsibility for the curriculum. Thus, the education committee does not attempt to prescribe what should be taught, although a member might occasionally query the unusual. But the education officer and his staff, and especially local inspectors and organizers, exert influence through their part in staffing and equipping the schools and Her Majesty's inspectors comment freely. Furthermore national examination systems, operated through regional boards, powerfully influence the teaching syllabus in each subject at the secondary school stage. Very recently, the Schools Council, a body representing local authorities and teachers' associations, has begun to provide specific guidance in curriculum development and teaching method. What is important is that the reaction to external stimuli of this nature by the head and the teachers in a school is not prescribed: at each stage it results from processes of consultation which extend far beyond the confines of any one local education authority. Where local education authorities as such exert decisive influence is in respect of developments, such as new approaches to science teaching, in-service television, and the institution of language laboratories, in which decisions are required as to the utilization of public money in large scale projects.

An approach to evaluation

Evaluation of the all-purpose local authority, as it exists in England and, indeed, in Great Britain generally, in either normative or operational terms, is a task beyond the scope of this paper, but it may be worth-while applying the test of three general propositions:

1. That the local authority system ensures a high level of participation in policy making by a wide cross-section of the population.

It is assumed that such participation is to be counted as a good, on the grounds that individuals and communities only attain full stature when they themselves have a substantial share in deciding how they shall live. The claim, I think, can be made that not only elected representatives and officers are concerned in consultations on policy matters, but literally thousands of teachers, parents, and indeed anyone who wishes to take an interest in current problems or reorganizations and expansion have opportunities to do so. Elected local authorities, like elected school boards, provide a focus around which individuals and pressure groups can make their influence felt.

This argument should not be taken too far. It can be shown that the dominance of party politics at one level and of professional autonomy at another restricts severely the effectiveness of all save a limited number of people. In many cases indeed, the defensive reaction of local politicians and officials is such that places not only on education committees but also on the governing bodies of schools are confined to members or supporters of political parties. Speaking of two authorities studied in some detail Pear writes:

Indeed, the "magic circle" of education policy makers seems very, and comfortably, small and cosy. Those who by tradition are in the circle (Chief Officers, their Deputies, Chairmen and committee members, Heads, some teachers and the N.U.T. representative) conduct their business face to face in the relaxed and friendly atmosphere of men and women in full control of all local activity.[17]

But, as shown in Croydon and Corby, the magic circle can be challenged, if not broken. Increasingly, in fact, lay participation is manifesting itself through *ad hoc* groups of parents and citizens.

2. That the local authority system provides a broader base for operational decisions *at national level* than that which would be provided by a central authority alone.

Elected local councils, and the officers to whom they assure independence from the central authority, provide a highly expert and varied stratum that, through its own functional associations, interacts both with the central authority and with individual local authorities in respect of a wide range of issues. The strength of this stratum lies in the authority it derives from its capacity to absorb and neutralize party political pressures and to represent the common interests of local authorities.

3. That the local authority system contributes to safeguarding the professional autonomy of the teacher.

The history of the past sixty years shows a keen determination on the part of the central authority not to allow heads and their schools to become completely subject to their local authorities and an equal determination on the part of local authorities to resist any domination of the schools by the central authority or its inspectorate.

The search for alternatives

Despite what has been said, the Royal Commission on Local Government at present sitting has revealed a very great discontent with the outdated structure and methods characteristic of very much local government. The Department of Education and Science and the Association of Education Committees both support the creation of fewer and larger authorities on the one hand and the strengthening of the managing and governing bodies of individual schools on the other.[18] This is in line with what has been done in recent years to give greater autonomy to technical colleges and colleges of education. It is felt that small authorities cannot command effective resources in terms of specialist administrative staff and, in some cases, inhibit the development of effective community relationships between individual schools and the areas they serve.

In view of the growing size and importance of education and of the significance attached to institutional autonomy it might be possible to challenge education's being viewed for the most part as a "service" within the general local government structure. There is, however, no suggestion that all-purpose local authorities should be replaced by school boards and other ad hoc bodies. On the contrary, the trend may be towards developing regional agencies that, without displacing local education authorities, will serve to coordinate their efforts in various directions.[19]

What does appear to be certain is that, as the proportion of highly educated men and women in the population increases and as school education becomes more and more decisive in fixing the "life chances" of each individual, lay concern with the making of policy in education at all levels is certain to grow. The extent to which various forms of local government, or regionalism, or of school and college government can satisfy this growing concern will be the major test of their appropriateness and acceptability.

Notes to Text

Chapter 1

1. Commonwealth of Australia, *Parliamentary Debates* (House of Representatives), Session 1965, H. of R. 45: 270.
2. Sir Robert Menzies, *Central Power in the Australian Commonwealth* (London: Cassell, 1967), p. 88.
3. *Ibid.*, pp. 88–89.
4. New South Wales, *Parliamentary Debates*, 3rd ser., Session 1967–68, 69: 2322.
5. *Ibid.*, pp. 2322–23.

Chapter 2

Thanks are due to McGraw-Hill Book Company for permission to reproduce Table 1, which is from W. G. Bennis, *Changing Organizations* (New York: McGraw-Hill, 1966).
1. C. I. Barnard, *The Functions of the Executive* (Cambridge, Mass.: Harvard University Press, 1938).
2. R. G. Corwin, "Education and the Sociology of Complex Organizations", in D. A. Hansen and J. E. Gerstl (eds.), *On Education: Sociological Perspectives* (New York: Wiley, 1967).
3. James G. Anderson, "Bureaucratic Rules: Bearers of Organizational Authority", *Educational Administration Quarterly* 2 (1966): 7–34. See also Jean Hills, "Some Comments on James G. Anderson's 'Bureaucratic Rules: Bearers of Organizational Authority'", *Educational Administration Quarterly* 2 (1966): 243–61.
4. A. W. Gouldner, *Patterns of Industrial Bureaucracy* (Glencoe, Ill.: Free Press, 1954).
5. Max Weber, *The Theory of Economic and Social Organization*, trans. A. M. Henderson and Talcott Parsons (New York: Free Press of Glencoe, 1954).
6. P. M. Blau, *Bureaucracy in Modern Society* (New York: Random House, 1965).
7. R. F. Campbell, L.L. Cunningham, and R. F. McPhee, *The Organization and Control of American Schools* (Columbus, Ohio: Merrill, 1965).
8. A. P. Rowe, *If the Gown Fits* (Melbourne: Melbourne University Press, 1960).
9. S. W. Cohen, "Internal Government and Administration of Universities" (Canberra: A.N.U. Research School of Social Sciences Administrative Studies Seminar, 1967. Typescript).
10. D. E. Griffiths, "The Nature and Meaning of Theory" in D.E. Griffiths (ed.), *Behavioral Science and Educational Administration* (Chicago: N.S.S.E., 63rd Yearbook, 1964).
11. J. W. Getzels, "Theory and Practice in Educational Administration" in R. F. Campbell and P.J. Lipham, *Administrative Theory as a Guide to Action* (Chicago: Midwest Administration Center, University of Chicago, 1960).
12. N. L. Gage, *Handbook of Research on Teaching* (Chicago: Rand McNally, 1963).
13. H. H. Remmers *et al.*, "Second Report of the Committee on the Criteria of Teacher Effectiveness", *Journal of Educational Research* 46 (1953): 641–58.
14. B. J. Biddle and W. J. Ellena (eds.), *Contemporary Research on Teacher Effectiveness* (New York: Holt, 1964).

15. N. A. Flanders, "Personal-Social Anxiety as a Factor in Experimental Learning Situations", *Journal of Educational Research* 45 (1951): 100–10. See also N. A. Flanders, *Interaction Analysis in the Classroom* (Minneapolis: University of Minnesota Press, 1960).
16. W. J. Campbell, "Excellence or Fear of Failure: The Teacher's Role in the Motivation of Learners", *Australian Journal of Education* 11 (1967): 1–12.
17. M. J. Dunkin, "Some Determinants of Teacher Warmth and Directiveness" (Ph. D. thesis, University of Queensland, 1966).
18. J. G. Withall, "Development of the Climate Index", *Journal of Educational Research* 45 (1951): 93–99.
19. H. F. Wright *et al.*, "Toward a Psychological Ecology of the Classroom", *Journal of Educational Research* 45 (1951): 187–200.
20. A. W. Halpin and D. B. Croft, *The Organizational Climate of Schools* (Chicago: Midwest Administration Center, University of Chicago, 1963).
21. A. F. Brown, "Research in Organizational Dynamics: Implications for School Administrators", *Journal of Educational Administration* 5 (1967): 36–49.
22. J. B. Miner, *The School Administrator and Organizational Character* (Eugene, Oregon: C.A.S.E.A., 1967).
23. F. Enns, "Rating Teacher Effectiveness: The Function of the Principal", *Journal of Educational Administration* 3 (1965): 81–95.
24. W. G. Bennis, *Changing Organizations* (New York: McGraw-Hill, 1966). Table 1 is on pp. 190–91.
25. *Ibid.*
26. J. M. Foskett, *The Normative World of the Elementary School Teacher* (Eugene, Oregon: C.A.S.E.A., 1967).
27. P. W. Jackson and E. G. Guba, "The Need Structure of In-Service Teachers: An Occupational Analysis", *School Review* 65, no. 2 (June 1957): 126–92.
28. Getzels, "Theory and Practice in Educational Administration".
29. R. K. Merton, *Social Theory and Social Structure* (Glencoe, New York: Free Press, 1949).
30. P. Selznick, *Leadership in Administration: A Sociological Interpretation* (Evanston, Ill.: Row, Peterson, 1957).
31. Talcott Parsons, "Some Ingredients of a General Theory of Formal Organization", in Andrew W. Halpin (ed.), *Administrative Theory in Education* (New York: Macmillan, 1967).
32. Weber, *Theory of Economic and Social Organization*.
33. F. W. Taylor, *Scientific Management* (New York: Harper and Row, 1948).
34. H. Fayol, *General and Industrial Management* (London: Pitman, 1949).
35. H. E. Metcalf and L. F. Urwick, *The Collected Papers of Mary Parker Follett* (London: Pitman, 1957).
36. Ordway Tead, *The Art of Administration* (New York: McGraw-Hill, 1951).
37. Chris Argyris, *Interpersonal Competence and Organizational Effectiveness* (Homewood, Ill.: Dorsey, 1962). See also Chris Argyris, *Personality and Organization* (New York: Harper and Row, 1957).
38. R. N. McMurray, "The Case for Benevolent Autocracy", *Harvard Business Review* 36, no. 1 (1958): 82–90.
39. G. W. Bassett, A. R. Crane, and W. G. Walker, *Headmasters for Better Schools* (2nd ed.; St. Lucia: University of Queensland Press, 1967).
40. R. F. Butts, *Assumptions Underlying Australian Education* (Melbourne: A.C.E.R., 1955).
41. I. L. Kandel, *Types of Administration* (2nd ed., Melbourne: A.C.E.R., 1961).
42. R. W. B. Jackson, *Emergent Needs in Australian Education* (Toronto: University of Toronto Department of Educational Research, 1961).
43. C. Sanders, "The Australian Universities" in R.W.T. Cowen (ed.), *Education for Australians* (Melbourne: Cheshire, 1964).
44. Elton Mayo, *The Social Problems of an Industrial Civilization* (Cambridge, Mass.: Harvard University Press, 1945).
45. F. J. Roethlisberger and W. J. Dickson, *Management and the Worker* (Cambridge, Mass.: Harvard University Press, 1939).
46. Halpin, *Administrative Theory in Education*.

47. J. K. Hemphill *et al.*, *Administrative Performance and Personality* (New York: Columbia University, Bureau of Publications, Teachers College, 1962).
48. N. Gross *et al.*, *Explorations in Role Analysis: Studies of the School Superintendency Role* (New York: Wiley, 1958).
49. R. V. Presthus, *The Organizational Society: An Analysis and a Theory* (New York: Knopf, 1962).
50. Griffiths, "Nature and Meaning of Theory".
51. Corwin, "Education and the Sociology of Complex Organizations".
52. Harmon Zeigler, *The Political World of the High School Teacher* (Eugene, Oregon: C.A.S.E.A., 1966).
53. P. 80.
54. D. E. Griffiths *et al.*, "Teacher Mobility in New York City", *Educational Administration Quarterly* 1, no. 1 (1965): 15–31.
55. N. Gross and R. E. Herriott, *Staff Leadership in Public Schools: A Sociological Enquiry* (New York: Wiley, 1965).
56. A. W. Gouldner, "Cosmopolitans and Locals: Toward an Analysis of Latent Social Roles", *Administrative Science Quarterly* 2 (1957): 281–306.
57. H. A. Simon, *Administrative Behavior: A Study of Decision Making Process in Administrative Organization* (New York: Macmillan, 1957).
58. Amitai Etzioni, *Modern Organizations* (Englewood Cliffs, N. J.: Prentice-Hall, 1964).
59. W. G. Walker, "Occupational Commitment in a Sample of Australian Teachers Five Years after Training", *Australian Journal of Higher Education* 3 (1967): 20–32.
60. Roland Pellegrin, "Community Power Structure and Educational Decision Making in the Local Community" (Eugene, Oregon: C.A.S.E.A., 1965. Mimeo).
61. P. H. Coombs, *The World Educational Crisis: A Systems Analysis* (Paris: I.I.E.P., 1967).
62. See Bennis, *Changing Organizations*.
63. D. E. Griffiths, "Nature and Meaning of Theory".
64. R. O. Carlson, *Executive Succession and Organizational Change: Place-Bound and Career-Bound Superintendents of Schools* (Chicago: Midwest Administration Center, University of Chicago, 1962).
65. R. R. Blake *et al.*, "Breakthrough in Organization Development", *Harvard Business Review* 46, no. 2 (November–December 1964): 133–55.
66. D. L. Clark and E. G. Guba, "An Examination of Potential Change Roles in Education" (Columbus, Ohio: U.C.E.A. Seminar on Innovation in Planning School Curricula, October 1965. Typescript). Fig. 1 is from this paper.
67. Sir Geoffrey Vickers, *The Art of Judgement* (London: Chapman and Hall, 1965), p. 87.

Chapter 3

1. D. G. Nugent, "Are Local Control and Lay Boards Obsolete?", *Educational Leadership*, November 1964.
2. R. G. Corwin, "Education and the Sociology of Complex Organizations", in D. A. Hansen and J. E. Gerstl (eds.), *On Education: Sociological Perspectives* (New York: Wiley, 1967).
3. B. Rhea, *Measure of Child Involvement and Alienation from the School*. Cooperative Research Project, 1966 programme, p. 3.
4. J. I. Goodlad, "Innovation in Education", *Educational Forum* 21, no. 5 (March 1967).
5. P. M. Blau, *Bureaucracy in Modern Society* (New York: Random House, 1965), p. 14.
6. V. A. Thompson, "Bureaucracy and Innovation", *Administrative Science Quarterly* 10, no. 1 (June 1965): 4.
7. H. A. Shephard and R. R. Blake, "Changing Behavior Through Cognitive Change" in W. G. Bennis, *Changing Organizations* (New York: McGraw-Hill, 1966), p. 118.

8. R. F. Butts, *Assumptions Underlying Australian Education* (Melbourne: A.C.E.R., 1955), p. 30.
9. M. N. Columbro, "Supervision and Action Research", *Educational Leadership* 21, no. 5 (February 1964): 298–300.
10. C. Argyris, "Interpersonal Barriers to Decision Making", *Harvard Business Review* 44 (March-April 1966): 84–97.
11. H. Strour, *Bureaucracy in Higher Education* (New York: Free Press, 1962), p. 221.
12. E. M. Dimock, "Bureaucracy Self-Examined", *Public Administration Review* 4 (1944): 205.

Chapter 4

1. K. S. Pinson, *Modern Germany* (2nd ed.; New York: Macmillan, 1966), p. 594.
2. *University of Oxford: Report of the Commission of Inquiry* (Oxford: Clarendon Press, 1966), vol. 1, para. 437.
3. *Ibid.*, para. 477.
4. J. A. L. Matheson, "The General Framework of University Government", in Ruth Atkins (ed.), *University Government* (Sydney: F.A.U.S.A., 1967), p. 10.
5. Nigel Walker, *Morale in the Civil Service* (Edinburgh: University Press, 1961), p. 260.
6. *Tertiary Education in Australia* (Report of the Committee on the Future of Tertiary Education in Australia to the Australian Universities Commission), vol. 3, August 1965, para. 16. 63.
7. R. V. Presthus, *The Organizational Society: An Analysis and a Theory* (New York: Knopf, 1962), p. 260.
8. *Ibid.*, p. 138.
9. F. Arnott, "The Teacher in the Fourth to Fourteenth Centuries", *Forum of Education* 16 (1957): 53.
10. A. G. Mitchell, "Changing University Concepts", *University of Sydney Gazette*, May 1965, p. 133.
11. Amitai Etzioni, *Modern Organizations* (Englewood Cliffs, N. J.: Prentice-Hall, 1964), p. 3.
12. F.M.G. Willson, *Administrators in Action* (London: Allen and Unwin, 1961), p. 275.
13. "Academic Structure and Government in a New University" (1964. Mimeo). Quotation from p. 14.
14. J. Hage and M. Aiken, "Relationship of Centralization to Other Structural Properties", *Administrative Science Quarterly* 12 (1967): 73–74.
15. J.J. Auchmuty (in collaboration with A. N. Jeffares), "Australian Universities: The Historical Background", in A. Grenfell Price (ed.), *The Humanities in Australia* (Sydney: Angus and Robertson, 1959), pp. 21–22.
16. Matheson, "General Framework of University Government", p. 11.
17. *Ibid.*
18. K. F. Walker, "Decisions, Democracy and Delegations", in Atkins, *University Government*, p. 28.
19. S. Hook, *Heresy, Yes: Conspiracy, No*, p. 154. Quoted by W.G.K. Duncan, "Freedom of the Mind", in *Liberty in Australia* (Sydney: Angus and Robertson, 1955), p. 28.
20. For an excellent survey, see L. N. Short, "Changes in Higher Education in Australia", *Australian University* 5, no. 1 (April 1967): 1–41.

Chapter 5

The help of Mr. A. G. Smith of Armidale Teachers' College in the preparation of the diagrams is gratefully acknowledged.

1. P. F. Lazarsfeld, *Radio and the Printed Page* (New York: Duell, Sloan, and Pearce, 1964), p. 134.
2. W. Schramm, "Procedures and Effects of Mass Communication", in N. B. Henry (ed.), *Mass Media in Education* (Chicago: N.S.S.E., 53rd Yearbook, 1954).
3. David K. Berlo, *The Process of Communication* (New York: Holt, Rinehart, and Winston, 1960).
4. Talcott Parsons, "Some Ingredients of a General Theory of Formal Organization", in Andrew W. Halpin (ed.), *Administrative Theory in Education* (Chicago: Midwest Administration Center, University of Chicago, 1958).
5. C. J. Haberstroh, "Organization Design and Systems Analysis", in J. G. March (ed.), *Handbook of Organizations* (Chicago: Rand McNally, 1965), pp. 1171–211.
6. R. V. Presthus, *The Organizational Society: An Analysis and a Theory* (New York: Knopf, 1962).
7. R. V. Presthus, *Behavioral Approaches to Public Administration* (Alabama: University of Alabama Press, 1965).
8. E. E. Jones, K. J. Gergen, and R. G. Jones, "Tactics of Ingratiation among Leaders and Subordinates in a Status Hierarchy", *Psychological Monographs* 77, no. 3 (1963).
9. E. E. Jones, *Ingratiation: A Social Psychological Analysis* (New York: Appleton Century, 1964).
10. A. R. Crane, "Communication Within a Bureaucratic Organizational Framework: Implications for the Educational Administrator of Some Recent Investigations", *Journal of Educational Administration* 5 (1967): 97–106.
11. A. W. Gouldner, "Cosmopolitans and Locals: Toward an Analysis of Latent Social Roles", *Administrative Science Quarterly* 2 (1957): 281–306.
12. D. E. Griffiths, S. Goldman, and W. J. McFarland, "Teacher Mobility in New York City", *Educational Administration Quarterly* 1, no. 1 (1965): 15–31.
13. *Report of the Committee Appointed to Survey Secondary Education in New South Wales* (Wyndham Report) (Sydney: Government Printer, 1957), p. 78.
14. J. R. Gibb, "Defensive Communication", *Journal of Communication* 11, no. 3 (1961).
15. R. Likert, *New Patterns of Management* (New York: McGraw-Hill, 1961).
16. R. Likert, *The Human Organization: Its Management and Value* (New York: McGraw-Hill, 1967).
17. G. W. Bassett, A. R. Crane, and W. G. Walker, *Headmasters for Better Schools* (St. Lucia: University of Queensland Press, 1961).
18. Dan C. Lortie, "The Teacher and Team Teaching: Suggestions for Long-range Research", in Judson T. Shaplin and Henry F. Olds, Jr. (eds.), *Team Teaching* (New York: Harper and Row, 1964), pp. 270–305.
19. J. W. Thibaut and H. H. Kelley, *The Social Psychology of Groups* (New York: Wiley, 1959).
20. E. Litwak and Henry J. Meyer, "Administrative Styles and Community Linkages" in Albert J. Reiss, Jr., *Schools in a Changing Society* (New York: Free Press, 1965).

Chapter 6

1. P. 73.
2. David K. Berlo, *The Process of Communication* (New York: Holt, Rinehart and Winston, 1960).
3. R. V. Presthus, *The Organizational Society: An Analysis and a Theory* (New York: Knopf, 1962).
4. Talcott Parsons, "Some Ingredients of a General Theory of Formal Organization", in Andrew W. Halpin (ed.), *Administrative Theory in Education* (Chicago: Midwest Administration Center, University of Chicago, 1958).

5. D. E. Griffiths, S. Goldman, and W. J. McFarland, "Teacher Mobility in New York City", *Educational Administration Quarterly* 1, no. 1 (1965): 15–31.
6. J. R. Gibb, "Defensive Communication", *Journal of Communication* 11, no. 3 (1961).
7. P. 75.
8. Parsons, "Ingredients of a General Theory of Formal Organization".
9. C. J. Haberstroh, "Organization Design and Systems Analysis", in J. G. March (ed.), *Handbook of Organizations* (Chicago: Rand McNally, 1965), pp. 1171–211.
10. P. 75.
11. P. 76.
12. Presthus, *Organizational Society*.
13. Griffiths, "Teacher Mobility".
14. A. W. Gouldner, "Cosmopolitans and Locals: Toward an Analysis of Latent Social Roles", *Administrative Science Quarterly* 2 (1957): 281–306.
15. Gibb, "Defensive Communication".
16. T. J. Sergiovanni, "Factors Which Affect Satisfaction and Dissatisfaction of Teachers", *Journal of Educational Administration* 5 (1967): 66–82.

Chapter 7

1. Herbert A. Simon, *Administrative Behavior: A Study of Decision Making Process in Administrative Organization* (New York: Macmillan, 1951), p. 1.
2. R. V. Presthus, *Behavioral Approaches to Public Administration* (Alabama: University of Alabama Press, 1965).
3. A. W. Gouldner, "Cosmopolitans and Locals: Toward an Analysis of Latent Social Roles", *Administrative Science Quarterly* 2 (1957): 281–306.
4. D. E. Griffiths, S. Goldman, and W. J. McFarland, "Teacher Mobility in New York City", *Educational Administration Quarterly* 1, no. 1 (1965): 15–31.
5. J. R. Gibb, "Defensive Communication", *Journal of Communication* 11, no. 3 (1961).
6. Talcott Parsons, "Some Ingredients of a General Theory of Formal Organization", in Andrew W. Halpin (ed.), *Administrative Theory in Education* (Chicago: Midwest Administration Center, University of Chicago, 1958).
7. C. J. Haberstroh, "Organization Design and Systems Analysis", in J. G. March (ed.), *Handbook of Organizations* (Chicago: Rand McNally, 1965), pp. 1171–211.
8. Griffiths, Goldman, and McFarland, "Teacher Mobility", pp. 15–31.
9. A. R. Crane, "Communication Within a Bureaucratic Organizational Framework: Implications for the Educational Administrator of Some Recent Investigations", *Journal of Educational Administration* 5 (1967): 105.
10. J. W. Thibaut and H. H. Kelley, *The Social Psychology of Groups* (New York: Wiley, 1959).
11. Presthus, *Behavioral Approaches*.
12. Parsons, "Ingredients of a General Theory of Formal Organization".
13. E. E. Jones, K. J. Gergen, and R. G. Jones, "Tactics of Ingratiation among Leaders and Subordinates in a Status Hierarchy", *Psychological Monographs* 77, no. 3 (1963).
14. M. A. Howell, "A Study of Communication Within a Private School" (Diploma in Educational Administration thesis, University of New England, Armidale, New South Wales).
15. G. C. Homans and H. A. Simon, "A Formal Theory of Interaction of Social Groups", *American Sociological Review* 17 (1952): 202–11.
16. Simon, *Administrative Behavior*, p. 1.
17. J. Wilson Hogg, "The Headmaster and His Public Relations", in P. J. McKeown and B. W. Hone (eds.), *The Independent School* (Melbourne: Oxford University Press, 1967), p. 121.

Chapter 8

1. R. G. Corwin, "Education and the Sociology of Complex Organizations", in D. A. Hansen and J. E. Gerstl (eds.), *On Education: Sociological Perspectives* (New York: Wiley, 1967), p. 173.
2. Sir Eric Ashby, *The Scientist as a University President* (Arthur Holly Compton Memorial Lecture) (Washington University, 1964).
3. A. V. Cicourel, "The Front and Back of Organizational Leadership", *Pacific Sociological Review* 1, no. 2 (1958): 54–59.
4. P. Selznick, *Leadership in Administration: A Sociological Interpretation* (Evanston, Ill.: Row- Peterson, 1957), p. 100.
5. N. Gross, "Organization Lag in American Universities", *Harvard Educational Review* 33 (1963): 63.
6. *Ibid.*, p. 67.
7. Cicourel, "Front and Back of Organizational Leadership".
8. D. C. Korten, "Situational Determinants of Leadership Structure", *Journal of Conflict Resolution* 6, no. 3 (1962): 224.
9. T. Caplow and R. J. McGee, *The Academic Marketplace* (New York: Basic Books, 1958).

Chapter 9

The research on which this paper is based was supported in part by a grant from the McKinsey Foundation for Management Research, which is gratefully acknowledged. The content and conclusions are wholly ours. This chapter appeared as an article in *Educational Administration Quarterly* 4, no. 1 (1968): 6–31.

1. Chester Barnard, *The Functions of the Executive* (Cambridge, Mass.: Harvard University Press, 1938); Herbert A. Simon, *Administrative Behavior: A Study of Decision Making Process in Administrative Organization* (New York: Macmillan, 1945); James G. March and Herbert A. Simon, *Organizations* (New York: Wiley, 1958).
2. For present purposes we are ignoring feather-bedding, political patronage, and similar devices which can lead to deviations from what we believe to be the central pattern.
3. We are indebted to Harold L. Wilensky for this distinction although he reserves the term "career" for the orderly variety and describes the disorderly as "work history". See his "Orderly Careers and Social Participation: The Impact of Work History on Social Integration in the Middle Mass", *American Sociological Review* 26 (1961): 521–39.
4. The distinction between salience and level of aspiration comes from William R. Dill, Thomas Hilton, and Walter Reitman, *The New Managers* (Englewood Cliffs, N. J.: Prentice-Hall, 1962).
5. See William A. Glaser, "Internship Appointments of Medical Students", *Administrative Science Quarterly* 4 (1959): 337–56.
6. The joint importance of career pattern and life cycle in the decision to change residences is revealed by Gerald R. Leslie and Arthur H. Richardson, "Life-Cycle, Career Pattern, and the Decision to Move", *American Sociological Review* 26 (1961): 894–902.
7. For a basic discussion of the reference group notion, see Robert K. Merton, *Social Theory and Social Structure* (Rev. ed.; New York: Free Press of Glencoe, 1957), Chapter 8.
8. See Dill, Hilton, and Reitman, *New Managers*.
9. Richard O. Carlson, *Executive Succession and Organizational Change: Place-Bound and Career-Bound Superintendents of Schools* (Chicago: Midwest Administration Center, University of Chicago, 1962). See also Carlson, "Succession and Performance among School Superintendents", *Administrative Science Quarterly* 6, no. 2 (1961): 210–27.

10. Dwaine Marvick finds the "hybrid" employee in government in *Career Perspectives in a Bureaucratic Setting* (Ann Arbor: University of Michigan Press, 1954); George K. Floro identifies the "floater" or "individualist" among city managers in "Types of City Managers", *Public Management*, October 1954. Dill, Hilton, and Reitman, studying aspiring industrial managers, find a "heuristic" orientation in "How Aspiring Managers Promote Their Own Careers", *California Management Review*, Summer 1960; Alvin Gouldner identifies the "company man" executive in *Patterns of Industrial Bureaucracy* (Glencoe, Ill.: Free Press, 1954).

11. Government employees labelled "specialist" in Marvick's study (*Career Perspectives*) seem to fit here. Floro ("Types of City Managers") terms city managers with this orientation "jumpers" or as those seeking "advancement-by-moving". In a study of a state government bureaucracy, Leonard Reissman identified the "functional" or "specialist" bureaucrat with this orientation in "A Study of Role Conception in a Bureaucracy", *Social Forces*, March 1949. Donald Pelz, studying a governmental research laboratory, identified this commitment as a "science orientation" in "Some Social Factors Related to Performance in a Research Organization", *Administrative Science Quarterly* 1 (1956): 310–25. Alvin Gouldner's identification of "cosmopolitans" on a college faculty also is similar in "Cosmopolitans and Locals: Toward an Analysis of Latent Social Roles", *Administrative Science Quarterly* 2 (1957–58): 281–306, 444–80. Carlson's identification of "career-bound" superintendents also fits here (*Executive Succession*).

12. Marvick (*Career Perspectives*) terms governmental employees with this orientation "institutionalists" and Reissman ("Role Conception in a Bureaucracy") calls them "job bureaucrats". Floro ("Types of City Managers") found the "one-city-manager", Carlson (*Executive Succession*), the "place-bound" school superintendent, and Gouldner (*Patterns of Industrial Bureaucracy*), the "local" college faculty member.

13. For identification of this variable, although with different emphasis, we are indebted to Raymond W. Mack and his concepts of "determinate and indeterminate occupations", in "Occupational Determinateness: A Problem and Hypotheses in Role Theory", *Social Forces* 35 (1956): 20–25. Roughly, Mack's "determinate" would correspond to our "collegial" category and his "indeterminate" to our "enterprise" category. We have chosen to give greater emphasis to the *source* of determinateness. See also Mack, "Occupational Ideology and the Determinate Role", *Social Forces*, October 1959, and Joseph R. Gusfield, "Occupational Roles and Forms of Enterprise", *American Journal of Sociology* 66 (1961): 571–80.

14. See Edward Goss, *Work and Society* (New York: Crowell, 1958), pp. 223–35.

15. Simon Marcson concludes that the scientist's training does not prepare him to be an industrial laboratory employee and that the industrial laboratory has the objective of adapting him to industrial research employment while at the same time not entirely destroying his self-conception. See his "The Professional Commitments of Scientists in Industry", *Research Management*, Winter 1961, pp. 271–75. See also Marcson, *The Scientist in American Industry* (Harper and Brothers, 1960), especially Chapter 5. For a description of how the adaptation proceeds, see Robert W. Avery, "Enculturation in Industrial Research", *IRE Transactions of the Professional Group on Engineering Management*, March 1960.

16. For an analysis which identifies "opportunity for advancement within the profession" as a crucial variable in determining commitment to professional skills versus aspirations for advancement, see Peter M. Blau and W. Richard Scott, *Formal Organizations* (San Francisco: Chandler, 1962), pp. 69–71.

17. This is especially true for those professions which may be practised in either context; medicine in private practice or as a staff physician; law in private or in corporate practice; art as a free-lancer or as an employed instructor.

18. Although our framework organizes material differently, much of the analysis of this section is derived from Theodore Caplow, *The Sociology of Work*

(Minneapolis: University of Minneapolis Press, 1954) and from Everett C. Hughes, *Men and Their Work* (Glencoe, Ill.: Free Press, 1958).

19. For evidence on the limitations to geographic mobility see Elizabeth Bott, *Family and Social Network* (London: Tavistock Publications, 1957), and Charles R. Walker, *Steeltown: An Industrial Case History of the Conflict between Progress and Security* (New York: Harper and Brothers, 1950).

20. See Robert H. Guest, "Work Careers and Aspirations of Automobile Workers", *American Sociological Review* 19 (1954): 155–63.

21. In a study of the Detroit Standard Metropolitan Area, Harold L. Wilensky reports that "in the middle mass—a relatively secure population, well off by American standards—only 30 percent can by any stretch of the imagination be said to act out half or more of their work histories in an orderly career. If we count the lower class, excluded from this sample, it is apparent that a vast majority of the labor force is going nowhere in an unordered way or can expect a worklife of thoroughly-unpredictable ups and downs." See Wilensky, "Orderly Careers and Social Participation". On the notion of job shopping see "The Trial Work Period", Chapter 18 in Delbert C. Miller and William H. Form, *Industrial Sociology* (New York: Harper Brothers, 1951).

22. Ely Chinoy, "The Tradition of Opportunity and the Aspirations of Automobile Workers", *American Journal of Sociology* 57 (1952): 453–59.

23. On this point see Wilbert E. Moore, "Occupational Structure and Industrial Conflict", in Arthur Kornhauser, Robert Dubin, and Arthur M. Ross, *Industrial Conflict* (New York: McGraw-Hill, 1954). Caplow, *Sociology of Work*, p. 258, observes that where education and experience requirements are "steeply graded", the overwhelming majority of employees occupy positions from which they cannot expect to be promoted.

24. That belief in the realities of opportunity for upward mobility is less strong among manual workers than among white collar workers is indicated by a number of studies. See, for example, Richard Centers, *The Psychology of Social Classes* (Princeton: Princeton University Press, 1949); Alfred W. Jones, *Life, Liberty and Property* (Philadelphia: Lippincott, 1941); Genevieve Knupfer, "Portrait of the Underdog", *Public Opinion Quarterly* 11, no. 1 (1947): 103–14.

25. See Harold L. Wilensky, "Life Cycle, Work Situation, and Participation in Formal Associations", in Robert W. Kleemeier (ed.), *Aging and Leisure* (New York: Oxford University Press); and Talcott Parsons, "A Revised Analytic Approach to the Theory of Social Stratification", in Reinhard Bendix and Seymour Lipset (eds.), *Class, Status, and Power* (Glencoe, Ill.: Free Press, 1953). Wilensky also points out that for the majority of employed persons the home and children come into focus, with mounting pressure for credit in the product market and income in the labor market before the peak in actual income and security is reached.

26. Reaching the ceiling before aspirations have stopped growing can have other consequences for job performance. There is some evidence that charge attendants in mental hospitals who have mobility aspirations despite the fact that they are blocked from the next stratum (registered nurse) are particularly sensitive to the racial status of patients and to maintaining status distinctions between themselves and patients. See Leonard I. Pearlin and Morris Rosenberg, "Nurse-Patient Social Distance and the Structural Context of a Mental Hospital", *American Sociological Review* 27 (1962): 56–65.

27. On the importance of visibility see Melville Dalton, *Men Who Manage* (New York: Wiley, 1959), Chapter 6. See also the developments of the concept "Getting the Attention of Superiors" as related to promotion in New York City schools in D.E. Griffiths *et al.*, "Teacher Mobility in New York City", *Educational Administration Quarterly* 1, no. 1 (1965): 15–31.

28. The prime example of such jobs, perhaps, is that of the "assistant-to". See Thomas L. Whisler, "The 'Assistant-to' in Four Administrative Settings", *Administrative Science Quarterly* 5 (1960): 181–216.

29. See Norman H. Martin and Anselm B. Strauss, "Patterns of Mobility Within Industrial Organizations", *Journal of Business*, April 1956, pp. 101–10.

30. This section also draws mainly on the analyses of Caplow, *Sociology of Work*, and Hughes, *Men and Their Work*.
31. See Gusfield, "Occupational Roles", and Arthur L. Stinchcombe, "Bureaucratic and Craft Administration of Production: A Comparative Study", *Administrative Science Quarterly* 4 (1959): 168–87.
    Studies of migration into Minneapolis and Duluth indicate that "professionals and managers" migrate longer distances than do "lower status migrants" and that the higher status migrants are likely to come from eastern urban centres while middle and lower status groups come from rural areas and small cities and towns west of the Mississippi. See Holger R. Stub, "The Occupational Characteristics of Migrants to Duluth: A Retest of Rose's Migration Hypothesis", *American Sociological Review* 27 (1962): 87–90.
32. Howard S. Becker found that the mobility pattern for Chicago public school teachers was from slums to middle-class neighbourhoods. See "The Career of the Chicago Public School-teacher", *American Journal of Sociology* 57 (1952): 470–77.
33. See Caplow, *Sociology of Work*, and Hughes, *Men and Their Work*.
34. The importance of sponsorship in building a medical career is brought out by Oswald Hall, "The Stages of a Medical Career", *American Journal of Sociology* 53 (1948): 327–36.
35. See Fred E. Katz, "Occupational Contact Networks", *Social Forces* 37 (1958): 52–55.
36. Families in these occupations learn to subordinate location preferences to professional attainment. See Bott, *Family and Social Network*, especially Chapter 4.
37. Fully vested retirement plans thus have considerable significance. Teachers Insurance Annuity Association, for example, permits the individual to move from one member organization to another without any forfeit. T.I.A.A. may well be more important than tenure in protecting the professionalism of individuals from the dictates of the particular enterprise. On the general point, see William M. Evan, "Organization Man and Due Process of Law", *American Sociological Review* 26 (1961): 540–47.
38. An important distinction among nurses emerges from a study by Ronald G. Corwin, who finds that graduates of degree programmes, offered in universities, have been highly exposed to professional conceptions, whereas graduates of diploma programmes, which are part of the hospital, have not. See "The Professional Employee: A Study of Conflict in Nursing Roles", *American Journal of Sociology* 66 (1961): 604–15.
39. See Warren G. Bennis, N. Berkowitz, M. Affinito, and M. Malone, "Reference Groups and Loyalties in the Out-patient Department", *Administrative Science Quarterly* 2 (1958): 481–500; Corwin, "Professional Employee"; and Becker, "Career of the Chicago Public School Schoolteacher".
40. See Eliot Freidson's distinction between participation in lay versus professional "referral systems", in "Client Control and Medical Practice", *American Journal of Sociology* 65 (1960): 374–82.
41. See Marcson, "Professional Commitments of Scientists in Industry", and *Scientist in American Industry*.
42. That the disrupted career prototype has achieved legitimacy in engineering occupations is suggested by the following prestige rankings provided by engineering faculty members: design engineer, project engineer, assistant chief engineer, chief engineer, vice-president, and president. Exactly how the question was posed is not clear, however. See Robert Perrucci, "The Significance of Intra-Occupational Mobility", *American Sociological Review* 26 (1961): 874–83.
43. See Howard M. Vollmer and Donald L. Mills, "Nuclear Technology and the Professionalization of Labor", *American Journal of Sociology* 67 (1962): 690–96, and Nelson N. Foote, "The Professionalization of Labor in Detroit", *American Journal of Sociology* 58 (1953): 371–80. On the impact of technological change on military occupations see Morris Janowitz, "Changing Patterns of Organizational Authority: The Military Establishment", *Administrative Science Quarterly* 3 (1959): 473–93.

44. See Edwin J. Thomas, "Role Conceptions and Organizational Size", *American Sociological Review* 24 (1959): 30–37.
45. For evidence in line with this proposition, see Charles H. Coates and Roland J. Pellegrin, "Executives and Supervisors: Contrasting Self-Conceptions and Conceptions of Each Other", *American Sociological Review* 22 (1957): 217–20, and "Executives and Supervisors: A Situational Theory of Differential Occupational Mobility", *Social Force* 35 (1956): 121–26.
46. Gouldner noted in the firm that calling an executive a "Company man" implicitly rated him as "high on loyalty to the company" and that company experts were less likely to be spoken of as "Company men" although there existed no conscious doubts about the expert's loyalty. See *Patterns of Industrial Bureaucracy*.
47. Howard S. Becker and Anselm Strauss suggest that "considerable switching . . . takes place . . . and is rationalized in institutional and occupational terms, both by candidates and by their colleagues. A significant consequence of this, undoubtedly, is subtle psychological strain, since the new positions and those preceding are both somewhat alike and different." See "Careers, Personality, and Adult Socialization", *American Journal of Sociology* 62 (1956): 253–63.
48. See William Goode, "Community Within a Community: The Professions", *American Sociological Review* 22 (1957): 194–200, and Rue Bucher and Anselm Strauss, "Professions in Process", *American Journal of Sociology* 66 (1961): 325–34.
49. For a specific illustration of this see James F. Downs, "Environment, Communication, and Status Change aboard an American Aircraft Carrier", *Human Organization*, Fall 1958.

Chapter 10

1. R. O. Carlson, "Environmental Constraints and Organizational Consequences: The Public School and Its Clients", in D. E. Griffiths (ed.), *Behavioral Science and Educational Administration* (Chicago: N.S.S.E., 63rd Yearbook, 1964).
2. R. O. Carlson, *Adoption of Educational Innovations* (Eugene, Oregon: University of Oregon, C.A.S.E.A., 1965).
3. R. K. Merton, *Social Theory and Social Structure* (New York: Free Press of Glencoe, 1957).
4. A. W. Gouldner, "Cosmopolitans and Locals: Toward an Analysis of Latent Social Roles", *Administrative Science Quarterly* 2 (1957–58): 281–306, 444–80.
5. R. O. Carlson, *Executive Succession and Organizational Change: Place-Bound and Career-Bound Superintendents of Schools* (Chicago: Midwest Administration Center, University of Chicago, 1962).
6. P. 135.
7. In the United States of America and other countries, on the other hand, there has been quite extensive research in this area. See, for example, T. J. Sergiovanni, "Factors Which Affect Satisfaction and Dissatisfaction of Teachers", *Journal of Educational Administration* 5 (1967): 66–82.
8. W. G. Walker, "Occupational Commitment in a Sample of Australian Teachers Five Years after Training", *Australian Journal of Higher Education* 3 (1967): 20–32.
9. R. V. Presthus, *The Organizational Society: An Analysis and a Theory* (New York: Knopf, 1962).
10. Pp. 124 and 132.
11. P. 117.

Chapter 11

1. R. O. Carlson, "Environmental Constraints and Organizational Consequences: The Public School and Its Clients", in D. E. Griffiths (ed.), *Behavioral Science and Educational Administration* (Chicago: N.S.S.E., 63rd Yearbook, 1964).

2. Richard C. Snyder, "The Preparation of Educational Administrators" (Columbus, Ohio: U.C.E.A. International Intervisitation Program, 1966), now published in G. Baron *et al.* (eds.), *Educational Administration: International Perspectives* (Chicago: Rand McNally, 1968).
3. *Ibid.*
4. P. 130.
5. R. M. Hartwell, "New Universities", *Vestes* 4, no. 4 (1961): 35–38.
6. W. M. O'Neil, "The Unsatisfactory Role of Non-Professorial Staff", *Vestes* 4, no. 4 (1961): 39–43.
7. Hartwell, "New Universities", pp. 36–37.
8. David Stenhouse, "Promotions: Gowns off the Peg", *Vestes* 6, no. 1 (1963):23.
9. H. Philp *et al.*, *The University and Its Community* (Sydney: Novak, 1964).
10. P. H. Partridge, "The Growth of the Universities", *Forum of Education* 18 (1959): 43.
11. *Tertiary Education in Australia* (Report of the Committee on the Future of Tertiary Education in Australia to the Australian Universities Commission), 1964, no. 1, p. 47.
12. A. P. Rowe, *If the Gown Fits* (Melbourne: Melbourne University Press, 1960), p. 46.
13. *Ibid.*, pp. 8–9.
14. J. H. Newman, *The Idea of a University* (New York: Holt, Rinehart, and Winston, 1964), p. 134.
15. A. G. Mitchell and J. A. Passmore, "The Nature of the Humanities", in A. Grenfell Price (ed.), *The Humanities in Australia* (Sydney: Angus and Robertson, 1959), pp. 12–13.

Chapter 12

1. J. A. Culbertson, "Trends and Issues in the Development of a Science of Administration" (Paper presented at Conference of the University of Oregon Center for the Advanced Study of Educational Administration, September 1964. Mimeo).
2. Sir John Crawford, quoted in K.S. Cunningham and W. C. Radford, *Training the Administrator* (Melbourne: A.C.E.R., 1963).
3. A. W. Halpin (ed.), *Administrative Theory in Education* (Chicago: Midwest Administration Center, University of Chicago, 1958), p. 184.
4. G. W. Bassett, "Training Educational Administrators in Australia", in E. L. French (ed.), *Melbourne Studies in Education 1964* (Melbourne: Melbourne University Press, 1965).
5. Cunningham and Radford, *Training the Administrator.*
6. R. C. Snyder, "The Preparation of Educational Administrators: Some Problems Revisited" (Columbus, Ohio: U.C.E.A. International Intervisitation Program, 1966), now published in G. Baron *et al.* (eds.), *Educational Administration: International Perspectives* (Chicago: Rand McNally, 1968).
7. R. V. Presthus, *The Organizational Society: An Analysis and a Theory* (New York: Knopf, 1962).
8. Chapter 5.
9. Talcott Parsons, "Some Ingredients of a General Theory of Formal Organization", in Andrew W. Halpin (ed.), *Administrative Theory in Education* (New York: Macmillan, 1967), p. 41.
10. C. J. Haberstroh, "Organization Design and Systems Analysis", in J. G. March (ed.), *Handbook of Organizations* (Chicago: Rand McNally, 1965), pp. 1171–211.
11. F. W. Taylor, *Principles of Scientific Management* (New York: Harper, 1911).
12. E. P. Cubberley, *Public School Administration* (Boston: Houghton Mifflin, 1916).
13. Elton Mayo, *The Social Problems of an Industrial Civilization* (Cambridge, Mass.: Harvard University Press, 1945).

14. J. B. Miner, *The School Administrator and Organizational Character* (Eugene, Oregon: C.A.S.E.A., 1967).
15. H. A. Simon, *Administrative Behavior: A Study of Decision Making Process in Administrative Organization* (New York: Macmillan, 1947).
16. Halpin, *Administrative Theory in Education*.
17. D. E. Griffiths, *Administrative Theory* (New York: Appleton, 1959).
18. Dwight Waldo, quoted by J. A. Culbertson, "The Preparation of Administrators", in D. E. Griffiths (ed.), *Behavioral Science and Educational Administration* (Chicago: N.S.S.E., 63rd Yearbook, 1964).
19. Presthus, *Organizational Society*.
20. A. W. Gouldner, "Cosmopolitans and Locals: Toward an Analysis of Latent Social Roles", *Administrative Science Quarterly* 2 (1957): 281–306.
21. D. E. Griffiths, "The Nature and Meaning of Theory" in Griffiths, *Behavioral Science and Educational Administration*.
22. N. Wiener, quoted in Culbertson, "Trends and Issues".
23. P. Lazarsfeld, quoted in Griffiths, "Nature and Meaning of Theory".
24. *Professional Administrators for America's Schools*, quoted in Griffiths, "Nature and Meaning of Theory".
25. Herbert Fiegl, quoted by Griffiths, "Nature and Meaning of Theory", p. 98.
26. J. G. March and H. A. Simon, *Organizations* (New York: Wiley, 1958).
27. J. Getzels, "Administration as a Social Process", in Halpin, *Administrative Theory in Education*.
28. W. G. Walker (ed.), *The Principal at Work: Case Studies in School Administration* (St. Lucia: University of Queensland Press, 1965).

Chapter 13

1. A. W. Reeves, H. C. Melsness, and J. E. Cheal, *Educational Administration: The Role of the Teacher* (Toronto: Macmillan, 1962).
2. O. Graff *et al.*, *Philosophic Theory and Practice in Educational Administration* (Belmont, Calif.: Wadsworth, 1966).
3. R. L. Saunders *et al.*, *A Theory of Educational Leadership* (Columbus, Ohio: Merrill, 1966).
4. A. W. Halpin, *Theory and Research in Administration* (New York: Macmillan, 1966).
5. F. Lutz and J. Azzarelli, *The Struggle for Power in Education* (including sections by Iannaccone) (New York: Library of Education, Center for Applied Research, 1966).
6. R. Carlson, *Adoption of Educational Innovations* (Eugene, Oregon: University of Oregon, C.A.S.E.A., 1965).
7. D. Griffiths, *Research and Theory in Educational Administration* (Eugene, Oregon: University of Oregon, C.A.S.E.A., 1965).
8. D. E. Griffiths *et al.*, *Taxonomies of Organizational Behaviour in Education* (Chicago: Rand McNally, 1967).
9. A. Etzioni, *Modern Organizations* (Englewood Cliffs, N. J.: Prentice-Hall, 1964).
10. J. G. March (ed.), *Handbook of Organizations* (Chicago: Rand McNally, 1965).
11. F. W. Taylor, *Principles of Scientific Management* (New York: Harper, 1911).
12. L. H. Gulick and L. Urwick (eds.), *Papers on the Science of Administration* (New York: Institute of Public Administration, 1937); L. F. Urwick, *The Elements of Administration* (London: Pitman, 1961).
13. R. F. Campbell and R. T. Gregg, *Administrative Behavior in Education* (New York: Harper, 1957).
14. R. F. Campbell, J. Corbally, and R. E. Ramseyer, *An Introduction to Educational Administration* (Boston: Allyn and Bacon, 1962).
15. A. W. Reeves, *The Skills of an Effective Administrator*, vol. 1 (Edmonton: University of Alberta).

16. A. W. Halpin, *The Leader Behavior of School Superintendents* (Chicago: Midwest Administration Center, University of Chicago).
17. L. W. Downey, *The Alberta School Principal* (Edmonton: University of Alberta, 1962); L. W. Downey and F. Enns, *The Social Sciences and Educational Administration* (Edmonton: University of Alberta, 1963).

Chapter 14

1. See G. W. Bassett, "Training Educational Administrators in Australia", in E. L. French (ed.), *Melbourne Studies in Education 1964* (Melbourne: Melbourne University Press, 1965).
2. H. A. Simon, *Administrative Behavior: A Study of Decision Making Process in Administrative Organization* (New York: Macmillan, 1960).
3. Bassett, "Training Educational Administrators", p. 39.
4. A. R. Crane. See Chapter 5.
5. See C. E. Blocker, "Clinical and Humanistic Training as a Foundation for Effective Administration", *Journal of Educational Administration* 4 (1966): 103.
6. J. A. Culbertson, "The Preparation of Administrators", in D. E. Griffiths (ed.), *Behavioral Science and Educational Administration* (Chicago: N.S.S.E., 63rd Yearbook, 1964), p. 309.
7. See A. W. Halpin, *Theory and Research in Administration* (New York: Macmillan, 1966).
8. W. G. Walker, "Theory and Practice in Educational Administration" (Paper presented at Third Conference on School Administration at University of Queensland, August 1964).
9. D. E. Griffiths, "Towards a Theory of Administrative Behavior in Education", in R. F. Campbell and R. T. Gregg (eds.), *Administrative Behavior in Education* (New York: Harper, 1957), p. 360.
10. Culbertson, "Preparation of Administrators", p. 314.
11. See D. E. Griffiths, "The Nature and Meaning of Theory" in Griffiths, *Behavioral Science and Educational Administration*, p. 98.
12. *Ibid.*, p. 101.
13. R. V. Presthus, *The Organizational Society: An Analysis and a Theory* (New York: Knopf, 1962).
14. See G. W. Muir, Chapter 12.
15. Blocker, "Clinical and Humanistic Training", p. 110.
16. Presthus, *Organizational Society*.
17. K. S. Cunningham and W. C. Radford, *Training the Administrator* (Melbourne: A.C.E.R., 1963).
18. *Education Gazette, South Australia* 83 (February 1967): 36.
19. Bassett, "Training Educational Administrators", p. 34.
20. See R. J. Hacon, *Management Training* (London: English Universities Press, 1961).
21. See A. P. Coladarci and J. W. Getzels, *The Use of Theory in Educational Administration* (Educational Administration Monograph no. 5, School of Education, Stanford University) (Stanford, Calif.: Stanford University Press, 1955).
22. W. G. Walker. See Chapter 2.
23. Cunningham and Radford, *Training the Administrator*, p. 33.
24. See R. Hall and K. McIntyre, "The Student Personnel Program", in Campbell and Gregg, *Administrative Behavior in Education*, pp. 396–97.

Appendix 1

1. This was recently demonstrated in one area (Enfield, one of the newly constituted London boroughs) in which, in pursuance of government policy of putting an end to selection for secondary education, the local authority decided to fuse an existing grammar school and a secondary modern school.

A group of parents objected and the matter went to the High Court. There it was ruled that the local education authority was, by its action, contravening the articles of government of the grammar school. On application from the authority the Secretary of State for Education and Science proposed (as he had power to do) the revision of the articles, but allowed only five days for objections to be made. An appeal to the High Court resulted in the Secretary of State's being required to extend the "wholly unreasonable" period of five days to one month and to pay the costs of the action.

It was pointed out during the hearings that the courts were not concerned with educational policy, but with ensuring that all parties, including the local education authority and the Secretary of State, should act within the terms of the law.

2. See Harry Eckstein, *Pressure Group Politics: The Case of the British Medical Association* (London: Allen and Unwin, 1960). Eckstein points out that in Britain the use of formal power is only acceptable if allied with consultation and negotiation with groups representing traditional, occupational, and other values. Indeed, the opening gambit in any dispute with a statutory authority is for the trade union, voluntary association, or citizen group to claim that consultation has either been non-existent or inadequate. If this claim can be validated the aggrieved party can develop its counter-argument with reinforced moral authority.

3. D. V. Donnison and Valerie Chapman, *Social Policy and Administration* (London: Allen and Unwin, 1965), Chapter 12, "Formulating a Policy for Secondary Education in Croydon".

4. At the time in question 5 per cent of Croydon children were being educated in these schools at the expense of the authority. Others, of course, were in attendance as fee payers. The part played by independent and direct grant schools in supplementing the provision made by local education authorities explains their continuing influence. A detailed study of another authority (R. Saran, "Decision-making by a Local Education Authority", *Public Administration* 46 (January 1968) has shown under what pressure a local education authority can be to retain places in such schools, even when it has adequate accommodation in its own.

5. S. J. Eggleston, "Going Comprehensive", *New Society*, 22 December 1966. This describes an investigation, carried out by a team of investigators, into policy formation in one area within a local education authority.

6. The composition of the committee and the leading part played by head teachers is interesting. Eggleston ("Going Comprehensive") writes: "All teachers' organizations were represented in proportion to their membership which gave the NUT 16 of the 24 places. The committee contained representatives of all types of school, both primary and secondary from all major centres of the country. But of particular interest was the proportion of headteachers—16 of the 24 members were heads. In the case of the primary representatives the proportion was even higher, six were heads and one was an assistant teacher."

7. George Baron and Asher Tropp, "Teachers in England and America" in A. H. Halsey, Jean Floud, and C. Arnold Anderson (eds.), *Education, Economy and Society* (New York: Free Press of Glencoe, 1961), pp. 527–44.

8. David Peschek and John Brand, *Policies and Politics in Secondary Education, Case Studies in West Ham and Reading* (Greater London Papers, No. 11) (London School of Economics and Political Science, 1966).

9. The phrase is borrowed from a chapter by Samuel H. Beer, entitled "The British Legislature and the Problem of Mobilizing Consent", in Bernard Crick (ed.), *Essays on Reform, 1967* (London: Oxford University Press, 1967).

10. Department of Education and Science, *The Organization of Secondary Education.* Circular 10/65, para. 40 (London: H.M.S.O.).

11. "All Through: Gloucestershire" by C. P. Milroy, an article in *The Times Educational Supplement*, 6 October 1967, p. 708.

12. J. A. G. Griffith, *Central Departments and Local Authorities* (London: Allen and Unwin, 1966), p. 117.

13. *Ibid.*

14. *Ibid.*, p. 128.
15. H. C. Dent, *The Educational System of England and Wales* (2nd ed.; London: University of London Press, 1963), p. 83.
16. See G. Baron, "Some Aspects of the 'Headmaster Tradition' ", *Researches and Studies*, University of Leeds Institute of Education, no. 14, June 1956.
17. See Peschek and Brand, *Policies and Politics*, p. 7.
18. "In the Department's view, managing and governing bodies of schools are particularly well fitted to express the local community interest in local schools. Their functions are not administrative but consist in part of friendly help and guidance to heads and other teachers and in part of taking certain decisions peculiar to the individual school—above all the appointment when necessary of a new head—which are the close concern of the local community and are within the proper scope of lay people with access to suitable professional advice." Royal Commission on Local Government in England, *Written Evidence of the Department of Education and Science* (London: H.M.S.O., 1967), para. 108.
19. This paper has been centred mainly upon policy making in respect of *schools*: whilst the overall pattern of shared responsibility is similar in respect of the further education provision made by local authorities, there are some differences of significance. The chief of these is that the functions performed by technical colleges and the courses they provide are already coordinated by some ten Regional Councils.

Author Index

General Index